Eye-Openers

Jim Feldbush

Nancy Beck Irland

Carolyn Rathbun-Sutton

REVIEW AND HERALD® PUBLISHING ASSOCIATION
HAGERSTOWN, MD 21740

This book was
Edited by Jeannette R. Johnson
Copyedited by Jocelyn Fay and James Cavil
Cover design by GenesisDesign/Bryan Gray
Interior design by Patricia S. Wegh
Cover photos by Stansin Clair
Typeset: 11/13 Palatino

PRINTED IN U.S.A.

02 01 00 99 98   5 4 3 2 1

R&H Cataloging Service
Feldbush, James Martin, 1958-
    Eye-openers, by Jim Feldbush, Nancy Beck Irland, and
Carolyn Rathbun-Sutton.
        1. Teenagers—Prayer-books and devotions—English.
2. Devotional calendars—Juvenile literature. I. Irland,
Nancy Beck, 1951-   joint author. II. Rathbun-Sutton,
Carolyn, 1944-   joint author. III. Title.

                242.6

ISBN 0-8280-1299-7

Dedication

To Angelika, Kristen, Christopher, and Michael,
whose love and generosity have made this project possible.
To my parents and grandparents,
who brought me up knowing what it means to serve.
To my students throughout the years,
who inspire creativity each day.
To Mark,
my first partner in youth ministry (we had fun!).
And most importantly, to Jesus,
whose grace is so amazing I still haven't figured it all out—
I just accept it.

Jim Feldbush

To Gary, Marc, Dave, and Holly,
who continue to open my eyes.

Nancy Beck Irland

To Andrew Kent Rathbun, son,
fellow traveler, and lover of fine stories . . .
May our favorites always be about Him.

Carolyn Rathbun-Sutton

Cheat the Worms

If you live in a place where it is now the middle of winter, take a moment and look outside. What do you see? Trees bare and black, reaching desperately toward the sky? Yellow grass in your neighbor's lawn? Dirty brown snow in the streets? No bright flowers and singing birds anywhere? Are you worried these things might never come back? Of course not! It doesn't concern you a bit. You know that come spring, the trees will sprout tender new leaves; tulips will thrust their brilliant heads through the earth and bob in the breeze; the lawns will turn green again; and you will plant a garden.

And when you plant that garden, does it seem incredible to you that those little dried brown things you push into the dirt are going to become thriving plants of various kinds from which you will pick something to eat? Of course not! And yet these are astounding miracles. If you had never seen them with your own eyes, you would have difficulty believing it if someone told you about it. Still, it would happen.

Even now, whether or not you believe anything will happen to the trees in the spring, it won't change a thing. Little green leaves are still going to pop out of the sides of those sturdy brown branches, whether or not you believe they will. And your bare garden will soon be filled with growing things. Your beliefs don't change the existence or power of God.

In the same way, whether or not you believe in Jesus, He's still coming! **Hebrews 9:27, 28** says, **Just as man is destined to die once, and after that to face judgment, so Christ was sacrificed once to take away the sins of many people; and he will appear a second time, not to bear sin, but to bring salvation to those who are waiting for him (NIV).** To "cheat the worms" means to live through something and not die. Some of us who believe in Jesus and accept His offer of everlasting life in heaven will cheat the worms. We'll be waiting for Jesus when He comes.

Which people are taking the bigger risk—those who don't believe the Bible, or those who do? Decide for yourself! It's one of the most important decisions you'll ever make. **Nancy**

5

Jan 2

Learning Your ABCs

It is to be with him, and he is to read it all the days of his life so that he may learn to revere the Lord his God. Deuteronomy 17:19, TLB.

When you learn to read, one of the very first things you must memorize is your ABCs. Without knowing your alphabet, you won't learn to read. Letters make up words, words make up sentences, and sentences make up stories.

It's the same way with any occupation. Let's say you want to become a physician. You have to know the basics before you can become a doctor. How would you like to be operated on by a doctor who hadn't learned where all your bones, muscles, and nerves are? If he's cutting into you, he had better know where all your parts are.

Being a Christian is like that too. If I say that I'm a follower of Jesus, I had better know what that means. If we really want to be true Christians, we need to learn our biblical ABCs.

When someone asks you why you believe in the Sabbath or in Jesus or in the Second Coming, can you tell them? Have you learned where to find these things in your Bible? Don't worry; you aren't expected to know everything now, but you can start learning. Jesus wants so much for us to tell others about His great love. He wants us to share His Word with others, but we need to know our ABCs before we can do that.

Why not start today? Take your Bible and look up in a concordance everything you can find out about the Sabbath, or what happens to a person when they die, or about the love of God. When you start doing this, you'll discover so many things that you never knew before. Sometimes we may think we know everything about the Bible, but even if we read it every day for the rest of our lives, we'll learn something new each time. So do it today—work on those biblical ABCs. **Jim**

The Spitting Tree

"Watch and pray so that you will not fall into temptation." Matthew 26:41, NIV.

Just as I was about to step under the shady relief of the tree's leafy branches, Alicia pushed me back into the hot sun with a sharp "Watch out, Madamu!"

"Why did you do that?" I objected.

"Madamu," explained Baluku, one of the students with whom I was on a Sabbath afternoon walk, "this dangerous tree will spit on you."

"Do you mean to tell me that this tree *spits?*"

A half-dollar-sized wad of something that looked like bubbly saliva plopped into the dust a few inches from my feet. Alicia gave a little scream and pulled me farther away from the shade. "Madamu, see this?" asked Baluku, bending his head forward and pointing to a bald spot about the circumference of the soupy wad on the ground. "If a tree spits on your head, your hair falls out. It can change you forever."

H'mmm, I thought, *maybe there is something to this.* I followed my students along the far side of the road, well away from the shady relief of the spitting trees.

Sure enough, while our sandaled feet left imprints in the blistering sand, blobs of "saliva" plopped regularly onto the road, stirring up tiny wisps of dust.

At this time of year, Alicia and Baluku explained, thousands of a certain kind of beetle inhabit these trees and manufacture so much "saliva" that it falls from the branches, making it appear that the trees spit.

Satan tries to lure us to within "spitting distance." He makes things such as alcohol, drugs, and off-color TV shows seem like refreshing shade—relief from life's "hot spots," such as low grades, family tensions, and other tough problems. But sooner or later his "shade trees" will spit on us, and we'll run the risk—like Baluku and his bald spots—of being changed forever.

The good news is that when we ask our powerful God, through prayer and Bible study, to give us minute-by-minute strength to walk in the Son, Jesus will eventually bring us *lasting* relief! **Carolyn**

Jan 4

Take in Tow

I grew up on the island of Ceylon. Sometimes I'd ride on the ferry with my parents out to the cruise ships to pick up visitors. Tied to each ship was a floating dock about the size of a large living room. The challenge was to climb the tall narrow flight of metal steps leading to the main deck, which clung to the outside of the towering ship. It always took my breath away to look down between the steps and see the heaving ocean, knowing one slip could land me there.

One day I got to take a two-day cruise on a small ship going to Bombay, India. Our cabin was down three flights of red metal stairs, in the very bottom of the boat. Our dining room wasn't fancy, and we served ourselves from a food bar. But hey, to me it was a cruise, and I enjoyed sitting out on the deck in the afternoons, licking salt spray from my lips.

The trip turned frightening as we approached Bombay, however, when one of the stabilizers fell off, pitching the ship at a crazy angle. Deck chairs slid, people screamed, and we all had to get our life vests on. The captain said we weren't in danger, but I didn't believe him. I thought about the sharks in the Indian Ocean as we continued toward Bombay. I breathed a sigh of relief as the tugboat towed us into the harbor, because I didn't trust my ship anymore. The tugboat captain knew exactly where the rocks were in the harbor.

Sometimes we can't wait until we're old enough so that our parents can't tell us what to do. But only after you leave home do you realize how good you had it when your parents were right there to talk things over with you. Like the tugboat that had my ship in tow, your parents know where the deep spots are and can help you avoid the rocks. What does **Proverbs 1:8** say about parents' advice? **Listen, my son, to your father's instruction and do not forsake your mother's teaching (NIV).** Your parents were once your age; they know the dangers that certain decisions may lead to. By taking their advice, you can stop fretting over the small things and use your energy to dream and plan your own future.
Nancy

8

Jan 5

Leapin' Lizards

But you, man of God, flee from all this, and pursue righteousness.
I Timothy 6:11, NIV.

It was a great day! The sun was out, the breeze was gently pushing its way through the trees, and the water was refreshing. We were enjoying a natural spring in Florida. On one end of the little body of water formed by the spring, a river flowed off into the weeds. Dan and I decided we'd do some exploring with our little vinyl boat.

We hopped in and began paddling toward the river. As we entered the crystal clear stream we found ourselves immediately surrounded by six-foot-high grasses. We paddled slowly, enjoying the sights and sounds of Florida wildlife.

Then, as we rounded the corner, I noticed a large tree that had fallen and was partially submerged in the stream. *No problem,* I thought, *we'll just paddle ourselves around this obstacle.* I was concentrating on the log as we approached it, making sure not to bump into it. I didn't want the sharp bark to puncture our small air-filled boat.

Suddenly, when we were about 15 feet from the waterlogged tree, something moved! Just beyond the tree was a seven-foot alligator! Several things flashed through my mind: vinyl boat, big teeth, sinking humans, me for lunch. All I could do was yell, "Dan, reverse!"

"Oh, I think we can get by him," Dan said.

But not wanting to take the chance, especially since I was sitting in the front, I said I wanted to turn around, and we left.

Sometimes we tend to float too close to sin. Sometimes we think we can get by without getting bitten. Don't be fooled; sin will get you. It may take a long time; it may take only a short time, but sin will eventually swallow you. Stay away from it! Run as fast as you can from it, right into the arms of Jesus.   **Jim**

Trapped in The Connection!

Commit everything you do to the Lord. Trust him to help you do it and he will. Psalm 37:5, TLB.

This is The Connection," said Marianne, my cave guide, as we hunkered down to the entrance of this narrow connecting passage. "The ceiling is low; you'll have to turn your head sideways and push through on your belly. I've done this a lot, so I'll go first."

Once through, she called back instructions. I tried to follow them but kept slipping toward a dark crack to my left. "I'm slipping!" I tried to sound brave.

"Keep pushing toward me and relax," she encouraged.

Suddenly my head hit a low-hanging rock that clamped the helmet tight over my face. "Mari-a-a-nne!" (The air was stuffy inside my helmet.) "You gotta help me!"

"But *you* gotta follow my directions."

But, I thought, *doing it your way will get me stuck in this cold muddy passageway for the rest of my life!* Yet doing it *my* way kept me sliding toward danger. Finally I got desperate enough to follow my guide's directions.

I did just as she had instructed me: I pushed . . . and relaxed . . . and then felt my whole body slip toward the crevice—and get stuck! *Panic!*

Unbelievably, Marianne, who was watching me in the beam of her headlamp, called back, "Good!"

Then the most amazing thing happened. My left leg and arm suddenly dropped through the tight crevice and hung free in some sort of vacuum. Also, sliding to the left like that had given my arm enough room to reach back and push the helmet off my face. I blinked at Marianne, smiling in the beam of my headlamp.

"That's better," she said. "Now find hand and footholds along that lower wall and push."

In seconds I'd found anchor points on the rough calcite wall and had quickly pushed my chilled body through The Connection's muddy ooze to join my cave guide at the other end.

Jesus successfully made it through the darkest cave of all—this world. As our all-knowing cave Guide, He has promised that when we push forward in obedience to His instructions, and then relax in perfect trust, He will get us through the tight places of our lives.   **Carolyn**

Fair-weather Friend

Steven was running for student body president, and he felt great! Sure, there were those who supported his opponent, but his supporters really made him feel popular. They cheered for him in class and made a fuss over him at the cafeteria. He wished the campaign would go on and on.

Election day came, and the students cast their votes. Steven didn't win. He was devastated. Many people he'd thought were his friends suddenly had no time for him. They were fair-weather friends—they pretended to be his friend when things were going well, but disappeared when he had troubles.

Fair-weather friends don't want to hear about your troubles. They don't really care about you. They want to be seen with someone, not because they like that person, but because they think associating with him or her makes *them* more important.

If you ask someone who seems to have everything how he or she feels, you'll hear that it's lonely at the top. This doesn't mean it isn't worth it to strive for leadership positions at school. Just be warned that if you think you won't be happy until you have power and position, you're in for a disappointment.

The Bible warns us about some other things that don't bring genuine happiness. You can read about them in **1 John 2:16. For all these worldly things, these evil desires—the craze for sex, the ambition to buy everything that appeals to you, and the pride that comes from wealth and importance—these are not from God. They are from this evil world itself (TLB).** Notice how these bad things take some very good things and twist them around to hurt us: the *craze* for sex, the ambition to buy everything that appeals to us (selfishness), the pride of wealth and importance. There's nothing wrong with sex between married people. It's not wrong to buy something nice for yourself. And it's not wrong to know you are important to someone. The Bible is simply urging us not to let these good things get out of hand. Stay in control, and the devil can't control you.

It's better to have one or two loyal friends than a whole classroom of fair-weather acquaintances. To be content with the good friends you have makes everyone happier—especially you!   **Nancy**

Jan 8

Alphabetical Confusion

"I am the Alpha and the Omega," says the Lord God. Revelation 1:8, NASB.

How many letters are there in your name? Go ahead, count. Who has the longest name in your family? Now, you might have a long name, but I'm sure your name isn't as long as the daughter of Arthur Pepper.

Back in 1883 Arthur and his wife had a baby girl. That's not so unusual, but the name Arthur gave his little girl is. Her name was Anna Bertha Cecilia Diana Emily Fanny Gertrude Hypatia Inez Jane Kate Louisa Maude Nora Ophelia Quince Rebecca Sarah Teresa Ulysses Venus Winifred Xenophon Yetty Zues Pepper. Wow! What a name! If you'll notice, Arthur had this thing for the alphabet. The first letter of each of his daughter's names is the entire alphabet, in order, with the exception of the letter P. He put that one at the end because he had to—his last name was Pepper. Little Anna had it covered from A to Z! I wonder if her mother used all of her names when she was upset with her. By the time she finished all those names, Mom might have forgotten what she was upset about. I guess there are some advantages to having that many names!

Jesus has a name like that too. No, He doesn't have 26 names, but in the book of Revelation Jesus says that He's the Alpha and the Omega. You see, alpha and omega are the first and last letters of the Greek alphabet. (Greek is the language in which the New Testament was originally written.) What did Jesus mean by that? Well, I think He meant that He's everything we need. For every problem, He is the solution. For every question, He is the answer.

We need to learn to trust in Jesus more each day. We would have much less reason to worry if we realized that Jesus is fully in control. I think little Anna may have been made fun of for having such a long name, but I'm surely glad that Jesus has it covered, from A to Z. **Jim**

The Monkey Deal

"He [Satan] is a liar and the father of lies." John 8:44, NIV.
"I [Jesus] am the way and the truth and the life." John 14:6, NIV.

Oh, what a sweet little thing!" I exclaimed.
"Nice monkey," said the smiling Zairian man at the back door.
"I'll sell him to you—cheap."

Why does he want to make me such a great deal? I wondered. I started to say no, but hesitated.

"OK, you take him—free! 'Bye!" And he was gone, and the monkey was now in my arms.

Wow! I owned an exotic pet—free. Too good to be true!

I'll cuddle the monkey for a couple days, I thought, *and then humanely release him back into the jungle.* His tiny hands grasped my wrists, and his little head pushed against my stomach, and—

Uh-oh! Its owner hadn't told me the little creature wasn't housetrained! I tried to set the monkey down so I could clean things up, but he clasped my ankle like a wraparound magnet.

Ouch! The previous owner hadn't told me the monkey was a *biter,* either! I limped into the kitchen for a cleanup rag.

Sighting Missy, our kitten, the monkey screamed, unsuctioned himself from my ankle, and pounced. Then, quick as lightning, the monkey flew onto the counter, slurped up a bowl of pablum I was cooling for the baby, and dived through the pantry door. There he planted himself on a stalk of bananas. Between bites he continued screeching while I ducked the banana peels he slung through the doorway.

Yep! My slight hesitation to say no to the monkey's owner had left me with a big problem on my hands. The man at the back door had lied to me. For sure, this was no "nice monkey."

Satan is constantly knocking at our back doors with "cuddly" temptations. But staying close to our truthful Saviour will give us the wisdom to know a lie when we hear it, see it, or feel it—and to stay away from the devil's "monkey" deals that are *always* too good to be true. **Carolyn**

Carry Water to the River

Harvey was finding it very difficult to believe in God. He prided himself on believing only in things he could see and touch. "And I have never seen or touched God," he told his friend. Then one day they came upon a rushing mountain stream and stopped for a cool drink.

"Ah, isn't it wonderful how the earth keeps the water cool in its caverns, then pours it out freely for our refreshment?" Harvey sighed.

"I'm surprised to hear you say that," his friend replied. "You have not seen the source of this water, and yet you believe there is a place from which it starts? None of us has seen God, the source of life, and yet we must believe there is a place from which life starts, for you and I are just as real as this water."

Harvey smiled slowly. "I am humbled. My friend is smarter than I."

You have a choice whether or not to believe that God exists as a kind and loving God. Some stories in the Old Testament may make you wonder how He is kind and loving, but consider this: It's very likely we don't know the entire story. All we have to remember is that Jesus came and died on this scary earth to show us He loves us.

The Old Testament stories of killing and plundering just don't seem to make sense. Probably not until we reach heaven and talk to God in person will we understand. Until then we continue to believe the best about God, because He is our friend.

To "carry water to the river" means to do something totally unnecessary. It is totally unnecessary to try to convince another Christian that God loves us. It is totally unnecessary to mistrust God, who is the only Person who has the power to keep all of His promises. But you must understand that His promises are lofty and long-term more often than they are short-term. God's promises are that He hurts with you and He laughs with you. And someday He wants to take you to a perfect world.

The next time you get a drink of cool water, remember God created it for you because you need it. And remember that someday He will answer all your questions. There's a promise in **Proverbs 15:33** for believers: **Humility and reverence for the Lord will make you both wise and honored (TLB).**   **Nancy**

14

Jan 11

Rattlesnake in the Rafters

Flee the evil desires of youth, and pursue righteousness, faith, love and peace, along with those who call on the Lord out of a pure heart. 2 Timothy 2:22, NIV.

As I crawled through a hole into the darkened attic, I couldn't help feeling like an archaeologist peering into an Egyptian pyramid. Who knew? Maybe I'd discover precious gems that someone had hidden years before. I switched on the only electric light in the attic of the abandoned house I was exploring. A pale light washed over the middle of the floor but left the far ends of the room dimly lit. I walked to a barely visible pile of leftover insulation. As my eyes adjusted to the darkness, I noticed a loop-shaped object sticking out of the pile. I didn't know what it was, but I thought it might be something important, so I reached down to pick it up.

Now let me stop right here and say this: Always use a flashlight in dark places, and don't grab objects whose identity you are unsure of. I reached down and grabbed onto the loop-shaped object. As I did so, it moved and then tightened up. It shook and made a noise like someone was shaking a baby's rattle very rapidly. I realized I was holding on to a rattlesnake.

I'm not afraid of many animals, but snakes—especially poisonous snakes—scare me to death. I ran out of the attic, hyperventilating. I had actually grabbed a rattlesnake with my bare hand! It looked innocent to me because its head and rattle were lying between layers of insulation. Only the middle of the snake's body was exposed.

You know, Satan is like that. He makes himself and his activities look innocent enough, but what he has in mind is no game. He makes his offer look exciting, but hides the part that will hurt us. He wants to destroy us. Stay as far away from sin and Satan as you can. His bite can kill!

Jim

15

Jan 12

True-blue Love

In my Father's house are many mansions: if it were not so, I would have told you. I go to prepare a place for you. And if I go and prepare a place for you, I will come again, and receive you unto myself; that where I am, there ye may be also. John 14:2, 3.

Just as human beings have certain ways they show love to one another, so do birds. Working for days, the male bowerbird builds an elaborate nest in preparation for his bride.* When he finishes, he doesn't have some ordinary brown bird's nest. Oh, no! He has built a *mansion*—several feet long, about four feet high, and decorated inside with brightly-colored flowers and berries.

Even *after* he has moved his lady in, the "man of the house" continues bringing her gifts—feathers, pebbles, flowers, snail shells, beetles, and anything else that catches his fancy. The fascinating thing about his gifts is that each one is blue—the color of his true love's eyes.

But wait! He has yet to put the final touch on this architectural masterpiece. Locating just the right berries (blue, of course), he painstakingly colors the inside walls with blue juice. Talk about true-blue love!

Have you ever prepared a "mansion" for a new pet coming to live at your house? Remember how good you felt when your new puppy curled up in the basket bed you'd prepared for it? Or when the turtle slid onto the blue-green gravel in its new bowl? Or when the parakeet began talking to its reflection in the shiny mirror you'd placed in its squeaky-clean cage?

Remember the warm excitement of waiting for the day your pet would come to live with you? Jesus feels that same kind of excitement as He prepares right now for the day of *your* arrival to His home.

The satin bowerbird may go to a whole lot of trouble preparing a new home for the one he loves. But our loving Saviour went to the trouble of dying a cruel death in our place, so that we may someday occupy a customized mansion at His.

Now that's *true*-blue love!

Carolyn

---

*Alan Devoe, "Animals in Love," *Marvels and Mysteries of Our Animal World* (Pleasantville, N.Y.: Coronet Books, Reader's Digest Assn., 1964), p. 282.

Know One's Beans

In England many, many years ago children were taught how to add and subtract by using beans. Each child was given a handful of beans and told to work out a problem written on the board, using the beans to get the answer. A person who knew his beans was considered knowledgeable.

It seemed there was always one child who had a more difficult time "knowing their beans" and figuring out the problems than their classmates did. People said this child "doesn't know beans" about it. Perhaps you've used this expression. Now *you* know beans about it!

We are warned in Matthew 24:4, 5 that in the last days Satan will try to deceive us. He may claim to be Jesus. He may work miracles right before our eyes. So how can we know he isn't really Jesus? How can we know beans about it? *By the way he comes.* **Matthew 24:27** gives us a clue: **"As lightning that comes from the east is visible even in the west, so will be the coming of the Son of Man" (NIV).** Satan may come with clouds around him. He may have angels tooting horns. He may even use the people's belief in UFOs to fool them. But when Satan comes, pretending to be Jesus, every eye will not see him at the same time—only Jesus is able to be seen by everyone at the same time when He comes.

Some people may tell you that events on TV are seen by the whole world at the same time. I consider that a dangerous approach to the Second Coming. I don't expect to see Jesus coming on the evening news—I expect to see Him live and in person! Jesus said His coming would be like lightning that seems to stretch from the east to the west. His coming will not be something that can be created in a movie studio and shown on television. Satan simply cannot re-create the real Second Coming, and don't you let anyone tell you he can.

Do you "know beans" about Jesus' return? Read about it in the Bible and ask questions so you won't be fooled. It's important to know as many of Satan's tricks as possible. **Nancy**

Jan 14

Let's Have a Barbecue!

Let us not give up meeting together, as some are in the habit of doing, but let us encourage one another—and all the more as you see the Day approaching. Hebrews 10:25, NIV.

Have you ever barbecued anything on the kind of grill that requires you to light the coals first? Keeping the coals burning can be a frustrating job! Let me tell you my secret. It works every time. Of course, don't ever do this yourself—leave that to your mom or dad.

First, take a number 10 can. (That's one of those really big cans you get at the grocery store with fruit or vegetables in it that holds about a gallon of liquid.) After your family has eaten what's in the can, cut the bottom out so you can see through the can from top to bottom. When it's time for a barbecue, place the can on top of the grate, dump in the coals, and Mom or Dad—not you—should pour in the lighter fluid and light it. In 20 minutes or so you'll have a mass of hot, glowing coals. Mom or Dad will need to use some pliers to remove the can (it'll be very hot), then they're ready to barbecue those fresh ears of corn.

Why do the coals light so well and get so hot this way? Because they were all packed together. If you would take one of the hot coals from the rest of the group, it wouldn't be long before it would be out cold. Why? Because it needs the others to keep it hot.

Church is like that. There are times when we may not feel like going to church, but meeting with others who are on fire for God will help keep our faith on fire. If we remove ourselves from the group too often, our faith will grow cold. I think that's why Paul said not to forget about meeting together. Fellow Christians will help encourage and strengthen you, so your light won't go out.

Jim

Fool's Gold

I counsel you to buy from me gold refined in the fire, so you can become rich. Revelation 3:18, NIV.

Gold in Alaska! The news spread through the United States during the months of 1897. Ironsmiths abandoned their anvils and farmers forgot their ripening crops. Preachers left pulpits empty to join the wild-eyed hopefuls heading northwest to the Klondike gold fields of the Yukon.

But the word these gold-hungry people did *not* receive was that hundreds had perished in the previous cruel winter. They had traveled by ship to Alaska, then made the 32-mile trek over the Chilkoot Pass. Therefore, in 1897 the Canadian Mounted Police were allowing no one to remain in gold country until he or she had transported *1,150 pounds* of survival goods (requiring about 30 round trips over the 3,700-foot-high pass). These provisions were to help them make it through the harsh winter. The last half mile of the pass sloped up at a steep 45-degree angle, so steps (now known as the Golden Staircase) had to be cut into the mountain. During winter months prospectors even cut steps into the icy snowpack. That winter 22,000 gold-desperate people struggled over the pass again and again.

Not only did many of them perish, but the cruel loads they placed on beasts of burden killed many pack animals. To this day the bones of 3,000 abandoned mules and horses lie in a huge ravine below a nearby trail known as Dead Horse Trail.

How many of the goldseekers, who gave up so much—professions, homes, family, even life itself—do you think actually struck it rich? Very few. What fools! Throwing away everything—for nothing! Most prospectors became so exhausted and desperate because of the severe climate and living conditions that within a few years they sold their mining stakes at very low prices to a few enterprising businesspeople. And *these* people got rich, instead of the prospectors who had sacrificed everything.

God has a special message about gold for those of us who are living at this time in earth's history. (The name He gave us is Laodicean. You can read about us in Revelation 3:14-22.) Before we go chasing after the fool's gold this world has to offer, our generous Father wants us to know that only He can give us the kind of gold that lasts forever. The only kind of gold that will make us truly rich.   **Carolyn**

Jan 16

Under One's Belt

Abby will never go to Oregon's Multnomah Falls again without feeling at least a little uncomfortable. On the night of February 7, 1992, she and three friends were hunted like animals for seven hours.

The moon shone like a fluorescent disk in the sky. The four friends decided to see what Multnomah Falls looked like by moonlight. Everything was peaceful along the wooded walkway until they came to the bridge that spans the mountain stream. There seven men in hooded coats held guns to their heads and robbed them. Then, pointing their guns at the four teens, the robbers laughed and ordered them to start running, following them and yelling threats.

The teens ran until they thought they couldn't take another step. At last they rounded a corner in the trail and quickly stepped into the woods, hiding behind trees. For several hours the robbers played a life-and-death game of hide-and-seek, muttering threats all the while. When dawn broke the next morning, the teens cautiously made their way back down the trail to the lodge. Abby knocked on the door. What relief when she and her friends were welcomed inside by the restaurant staff!

Later, when interviewed for the *Oregonian* newspaper, Abby said, "I never thought that at age 18 I'd be saying all I wanted was to be with my mom and dad. But that's exactly who I wanted to be with the most. They make me feel so safe."

Abby and her friends will never forget their experience. It has become part of them, affecting their belief system and their values. Every experience you have affects you this way. To have something "under your belt" means it has become part of you, just as the food you eat becomes part of you. Jesus is the only supernatural being who has life's experiences "under His belt" too. You can tell Him your worries, concerns, and all your joys; He will understand. If you have trouble trusting people because of some experiences you've had, Jesus will understand. You can learn to trust again—that is the work of healing. Remember the promise of **Romans 8:28: "And we know that in all things God works for the good of those who love him, who have been called according to his purpose" (NIV).**   **Nancy**

Jan 17

Batter's Out!

Therefore, there is now no condemnation for those who are in Christ Jesus, because through Christ Jesus the law of the Spirit of life set me free from the law of sin and death. Romans 8:1, 2, NIV.

W hen I was 14, we lived on a farm. It was a great place to explore—all kinds of dark little rooms in farm buildings, animals hiding here and there, and plenty of woods to sneak around in and play commando.

One day my friend and I were exploring some of the old farm buildings. We went into a building with horse stalls, shut the door behind us, and suddenly heard a hissing noise. We turned around to see a very angry bat on the floor. He had pushed himself up on his wings and was hissing at us with fangs bared. We were pretty scared at first, but as we watched the bat we realized it wasn't going to attack.

I carefully stepped over the angry mammal and hurried into my house to find an empty mouse cage. Putting on gloves, I ran back to the horse stalls and gently guided the bat into the cage. I had done it! I'd caught a bat! Proudly I walked back to my house and showed my mom.

"You get that thing out of this house right now!" she screeched.

"Please, Mom, at least let me keep it on the porch," I pleaded. "I want to watch it."

She reluctantly agreed, and I spent the rest of the afternoon watching what seemed like a very lazy bat. It really didn't do much. The next morning it was gone. Somehow it had slipped through the narrow openings between the cage bars.

Some people think being a Christian is like living in a cage—no freedom; confined behind bars. In reality, Jesus sets us free; free from the cage of sin Satan would like to keep us in.　　　　**Jim**

Jan 18

Go, Team, Go!

His banner over me was love. Song of Solomon 2:4.

The year the Dodgers baseball team left Brooklyn, New York, to move west, I was one among thousands of junior high kids who came down with Dodger fever. I talked baseball, collected baseball cards, and even considered running away from home to become a bat boy (which really would have been something, since I was a girl)!

I'll always remember the first game Dad took me to: the Los Angeles Dodgers versus the Chicago Cubs. Dad bought me a triangular felt L.A. Dodgers pennant. When "the boys in blue" took the field, I cheered with thousands of other Dodger fans, waving the new pennant while my stomach tightened in anticipation. But no matter how much I yelled those first few innings, the Cubs—not my Dodgers—racked up the runs. I found myself wishing I could use my pennant like a magic wand to empower Duke Snider with a grand slam or Don Demeter with strikeouts for the next six batters. No such luck.

Yet God once did that very thing for the children of Israel! You can read about it in Exodus 17:9-16. During the land-of-Canaan pennant race, an enemy nation, the Amalekites, challenged the Israelites to fight. During the battle Moses stood on "the top of the hill with the rod of God" in his hand (verse 9). When Moses held it up, Israel prevailed (verse 11), but when he lowered the "pennant," the Amalekites pulled ahead. With the help of a couple other Israelite "fans" Moses kept the pennant up long enough for Israel to win the game. (By the way, the Dodgers won the game I went to, but without any help from my pennant.)

Did you know that God has a pennant—or banner—He has promised to wave over us right now on the playing field as we struggle against Satan's opposing team? That powerful pennant is His love for us. With a Supporter like that, "our side" can't help but win! (see Isaiah 59:19).

Carolyn

22

Fly in the Face of Danger

There once was a cobra who was the terror of a small village. Hoping to make things better, the holy man decided to visit the snake. The snake was no idiot. It knew it couldn't hurt a holy man, so it had to listen to his long lecture about how things had to change. Reluctantly it agreed to stop biting people.

When the villagers learned that the snake had stopped biting, they thought it was too old to fight anymore and threw rocks at it and jabbed it with sticks. Although the snake didn't retaliate, it was angry inside. When the holy man returned a few months later, the snake, tattered and exhausted, complained bitterly. "You and your ideas! Do you know what I've been through since I followed your advice?"

"Calm down," the holy man said. "It's true I told you not to bite anyone, but I didn't forbid you to hiss!"

The term "fly in the face of danger" is taken from the animal kingdom. Stories abound of insects and birds who disregard their instincts and literally fly in the face of their enemies. Sometimes young people fly in the face of danger too, and tempt themselves by making wrong choices. Maybe they start kissing each other and go too far, or hang out with kids they know are drinking or taking drugs. They may do other things just because their "friends" are doing them. God has some advice for us in **Genesis 4:6 and 7** about choosing to do what's right: **"Why are you angry?" the Lord asked [Cain]. "Why is your face so dark with rage? It can be bright with joy if you will do what you should! But if you refuse to obey, watch out. Sin is waiting to attack you, longing to destroy you. But you can conquer it!" (TLB).**

We can feel joyous if we do what we know is right. Unless we do what we know we *should* do, we'll experience dark, uncomfortable emotions. It's a choice we can control. What will you do when faced with an uncomfortable situation? Let others flog you, as the snake did? Or will you hiss and take a stand? Better yet, get out of there and leave those bad influences alone. **Nancy**

Jan 20

Bears and Midnight Snacks

"We have left everything to follow you!" Mark 10:28, NIV.

Backpacking in the mountains gives you exercise and a view of mountains, lakes, and trees that can inspire you. But the trip can kill you if you don't know what you're doing.

There's a story about a backpacker who was mauled to death by a bear. It happened in his tent in the middle of the night. The sad thing is the bear wasn't really after the man; it only wanted the food in his tent. It was a death that could have been avoided with proper planning.

It's important to store your food in a place where *you* won't be mistaken for lunch. At night most knowledgeable backpackers place their food in a bag, tie a rope to the bag, and hang it from a tree. That way the bear can't get it, and you won't be eaten for supper. True; you can't have your midnight snack in the tent. But would you rather *have* a midnight snack or *be* a midnight snack? You give up eating in your tent so you won't be eaten in your tent. It's called self-denial.

Sometimes we feel as though God is restricting us with commandments that say "Thou shalt not." However, God knows that certain things can destroy our lives. It may not be much fun going without your midnight snack in the mountains, but there's a very good reason for denying yourself.

Jesus often denied Himself for you and me when He walked this earth. He didn't really want to die, but He did it for us. When God asks us to deny ourselves, it's for a very good reason—a reason that makes the difference between life and death. I'm so glad God has warned us about these things, just as I'm glad someone warned me about bears and midnight snacks.
                                                                    Jim

Bungling Burglars

Be sure your sin will find you out. Numbers 32:23.

Many people think their crimes will never be found out, but here's what international police records show:

A French burglar interrupted his robbery to snack on cheese, biscuits, and three bottles of champagne he'd found in the absent family's refrigerator. Local police arrested him the next morning after the homeowners found him fast asleep in the guest bedroom.

A British burglar decided to steal money from the cash register of a Chinese restaurant. Climbing through a kitchen window, he fell into the cooling deep fat fryer. He crawled out, but found only about $40 in loose change—and promptly slid right into the arms of a waiting police officer.

Three Scottish burglars became stuck in the revolving doors of the Royal Bank of Scotland. After untangling themselves and regaining composure, they continued the burglary. When the head cashier laughed at their demand to turn over 5,000 pounds, the leader reduced his demand to 500 pounds . . . before reducing it to 50 pounds . . . before finally pleading for even a 50-pence piece. Then, deciding to show they meant business, one of the burglars leaped over the counter but fell to the floor, grabbing his ankle. The other two decided to split but got trapped—for the second time—in the bank's revolving doors.*

TV shows, such as *Unsolved Mysteries*, may give us the impression that people who are "good" enough at sin don't ever have to pay for their choices. We may be tempted to think, *How unfair that one person can cause all that misery and never get caught!*

Yet our wonderful and *fair* God has promised that one day all things will be made right, and each person will meet "what he has done" (Revelation 22:12, NIV). We know that those who continue to hurt others by their sinful deeds eventually *will* get caught—not just by God, but especially by their own choices. **Carolyn**

---

*Stephen Pile, "Law and Order," *The Incomplete Book of Failures* (New York: E. P. Dutton, 1979), pp. 58, 59.

Out on a Limb

Sara and Tim were enjoying a weekend camping trip in a remote area of Minnesota. As Sara prepared lunch at their tent, Tim hunted for firewood in the woods. Suddenly a bear attacked him, mauling his arm badly. He broke free and started to run toward the lake, then collapsed. Sara knew she had to distract the bear, so she grabbed the nearest kettle and began hammering on it. The bear paused to look at her, then, to her horror, came toward her.

She ran into the forest, thinking she would be safer in a tree than in the cold lake. The bear followed her. Swinging herself up into the branches of the nearest tree, she scrambled to the top. The bear followed her but, to her relief, stopped climbing before it reached her. Not wanting to go "out on a limb," for fear that would put her in more danger, she stayed still until the bear lost interest and lumbered back down the tree.

By then Tim had found the strength to wade into the water. Losing Tim's scent and being unable to reach Sara, the bear ambled into the forest, giving the couple time to break camp and paddle across the lake to a safer spot.

"Going out on a limb" means putting yourself in a vulnerable position. A treed animal who's "out on a limb" has no escape. The limb may break, or a predator may come after it. Sometimes we lie to save face or to avoid punishment, but lying doesn't make us feel safe. We can sometimes get away with being dishonest to people; but we can never lie to God. He knows our hearts. As it says in **1 Samuel 16:7, Man looks at the outward appearance, but the Lord looks at the heart (NIV).**

God is the only person you can be completely open with. You can tell Him you're feeling mad at Him, or that you don't feel sorry about something unkind you may have said to someone. You can tell Him where your heart really is, and He will still love you and accept you, because He made you. Most important, by becoming God's friend you will live a life you don't have to lie about. As you practice telling the truth, honesty will become second nature, and you'll respect yourself. Give it a try!   **Nancy**

What's a Billion?

With the Lord a day is like a thousand years, and a thousand years are like a day. 2 Peter 3:8.

How many zeros does a billion have? Before you answer that question, it makes a difference where you live. In Great Britain a billion has 12 zeros; in France and the United States a billion has nine zeros. Confusing, isn't it?

Then, of course, there are the metric and the English systems of measuring. In the metric system you use terms like liter, meter, and gram. In the English system of measurement you'll hear things like quart, yard, and ounce. Which one is the right system of measurement? Some think one is better, and some prefer the other. It seems that if you were taught one way, that's the way that seems easiest.

And don't forget there's 12-hour time and 24-hour time. If you keep time with the 12-hour system, you say it's 1:00 in the afternoon. If you keep time with the 24-hour method, you say it's 1300 hours. Now, are you all mixed up?

How does God keep track of time and numbers? To Him it makes no difference. God has always existed. He had no beginning and will have no end. A day is like a thousand years, and a thousand years are like a day. That's the Bible's way of saying that time makes no difference to God. He does things in His own timing. He fulfills His promises when it's best to fulfill them. He doesn't follow our calendars or schedules.

That means we need to learn to be patient. Sometimes God will work things out when we think He should, and sometimes He won't. We may wonder why God doesn't hurry up. We may question why He's taking so long to do what needs to be done. And sometimes He won't even do what we think would be the best thing.

God knows what's best for us, and He knows when the best time to do it will be. Sometimes it's difficult, but let's trust Him to do the right thing at the right time.   **Jim**

Jan 24

Parachuting Cats

Thank you for making me so wonderfully complex! It is amazing to think about. Your workmanship is marvelous—and how well I know it. Psalm 139:14, TLB.

Parachuting cats? You're kidding! But it's true. Two cats were "drafted" into the British Royal Air Force (RAF) in 1954 and made a test parachute jump—from an altitude of 350 feet.

It seems that deep in the Malayan jungle, mice were overrunning a British fort. Leaders of the garrison relayed an urgent call for help as the tiny rodents threatened to destroy the fort's food supply. So the RAF laid plans to airlift feline paratroopers into the "battle zone" to end the conflict over food supplies.

Cats have unique characteristics: they move silently, they are excellent predators, and they seem to live through dangerous encounters. (Some people say they have "nine lives.") These unique characteristics, however, have made them among the most misunderstood of any creatures in the animal kingdom.

For example, ancient Britons believed cats could cure blindness, while Russians used cat skins to treat stomach cramps. European sailors avoided sending a cat overboard, fearing that this action would result in shipwreck. During the Dark Ages—again because of their special characteristics—cats were associated with witchcraft, hunted down, and killed along with their owners.

Yet the very characteristics that made some people misunderstand cats (their silence, their predatory skills, their survival instincts) were the *very* characteristics that made them the perfect choice to execute a special mission for the RAF.

We don't know how many mice the parachuting cats actually caught, but one air dispatch officer involved with the operation described the cats as being "quite jolly about the whole thing."

Do you have a special characteristic? Even one that your classmates have misunderstood or made fun of, perhaps? Our loving Creator gave each of us unique characteristics. Maybe a characteristic of yours will some day be what makes *you* the perfect choice for one of God's special missions.

Carolyn

One-track Mind

A kindergarten class toured the Alpenrose Dairy in Portland, Oregon. They saw cows lined up for the milking machines. They saw the bottling room, where the cartons were filled with the foaming liquid, and the old museum, where the owners' collection of antique dolls and cars were on display. Throughout the tour one little girl kept looking down at her dress and smoothing it out, paying more attention to it than to the tour guide.

Then the group sat down in a cozy room and munched on ice cream and cookies. When the tour guide asked if they had any questions about the dairy, the little girl was quick to raise her hand. "Did you notice my new dress?"

Her dress was the only thing on her mind. You might say she had a "one-track mind." Like a train moving in only one direction, a person with a one-track mind is considered narrow-minded, obsessed with only one thought or opinion.

Sometimes we "one-track" our mistakes. We keep going over and over what we said "wrong" or what we forgot to do. We think that because we did that "wrong" thing, we are bad, and God can never love us.

Maybe you're angry because someone you trust has treated you unfairly. Is that wrong? Not for a survivor—just don't stay angry, because a simmering anger hurts you, not the abuser. Anger can separate you from God, and separation from God is considered a sin.

Read **Micah 7:18 and 19** to see what God says about survivors: **Where is another God like you, who pardons the sins of the survivors among his people? You cannot stay angry with your people, for you love to be merciful. Once again you will have compassion on us. You will tread our sins beneath your feet; you will throw them into the depths of the ocean! (TLB).** God "pardons the sins of the survivors among His people." You're a survivor! You're pardoned for being angry! Use that anger for energy as you heal, but find ways to release it, using your energy for good feelings. (If you can't stop feeling angry, please talk to a professional.)

How about having some ice cream today? And as you eat it, remember God's attitude toward you. He loves you, and that gives you permission to love yourself. **Nancy**

How Do You Like Your Eggs?

Blessed are you when people insult you, persecute you and falsely say all kinds of evil against you because of me. Matthew 5:11, NIV.

Do you have any idea why birds' eggs are round? Well, actually they aren't quite round, are they? And for good reason. If they were perfectly round they might roll away and smash if they were laid on a hard surface. That's why God designed them with one end smaller than the other. When they roll, they roll in circles.

Another reason birds' eggs are shaped like they are is so they're tough and sensitive at the same time. How can that be? Well, round objects are designed so they are difficult to break from the *outside*. Think about it: when an egg is knocked from its nest, it sometimes breaks if it's had a long fall, but some eggs fall from the nest without breaking. That's because of their shape.

On the other hand, hollow, egg-shaped objects are very easy to break from the *inside*. God designed the egg that way too. Just think of how you'd feel if you were a ready-to-hatch baby bird and were trapped inside an egg you couldn't get out of. God designed the egg so that with the gentlest of tapping the baby bird can break out when the time is right.

Did you know that God wants us to be both tough and sensitive like a bird egg? When soldiers put nails through Jesus' hands and feet, did He stop loving them? No! In fact, He asked His Father to forgive them. Jesus was tough because He endured their cruelty. Jesus was also sensitive because He continued to love them and asked His Father to forgive them.

Has anyone ever done something cruel to you? It's hard to take, isn't it? It's difficult to love that person as Jesus does. Let's ask God for the power to be an egghead—tough and sensitive at the same time. **Jim**

Holding Hands

I will help thee; yea, I will uphold thee with the right hand of my righteousness. Isaiah 41:10.

On a steep sideways slope of a cave trail, my feet began to slip in the thick oozy mud. In seconds I could be disappearing into the black ravine on my right, for no handholds existed along the slick wall to my left.

A guest on this adventure, I was midway in the single-file line of 20 Pathfinders and several adults. Suddenly we had to stop, and I was slipping off this dangerous section of trail. In a matter of seconds I decided how I would meet my death.

First of all, in order not to frighten the Pathfinders unnecessarily, I would wait until my feet were actually going over the edge, and then as quickly (and as casually) as possible say something like, "Kids, I'm going now." And just before my body hit the first shelf below and dropped out of sight for good, I'd call out one final time to my husband at the end of the line, "Honey, I love you!" Then it would be all over.

As my boots slid closer and closer to the ledge, from my throat came a plea for help that sounded something like "Who-o-o-o-oa!" In that instant—just ahead of me on the trail—little Trina turned around and calmly said, "Here, take my hand."

I made a desperate grab, and that small hand steadied me before both her hands pulled me quickly to the dry rock on which she was standing. Even after I was safe, my knees kept shaking. I just didn't want to let go of Trina's hand—ever.

Don't you imagine that's how Peter felt when, drowning in a stormy sea, he called out and "immediately Jesus stretched out His hand and took hold of him" (Matthew 14:31, NRSV) and saved him? (You can read the whole story in Matthew 14:22-34.)

When I was in a dangerous situation, Trina offered me her hand. Jesus is that kind of friend—offering His strong hand to help us through impossible situations we'd never get out of by ourselves. **Carolyn**

31

Jan 28

Pave the Way

We were the last visitors to leave Washington, D.C.'s Smithsonian Institution Museum of Natural History. It was getting dark as my parents stood on the sidewalk, trying to figure out how to get to the bus stop. Just then a tall man strode up, smiling broadly. "Good evening. Do you folks need some help?"

My dad returned the smile, though Mom was a bit hesitant to be too friendly to a stranger. "We're wondering how to get to the bus stop. Do you know?"

"Sure! But it's not the best area to walk in at this time of the day. Why don't I take you in my car?"

Cautious Mom frowned at Dad nervously, but he gave her a reassuring nod. Minutes later we pulled up in front of a lighted bus stop. Dad offered the kind man $5.

"No, keep your money," the man said graciously.

"But we'd like to give you something," Dad insisted.

The man scratched his head. "Well, I'm a security guard at the Smithsonian. Here's my card. The best gift you can give me would be to write a letter of thanks to my employer to put in my file."

The security guard must have known about the good advice in **Proverbs 11:18: The evil man gets rich for the moment, but the good man's reward lasts forever (TLB).** Five dollars was nothing compared to a written commendation from museum visitors. That could "pave the way" to a better job in the future, making things smoother in the same way that a paved road is smoother than a gravel road. And that's just what my parents did!

Right now you're establishing your future reputation, leaving a "paper trail" that follows you everywhere. Your birth certificate and Social Security number were the beginning of your personal paper trail. Then came grades, behavior, and attendance in school. Some companies won't hire people who didn't attend class faithfully. They figure that person might not come to work faithfully either. If your paper trail remains good, it will pave the way for endless choices and happinesses to come.

Make the choice to maintain your integrity—the confidence that you have nothing to hide or to be ashamed about. **Nancy**

Blood-bought!

In him we have redemption through his blood. Ephesians 1:7, NIV.

Bloodletting was a medical treatment used by doctors hundreds of years ago. If a patient had a disease, doctors thought the best way to get the disease out of the system was to cut the patient open and just let the blood run.

Doctors also thought there were fluids in the body that controlled the personality. If a person had a bad temper, they had too much of the wrong kind of fluid in their body. So the doctors would recommend that more blood be let out and figured the bad temper would just go away. And to keep worldly thoughts out of a monk's mind—you guessed it— let out more blood.

Actually, it wasn't the doctors who let the blood out. They only prescribed the treatment. Barbers—you know, the ones with the big razors—did the actual bloodletting. Have you ever seen the red-and-white-striped post at a barber shop? It's said this came from the time of bloodletting. The red stripes symbolized the blood; the white stripes represent the bandages that were used; and the knob at the end of the pole is like the little cup they used to catch the blood.

It seems sort of crazy that anyone would believe letting the blood out of a person would cure them of all these things. Many patients died because too much blood had been taken from their bodies. The supposed "cure" actually killed them.

Did you know there really is a form of bloodletting that works? It happened about 2,000 years ago when Jesus let His blood flow out for you and me. What did it cure? It was the only cure for the problem of sin. Accept Jesus' cure for you today and spend the rest of eternity with the one who let His blood out for you.   **Jim**

Jan 30

Bad Habit Busting

Greater is he that is in you, than he that is in the world. I John 4:4.

I don't know exactly how it became a habit. But I do remember blinking my eyelids during a fifth-grade spelling test and feeling them kind of "stick" to themselves before shutting normally again. It felt kind of fun, in a weird sort of way. On the walk home from school I asked Marilyn, "Do your eyelids ever, you know, *stick* to themselves?" The are-you-for-real look in her eyes made me quickly add, "Never mind."

That night at supper my little brother suddenly blurted out, "Look at sis! She's doing something really *bizarre* with her eyes!"

"I was noticing," Daddy agreed. Then he warned, "Making silly faces isn't a very good habit to have."

Habit? Surely a few harmless blinks haven't turned into a habit, I thought. Just then I felt an uncontrollable urge to do a big eyeball-squeezing blink. . . . *Whoa!*

A strange silence descended on our small math study group the next day. When I looked up, the others were just sitting there, staring at me.

"What are you doing with your eyes and nose and forehead?" asked Freddy.

At that moment I realized I'd allowed a very embarrassing habit to sneak up on me. It took me at least a week of remembering not to blink weird—and of my classmates mimicking me when I forgot—to break that habit.

The children of Israel had a bad habit too—allowing idol worship to sneak up on them. After worshiping God for a while, they'd try something "harmless" that nearby worldly nations were doing. And before they knew it, they were slaves to the pain, impurity, and violence that were all part of their bad habit. The only times they could ever break their bad habit were the times they cried to God for help.

Jesus is the only surefire way for us to get complete, lasting control of a bad habit. That's because when He was on this earth, He never allowed a bad habit to sneak up on Him—which makes Him the ultimate Expert on bad-habit busting.

Just as God gave the children of Israel strength when they asked, He'll give us the strength to bust our bad habits too.　　　**Carolyn**

Jan 31

Know Which Side of One's Bread Is Buttered

I took a quick bite of my toast, then, balancing it precariously in one hand, I pulled open the refrigerator door to take out the milk. At that moment the toast teetered and landed on the floor—buttered side down. Little bits of dirt and debris were embedded in the sticky butter (the dog had just walked in). So I had to settle for only a glass of milk for breakfast.

Knowing which side your bread is buttered on means you know what is, or is not, to your best advantage. If you come from a loving family, you know that running away from home would not be to your best advantage, since your parents are the ones who "butter your bread" and make things good for you. You take care of your relationship with them not only because you love them, but you want things to remain good for you. So you prevent anxiety for your parents, if you can.

Sometimes we don't appreciate what we've got till we lose it. Read **Isaiah 1:3** and see what God has to say about appreciation: **Even the animals—the donkey and the ox—know their owner and appreciate his care for them, but not my people Israel. No matter what I do for them, they still don't care (TLB).**

It seems the people of Israel didn't know which side of their bread was buttered. They didn't appreciate all the good things that came from God and became careless with that relationship.

Sometimes a person gets to feel that way about the Bible. You've heard the stories so many times; you know how they end. Maybe they don't even seem that miraculous anymore or "speak" to you as they do to someone hearing them for the first time.

Try this: imagine yourself in that situation. What if you and Daniel were kidnapped and taken to live in Saddam Hussein's palace? Would your faith in God survive? What if you saw animals walking into a huge ship as a man on the ramp, using a bullhorn, urged you to enter and be safe? Would you leave your family and walk in?

Make the Bible personal and you'll have a stronger relationship with God, the person who butters your bread. **Nancy**

The Most Annoying Bird

Do not revile the king even in your thoughts, or curse the rich in your bedroom, because a bird of the air may carry your words, and a bird on the wing may report what you say. Ecclesiastes 10:20, NIV.

There isn't a category in a book of world records for the most annoying bird, but if there was, my vote would be for the blue jay. Imagine a peaceful summer day. The sky is blue. The breeze rustles the leaves. . . . Suddenly everything is interrupted by the squawking and screeching of a blue jay. There's no doubt that the blue jay is one of the prettier birds in the neighborhood, but it's all spoiled when it opens its mouth. It annoys people and other animals. I've seen blue jays run other birds out of their nests, cause squirrels to move to another tree, and ruin a peaceful afternoon for a sleeping human being.

Did you know some people are like blue jays? They interrupt other people's conversations; they have to know everybody's business; and often they make a nuisance of themselves. Oh, they probably don't mean to. But if they'd do more listening than talking, and tune in to other people's feelings, they might see some of the harm they do. It's a shame, but you have to be careful about what you say around these people. You may find out that your words are being broadcast all over town.

But rather than hate people who gossip, you need to do three things. First, make sure that *you* don't gossip. Gossiping can ruin your reputation, as well as others. Second, it may be difficult, but being honest with gossipers may help them stop hurting themselves and others. Let them know, in a kind way, they've hurt you with their words. Third, pray. Pray for those who hurt others by gossiping, and pray for yourself. Pray that you won't be a blue jay by sticking your nose in other people's business and broadcasting it all over town. Gossiping is annoying, and it hurts. Don't do it yourself, and help those who do to stop.   **Jim**

Cave Bait

Your words are a flashlight to light the path ahead of me . . . I will obey these wonderful laws of yours. Psalm 119:105, TLB.

Everything had seemed just fine until their only flashlight went dead, leaving them in total darkness. The three friends had told no one they were going to explore caves that afternoon. And now, deep in a cavern chamber, they huddled together, attempting to warm themselves over a tiny fire they'd lit with a match one had found in his pocket. The only fuel they had for the fire was their one rope and the shirts off their backs.

In vain the boys raised their eyes, searching the murky atmosphere for an exit passage. Then the flickering flames consumed the last fibers of the rope, faded into a short-lived glow, and died, plunging the boys into dank, silent darkness.

The three shivering spelunkers, clad only in jeans and tennis shoes, were actually well acquainted with the basic rules for safe caving:

1. Never cave alone.
2. Always tell someone where you're going and when you'll be back.
3. Take three light sources per person on any caving trip.

But being in a hurry to start exploring, the three cavers hadn't bothered to consider the consequences of their choices. And by not prethinking the consequences, the young explorers had become "cave bait."

When the cavers didn't come home that night, the worried families notified the authorities. Since the boys had previously gone caving together, search-and-rescue volunteers began searching in surrounding caves. Then, two days after the missing persons report had gone out, the persistent rescuers located and rescued the hypothermic, nearly dead spelunkers.

The Bible contains many stories of people who, like the three cavers, chose to turn away from God's "safe caving" rules and ended up in darkness. Samson experienced the darkness of being blind; Jonah found his darkness in the belly of a whale; and Lot's wife looked back into the darkness of death.

Long ago our far-seeing God prethought the consequences of our poor choices. That's why a choice to cooperate with Him in keeping His loving law enables us to avoid becoming "cave bait" and to walk safely in the warmth of His light.   **Carolyn**

Feb 3

You Catch a Lot of Fish in Troubled Waters

My sons, Marc and Dave, had been fishing for almost a month in a large pond not far from our house. They'd had enough "bites" to keep them coming back. Sometimes the bites were curious toads; sometimes they were catfish with stinging tentacles. Still, the boys returned to the pond, hoping to catch the elusive sunfish that only experienced fishermen seemed to catch.

One particularly gray day they were surprised to find some of these fishermen at the pond. They thought that fishing was done only on sunny days. So when rain began to fall, the boys wrapped up their lines.

"Going so soon?" the fishermen asked.

"Well, yeah; it's raining!"

"You catch a lot of fish in troubled waters," one old man said sagely.

"What do you mean?"

"When it's cold and rainy, the fish come up to the surface of the water, where it's warmer. They'll bite at just about anything when the rain confuses them."

So the boys stayed and caught their first sunfish.

Have you been fishing in troubled waters lately? Even though things may be troubled all around you, something good can come out of it if you look for it. Read **Luke 21:34 and 35** to find out God's warning to people who get too absorbed in living down here on earth: **Watch out! Don't let my sudden coming catch you unawares; don't let me find you living in careless ease, carousing and drinking, and occupied with the problems of this life, like all the rest of the world. Keep a constant watch (TLB).** People who are living in "careless ease" will be caught, unaware, by Jesus' coming. Others will be occupied so completely with the troubles of this life that they won't expect anything good to happen. They'll be caught too.

Christians, on the other hand, have the peace of knowing that no matter how horrifying things can get in this life, something good is going to happen after the awful stuff is over. Looking for the benefits of troubled waters is the attitude that makes life an adventure, not an endurance test.

Nancy

38

Books, Books, Books

Jesus did many other things as well. If every one of them were written down, I suppose that even the whole world would not have room for the books that would be written. John 21:25, NIV.

I like books. But I don't like them as much as Joseph Feldman did. One day there was a fire in Joseph's New York apartment building. After the fire department had put the fire out, they checked all the other apartments in the building to make sure it was completely out.

During their inspection the firefighters came to check Joseph's apartment. When they walked through the door, they would have fallen over if there had been a place to fall. Except for a two-foot-wide path, every space was taken up by books. They were in the sink and the bathtub, on top of the stove, and everywhere else a book could be put. In all, there were more than 15,000 books in Joseph Feldman's apartment. Joseph simply liked to read.

Now, 15,000 books is a lot of books, but there are a whole lot more books than that in the world today. There are millions of books. The most important one of all is the Bible. For me, the most exciting books of the Bible are the Gospels: Matthew, Mark, Luke, and John. They tell us the story of Jesus, but they don't tell us everything. Why not? Because there wasn't enough room. In fact, John says there wouldn't be enough room in all the books in the world to tell us about all the good things that Jesus did here on earth.

The story didn't end there, either. Jesus died, rose again, and then went to heaven. Now He's preparing a place for us to live with Him. I think I'd get pretty tired if I had to read all the books in the world, but fortunately you and I have the opportunity to spend eternity with Jesus. He'll never run out of time to tell us all the stories of how He lived and died for us!   **Jim**

Caught in the Clutch

Little children, let no man deceive you. I John 3:7.

The outer wall of the Department of Motor Vehicles building approached at sickening speed. The DMV driving examiner in Auburn, California, threw his arms protectively about his head as Helen, a woman taking her driving test, crashed through the wall into the building. She had failed her driving test within the first five seconds. Why? Because she had confused the gas pedal with the clutch.*

Beatrice, a driver's license candidate in Guilford, England, made the same mistake a year earlier. When Beatrice confused the clutch with the gas pedal, she and her examiner soon found themselves sitting in the River Wey. The two managed to climb onto the roof of the car to await rescue.

After the rescue the poor examiner went home in a state of shock with the testing clipboard still clutched tightly in his hands. Beatrice, however, wasn't as ruffled. After being pulled onto shore she asked, "So, did I pass the driving test?"

Can you imagine someone going to a driving test without knowing the difference between the clutch and the gas pedals? Oops! I almost forgot that when Dad first started teaching me to drive (in an old stick-shift World War II-vintage Jeep) I complained, "But those two pedals look exactly alike!"

Satan does everything he can to get our foot off the gas pedal during our drive to God's kingdom, and to go for the clutch—which would send us coasting in the opposite direction. One way he does this is through certain magazines, TV shows, and movies, suggesting there are no *real* rights and wrongs—that it's all the same difference. Jesus foretold that in the end-times this deception will be so bad that "if it were possible, even God's chosen ones would be deceived" (Matthew 24:24, TLB).

Being well acquainted with God's *unchanging* Bible truth is the only way not to get caught in the clutch.   **Carolyn**

---

*Anecdotes from Stephen Pile, "Off Duty," *The Book of Failures* (New York: E. P. Dutton, 1979), p. 39.

In the Long Run

A college professor was puzzled when a certain student enrolled in his algebra class for the fourth year in a row, though she had passed the course the first time she took it. "Why do you take my course every year?" he asked her.

"Because it gives me security," she said. "I'm so tired of arguing about everything with my roommates and discovering that what I learned in biology last year is already out-of-date, along with everything else. I just needed something in my life that was constant."

"What do you mean?" the professor asked.

"Two plus two equals four," she replied. "Nobody can argue about it; nobody can change it. Two plus two will always equal four."

Recently I went back to college. One of my classes was algebra. I was reminded that when multiplying a negative number by a negative number, the answer is a positive number. That reminded me that God is a mathematician: doesn't the Bible promise us that negative things will work out positively in the end—in the long run? People who endure difficult situations in life learn to keep plodding along like a long-distance runner who conserves his energy till the end. If he drops out too soon, he'll never know the thrill of finishing. And when life's race is over, and we know the end from the beginning, we'll know that in the long run God can be trusted. All our negatives can turn out positively if we give God enough time.

Whenever you see numbers today, remind yourself that there's a lesson to be learned in the darkest of situations. Sometimes the lesson is simply that the things of this world are second in importance. If you take the attitude of "living on purpose" and trying to discover something helpful about each of your challenges, you reduce the feeling of helplessness. "What can I learn through this challenge?" is better for your emotional health than "Why is this happening to me?"

God wants you to steer your life in the right direction, whether or not you can see over the top of the next hill. Just keep going His way, and it will turn out positive in the end. King David learned to live that way. Read about how he bolstered his courage in **Psalm 91:2: I will say of the Lord, He is my refuge and my fortress: my God; in him will I trust.**

Nancy

Quick, Call 911!

"Now is the time for judgment on this world; now the prince of this world will be driven out." John 12:31, NIV.

Jim was getting to bed late one summer night. As he was about to start his journey into dreamland, he heard the sound of breaking glass. Looking out the back window, he spotted a figure coming from a shed in the back lot of the school next to his yard.

Moving quickly from the bedroom to the dining room, he dialed 911. The operator asked for Jim's name and what she could do to help. "I'd like to report a burglary in progress." (Jim had always wanted to say those words. They sounded very police-like.) The operator asked for the address and told Jim to stay on the phone until the police arrived. Jim watched as the man moved across the parking lot, carefully wrapped a shirt around his hand, and smashed the gymnasium window. Reaching in, he opened the door and disappeared.

Getting a little braver now that the burglar was in the building, Jim handed the phone to his wife and quietly crept outside just as the police came running into the parking lot. Jim moved quickly toward the officers and told them that their man was in the gym. The police crouched around the gym door, pulled their guns, then quickly moved into the building. Five minutes later the men in blue emerged from the gym with the handcuffed suspect. How had they caught him? Jim wanted to know. It turned out to be a not-so-exciting story.

When the police arrived on the scene, everyone in the neighborhood, awakened by the commotion, seemed to be afraid that there was a burglar in the area. But the big bad burglar was hiding in a cupboard.

Did you know that Satan is a lot like that burglar? When Jesus came to die for our sins, He did what was necessary to set us free from Satan's chains. Satan has lost the battle, so let's act like children of the King; children of King Jesus, who is victorious over death and has sent Satan running.

Jim

Letting Go

I count all things but loss for the excellency of the knowledge of Christ Jesus my Lord. Philippians 3:8.

Not with all those balloons are you riding in my cab!" shouted the frustrated taxi driver. "We'd have an accident."

Reluctantly Harvey released three balloons.

"OK," agreed the cabbie. "Get in. Where to?"

"The dock," answered Harvey, squeezing into the back seat with his remaining balloons.

As a child Harvey had two loves: ships and balloons. His dream in life was to meet the captain of a ship and sail with him. But Harvey had a problem. Even as an adult he never went anywhere without a bunch of balloons. Eventually Harvey landed a job in a toy store. One day Harvey learned he'd won a contest. The prize? A week's trip on a small cruise line! On the day he was to sail he left his apartment, clutching a suitcase in one hand and the strings of a week's worth of balloons in the other. Those balloons were what had caused the argument with the cabbie.

Once aboard ship Harvey's balloons kept him from going down the narrow hallway to his luxurious stateroom. So he slept up on deck that night. The next morning a dew-covered Harvey tried to enter the dining room for breakfast, but the waiter informed him he couldn't come in with his balloons.

Then a junior officer approached him. "Excuse me, sir, are you Harvey Hiscock?"

Harvey nodded his head weakly.

"The captain requests the honor of your presence at his table this week and wants to do anything he can to make your voyage a good one."

Harvey felt a stab of joy shoot through him

"Of course," continued the officer, "you can't bring your balloons. They'd get between you and the captain."

Know what? You and I are Harvey, and the worthless sins we hold on to can keep us from getting close to Jesus, our patiently waiting Captain.

Paul said that everything in this world is worthless compared to knowing Jesus. I guess that means that if Harvey and you and I let go of our balloons, we'll have nothing to lose and everything to gain. **Carolyn**

43

Trade Off the Orchard for an Apple

Everyone could see that Jake's girlfriend, Kelly, was making all his decisions—who his friends could be, what he should wear, how he should spend his money—and Jake did it. Before long Jake's only friend was Kelly. He was in danger of flunking several classes, and his dreams of going to college were replaced with dreams of touring the country on motorbikes with Kelly after he graduated from high school.

Jake's parents pleaded with him to wake up. "Don't trade the orchard for an apple," they said. "Don't trade the larger, more valuable thing (your future happiness) for the smaller thing (your friendship with one person)."

One day Jake came home to find his mother on her knees in the living room, her face buried in her Bible, crying. Seeing her in such obvious distress startled him. He suddenly realized how much his life had changed, how little happiness he felt. How could he get back the friends he had dropped? What would Kelly do when he broke up with her?

He had to try. First he showed up at a church-sponsored volleyball game and began to reconnect with his old friends. Then he told Kelly he'd changed and thought it was best they make other friends. When Kelly said she'd kill herself if he walked away, Jake told her, "I'm not worth killing yourself over. But if you really feel that way, you need to talk to a counselor."

Jake felt a strange sense of emptiness, yet he knew it was the right thing to do. His mother advised him to take one day at a time, to think of his loneliness as tissue paper he could step through by reaching out to others. Every day he found one thing to look forward to—a favorite food, a walk in the sun, a phone call to a friend, a special song to listen to, a chat with his favorite teacher. And in a matter of weeks his feelings had changed from despair to hope.

It's important to remember that feelings come and go; each one is temporary. **Matthew 6:34** is not only comforting, but a wise way to live your life: **"Don't be anxious about tomorrow. God will take care of your tomorrow too. Live one day at a time" (TLB).**   **Nancy**

What's Under There?

It is God who arms me with strength. 2 Samuel 22:33, NIV.

Did you ever wonder what was under a camel's hump? Do you think that's where it carries extra clothes for long trips? Or maybe it's like a trunk where the camel's owner keeps extra camel shoes. Some people think the camel stores water there for long trips through the desert. Well that's close, but not quite the truth. Do you give up?

Actually, camels have a whole bunch of fat under those humps. A chemical process in the camel's body allows the camel to change the fat into water. Because of this process the camel can survive for as long as 17 days without water in the dryest of deserts. When the camel is really thirsty and has gone for many days without water, it can drink 25 gallons of water in about 10 minutes and fill its tank back up. Amazingly, God has given the camel the power to survive in the worst of conditions.

Job was a man in the Bible who had a pretty good life—that is, until disaster struck. He lost his servants, his animals, and even his family. As if that wasn't bad enough, Satan caused Job's body to be covered with painful sores from the top of his head to the soles of his feet. How could anyone take all that? Job's friends and even his own wife didn't understand. They thought Job should just give up on God. But Job wouldn't give up. He said if he was thankful to God in the good times, then he would continue to serve Him in the bad times. When Job chose to be faithful to God, he was given special strength from heaven.

Sometimes hard times will come to you and your family. You might even wonder how you can possibly survive. Don't worry; in heaven, like in the camel's hump, there's an extra supply of strength. God will give you all you need if you'll only choose to be faithful to Him.   **Jim**

Houn' Dawg

And we know that all things work together for good to them that love God. Romans 8:28.

He was just a stray black "houn' dawg" pup that someone took in. And when the family moved out of state onto a large ranch, Sam seemed to think he was in a sort of dog paradise with dozens of acres to roam. But Sam had one problem—he roamed too far.

Being the friendly sort, he liked to drop in on the neighbors. One Sabbath afternoon, when Sam's master was sitting on the front porch reading his Bible, Sam slipped away. Soon he was back with a woman's shoe in his mouth.

Sam's master returned the shoe and apologized, then returned home to his Bible reading. An hour later he looked up to see Sam rolling on the front lawn and tossing another shoe up in the air. This one was a man's shoe.

After scolding Sam, they both went to return the shoe. The neighbor's daughter approached Sam's owner and said, "One time you invited us to go with you to your church on Saturday. I want to go sometime."

"Anytime you want to go!" answered Sam's master.

As the months passed, Sam learned not to bring home the neighbors' shoes. But you know what? They kept showing up on Sam's front porch anyway—with the owners in them! For after attending Sam's master's church a few times, the neighbors decided to take Bible studies.

Eighteen months after Sam stole that first shoe from the neighbors' house the young woman to whom it belonged was baptized into the Seventh-day Adventist Church. Five months after her baptism her father, the owner of the second shoe Sam had stolen, was baptized, along with his wife.

And Sam hasn't stolen one shoe since!

Carolyn

An Empty Kettle Makes the Most Noise

Two painters once had a contest to see who could best produce on canvas his impression of what peace means. Thinking this an easy win, the first painter went quickly to work, sketching a mountain lake surrounded by graceful trees. Two birds winged their way across the sky. "This is peace," he said.

The second painter chose a much different scene. He portrayed a massive waterfall, thundering over gray rocks before crashing into the churning waters below.

"This is peace?" the judges asked skeptically.

Then the artist added the final touch: a flowering apple tree branch that bent out over the water. In a crook of the branch a mother robin sat peacefully on a nest, unaffected by the danger around her. The artist smiled smugly. "This is peace," he insisted. "Peace is the ability to rest in the Lord in spite of the noise and danger around you."

Everybody has times when so much is happening that we don't know what to do first. Homework piles up. Your room is a mess, and your mother's mad about it. Then your best friend calls to invite you to go skiing. You *have* to find peace in the middle of all this!

Here's what I'd recommend. Make a list, giving each task a time limit. Take three minutes to make your bed. Then find the floor by piling all the clothes on the bed. (That will make Mom feel better—but don't forget to finish the job before tomorrow.) Homework? Do the most difficult first, saving the easy stuff for when you're getting tired. Skiing with your friend might have to wait until another time.

"An empty kettle makes the most noise." Sometimes the best prayer might be "I don't even know what to say. Please come and be close to me. I need You." The Holy Spirit will pray for you, and in the middle of your chaotic life you can find peace when you lean on Him. **Romans 8:26 says: And in the same way—by our faith—the Holy Spirit helps us with our daily problems and in our praying. For we don't even know what we should pray for, nor how to pray as we should; but the Holy Spirit prays for us with such feeling that it cannot be expressed in words (TLB).**   **Nancy**

Reach Out and Touch Someone

But Jesus took him by the hand and lifted him to his feet, and he stood up. Mark 9:27, NIV.

What a beautiful day to canoe! I had canoed several times before and so had Edie, my partner, but she had never been the rudder person. (The rudder person sits in the back of the canoe and steers.) Edie told me she'd never done it before, but I figured it was a nice day to learn, so I sat up front.

We headed out on Michigan's Pine River. We had fun splashing the other canoers and watching the sights along the bank. Some time later I looked up to see a very angry-looking sky above. I remember thinking that it looked like it might rain, but I never thought about switching positions with Edie. I should have been more thoughtful, because it soon began to rain harder than I had ever seen before.

The river began to rise swiftly as the rain came down harder, and visibility was cut to just a few feet. As we came around a corner, we didn't see that we were headed straight for a logjam. The next thing I remember was being thrown out of the boat and into the raging water. I was sucked under by the strong current and pulled beneath the logjam. When I couldn't get my head above the logs, I swung my arms around but couldn't find anything but smooth, slippery surfaces. It occurred to me then that I might drown. "Lord," I prayed, "help me."

I swung my arms once more and found a branch I had missed before, one I could actually grab on to. As I pulled my way up, I was suddenly above the water, gasping for breath. It seemed as though God had reached down His arm and helped me out of the swirling waters.

God is reaching out His hand right now to help you. He wants to save you and take you through whatever circumstance you're in. Won't you reach out your hand and grab on to His?   **Jim**

Your Legs Just Crack Me Up!

But speaking the truth in love, may grow up into him in all things, which is the head, even Christ. Ephesians 4:15.

Here's the mathematical equation for friendship-building communication: Honesty + being sensitive to another's feelings = TACT.

Honesty without *sensitivity* is what my 3-year-old son demonstrated one day when he came upon me doing my exercises in gym shorts.

"Mom!" he blurted out. "Up to the knees your legs look like—well, just like regular legs. But after that they get big and fat . . . just like the rest of your body!"

Thanks a lot, sonny! That's honesty, but without sensitivity.

Now, sensitivity without *honesty* is what Tony told Richie after Richie hit only a single during the entire softball season.

"Hey, man, you just get better all the time!" But of course when Tony griped to the rest of the team that Richie had caused them to lose the playoffs (and word got back to Richie), hard feelings resulted—big-time. See how leaving out one of those necessary ingredients can cause long-term problems?

My Rwandan students in Africa were among the most tactful kids I've ever known. Once I tried to say a sentence in their language and then asked if I'd said it right (pretty certain that I'd massacred the grammar). Eliel answered, "Not too bad. It's just that *I'm* not in the *habit* of hearing it *said* like that."

Then there was Cassie, who groaned inwardly when little sister Beth Ann interrupted her and best friend Sara.

"Can I play?" Beth Ann asked.

Cassie thought quickly and then answered, "Sure. I'm the mother, and Sara is the daughter. So you can be the maid—and guess what? This is your afternoon off!" And Beth Ann left happily for her afternoon off. Now, *that's* tact—sort of.

But you get the point, don't you? Tact. That's what the apostle Paul was talking about when he reminded us about "speaking the truth in love." Today, at home, why not apply the tact math equation and see if things don't add up just a bit easier than usual? **Carolyn**

Feb 15

Sit Tight

A man once did something that angered the king so much he was condemned to death. At his hearing the man pleaded, "Let me have a year, and during that year I will teach the king's horse to fly."

Now, if it hadn't been for the king's silly pride, the man wouldn't have had a chance. But the king was rather taken by the idea of having the first flying horse in the kingdom. So he agreed that the horse would be brought to the man's house every day for a year and be taught to fly. There would be a demonstration on the last day of the year.

The man was elated, but his friends worried. "What kind of deal have you made?" they cried. "Nobody can teach a horse to fly!"

The man shrugged. "A lot can happen in a year. The king may die. I may die. Even the horse may die, and the deal will be off. And if none of those things happen, it's also possible that maybe the horse *will* fly."

It's not clear what he meant by his last statement. Perhaps he intended to take off with the horse at a flying gallop and get out of the kingdom. Whatever, this man had learned a good attitude to take toward life: things can change if you give them enough time. Many of us need to learn to "sit tight," an old card game term that means we don't decide the outcome of the game before it's over. We play cautiously, tightly glued to our chairs, not giving up too soon, since things can change.

When we pray "Thy will be done," we give God the benefit of time too. Sit tight. God will work things out to our benefit *in the end*. Satan torments us now and brings pain and suffering, but *in the end* God's will is going to rule. And God's will is that you be with Him in heaven. Think about that flying horse. Remember to take the attitude that God's children *will* win in God's time. Sit tight and watch it happen. And pray Jesus' prayer from **Matthew 6:9 and 10: "Our Father in heaven, we honor your holy name. We ask that your kingdom will come now. May your will be done here on earth, just as it is in heaven"** (TLB).

Nancy

50

Be Devoted

Be devoted to one another in brotherly love. Romans 12:10, NIV.

One evening on my way home from the grocery store I found myself heading for a parked car on the side of the road, almost unable to steer away. Actually, my steering wheel would turn, but it was very difficult. Something was definitely wrong.

I discovered the next day that a long snakelike belt on the engine had come off. I drove down to the auto parts store. I figured someone there could take a quick look at my problem, sell me a part, and I'd be able to fix it. I really don't know anything about fixing cars, but I figured someone could just tell me what do to. I can follow directions, and I really didn't want to pay what the repair shop was going to charge me.

So I walked into the store, and the assistant manager, Gary, asked if he could help. I told him what my problem was, and we went outside to look at my car. We spent the next hour in nearly freezing weather, in the dark, with a flashlight, trying to put my belt back on. Gary didn't have to do that; he only sold car parts. I was freezing, but he didn't even have a coat on. When I tried to pay him, he wouldn't accept any money. Why did he do that for me?

The next day my next-door neighbor, Roger, who had noticed I was driving someone else's car, knocked on my door. "Somethin' wrong with your car?" he questioned.

I told him what had happened. "Let's go take a look at it," he said. And Roger spent the next five hours working on my car. Why did he do that for me?

I think I know why. Both Gary and Roger were doing what Paul said to do in Romans 12:10. Do you think I'll buy my parts from Gary in the future? Yes, I will! Do you think I'll help Roger whenever he needs help? Yes, I will! I guess God knows that kindness is contagious. What a happy place this world would be if we were all Romans 12 people.   **Jim**

Customized Witnessing

It is better not to eat meat or drink wine or to do anything else that will cause your brother to fall. Romans 14:21, NIV.

No, I didn't call you to the door," I said, perplexed, as Salathiel and eight other tall Africans stood in respectful silence on my front porch.

"Yes, you did, Madamu!" the school construction foreman insisted. "You looked at me through the window and waved your hand like this." He flopped his hand up and down from the wrist.

"I know I did," I answered, "but that was to just say hi."

"In our culture the way we say hi is to move a hand from side to side. Moving your hand up and down means 'Come here immediately!'"

I thanked Salathiel for the lesson in local customs and was very careful after that to wave my hand from side to side so I wouldn't be sending any wrong messages.

I learned about other customs too. For example, I avoided placing my hand in front of my mouth while I was eating. That would signal the cook that her food tasted bad. Waving to someone with my *left* hand would be an obscene gesture, but waving with *both* hands was a sign of great respect. As a woman, I did not jump across creeks, whistle, or climb a ladder, as those activities were reserved strictly for men and boys. My doing so in their presence would have given the message "I don't respect you."

My custom of American-style waving sent the wrong message to Salathiel and his coworkers. Likewise, we Christians can send the wrong message to others about what God is like. How? By what we wear, the entertainment we choose, and the things we eat and drink. Or even worse, by making poor choices in these areas we can actually discourage a fellow Christian who is struggling to do what's right.

Jesus took responsibility for us at the cross. Then He made us responsible not only for ourselves, but for those around us. That's why the apostle Paul cautioned us to customize our witness and not do anything that would cause someone to fall.   **Carolyn**

A Rift in the Flute

It was just a tiny crack in the body of her wooden recorder when Judy first noticed it—probably caused by temperature changes from all the trips she'd taken with the school band. At first it made no difference; the notes came out just fine. But when the crack became larger, the whole instrument was ruined. Judy couldn't control which holes the air escaped from; she could no longer make music.

When someone says there's a "rift in the flute," it means there's one flaw that affects the integrity of the whole thing. One tiny crack in Judy's flute affected her ability to play.

Sometimes we allow little things to affect our relationships with our friends and with God. When a friend chooses to do something with another friend sometimes, we may decide she doesn't like us. Is that fair? When bad things happen to us, we may be tempted to think God doesn't love us anymore—or that He doesn't exist. Is that fair?

What if everyone who became a Christian lived a charmed life, untouched by fear, hunger, or cold? Psychological studies have shown that the first generation that is brought out of fear and given peace and safety is very appreciative. But following generations, knowing nothing except peace and safety, think they deserve it and begin to fight with those who don't give it to them. Christians would lose the kindness and appreciation that characterizes Christianity. We would be Christians only for what we could get out of it. We would be Christians for the wrong reasons.

The best reason for being a Christian is that Christianity gives us hope, not hopelessness, so that our days on earth are mostly positive ones. God doesn't bring bad things to us. Read it for yourself in **James 1:13: Remember, when someone wants to do wrong it is never God who is tempting him, for God never wants to do wrong and never tempts anyone else to do it (TLB).** Put the blame where it belongs: on Satan. And when you hear flute music today, let that be the moment you lift up a silent prayer to God, telling Him you trust Him, even when Satan tempts you not to believe. Make the choice not to let Satan put a rift between you and God. You do have only one life to live, and your beliefs—your hopes—will determine whether that life is joyous or full of despair.

Nancy

Journey to the Center of the Earth

"No eye has seen, no ear has heard, no mind has conceived what God has prepared for those who love him." I Corinthians 2:9, NIV.

In the old movie *Journey to the Center of the Earth* a group of explorers discover a whole new world in the center of our earth. Now, you know from your science textbooks that the center of the earth is made up of rock and molten lava, but there were actually people back in the 1800s who believed there was another world down below.

Captain John Symmes was one of these people. In fact, he was so convinced that he went to the Congress of the United States. He tried to persuade our country's leaders to give him money so he could start on an expedition to find this other world. He asked for a ship and a few courageous scientists to come with him to the North Pole. Once there, he believed he would find a hole in the ground that would lead them to this unbelievable new world. Even though Congress defeated his plan, there were still 25 people who voted for the Captain.

We know there's no world in the center of our earth, but there is another world none of us has ever seen. Think of the great time you and I can have exploring heaven! It'll be unbelievable, but it'll be real! We don't have to go to Congress to get permission to go. All we need to do is to give our hearts to Jesus and accept His gift of salvation. He'll save us and change us every day to be more like Him.

I've always wanted to be an explorer. You and I can explore the most exciting new world ever. Trust in Jesus today, and get ready for the journey.

Jim

Don't Get Burned!

There is a way that seemeth right unto a man, but the end thereof are the ways of death. Proverbs 16:25.

A man's up there!" screamed frenzied onlookers. "There's a man on the third floor of that burning building!"

A bucket brigade quickly passed pails of sloshing water along the line from the horse-drawn water wagon to the end nearest the burning boardinghouse. Firebells rang and horses neighed as everyone within smoke-smelling distance rushed to the scene.

"Why, that's old man Jenkins up there!" someone yelled. Jenkins's jerky gestures and lack of balance made it obvious he'd had his nose in the wine bottle again.

"Can you come down the inside steps?" a firefighter called up.

The man on the balcony seemed not to understand.

"Jump, man!" Several volunteers, shielding their faces from the intense heat, stretched a wool blanket between them as a landing spot.

Old man Jenkins just shook his head.

"Hey, Jenks!" roared Billy, Jenkins's most frequent drinking buddy. "I gotta idea that'll git ya down. Catch this!" He threw the weighted end of a rope up over the railing of the third floor balcony.

Jenkins dove down and came up triumphantly with the rope's end. The crowd waited in eager anticipation.

"All right, ol' buddy boy," Billy yelled, swaying slightly, "tie the end there 'round yer waist."

With trembling hands, old Jenkins tied the rope about his waist.

"Now sit on the railing, and I'll git ya down!" Billy hollered. True to his word, Billy yanked on the rope—and pulled him down! (Or so goes the *fictitious* story by American humorist Mark Twain.)

The Bible cautions that people get burned when they leave God out and live life according to what seems "right" to them. Daily Bible reading will show us the clear difference between "the ways of death" and *God's* right way.   **Carolyn**

55

Feb 21

Hand on the Torch

Before there ever was an Olympics race, the Greeks enjoyed relay races with lighted torches. How exciting those races must have been at dusk . . . powder clouds of dust puffing around the runners' feet, flickering yellow torch flames being pushed back by the wind. And then the moment—that critical moment—when, without breaking stride, one runner passed the torch to the other.

I was a regular relay racer at school. And from a few heartbreaking experiences I learned that "passing on the torch" is a finely tuned skill. There is a point at which the runner who receives the torch must start running, even before her teammate has approached. I can still remember the feel of the gravel spitting beneath my shoes as I took off, one hand held behind my back to receive the torch. I knew my teammate was approaching by the sound of her breathing, her feet pounding the track. My feet pounded in the same cadence, and I opened my hand without looking back. Then she was right behind me, pressing the torch into my hand. Only when I had a good grip on it did I pick up speed, imagining my feet like pistons, carrying me to the finish.

What does Jesus say about passing on the torch? Read **Mark 1:17: Jesus called out to them, "Come, follow me!" (TLB).** Jesus wants us to follow His example. He wants to pass on the torch of integrity. To do so we must follow in His footsteps, matching our lives to the cadence, the rhythm, of His. By having worship, your parents or teachers are passing on the torch. By church attendance and morality, they teach you. By ethics and example, you learn. Don't drop the torch. Keep your focus and hold on to the torch until your race is over and Jesus says, "Well done!"

Nancy

Hide-and-seek

Now it is required that those who have been given a trust must prove faithful. I Corinthians 4:2, NIV.

I've always liked to play hide-and-seek. I especially like to play manhunt. Manhunt is hide-and-seek played outside at night. I used to pretend I was a spy. It was fun hiding under bushes and up in trees. It's like being invisible. My friends could walk right by me and never see me. That's what was fun about playing at night.

Did you know there's a kind of lizard that can hide in bushes in broad daylight and never be seen? It's the chameleon. God gave the chameleon the ability to change the color of its skin when it needs to hide from enemies. It can become yellow or cream, green or dark brown. The chameleon can even produce spots on its body if it's sitting on a spotty background. Pretty amazing, isn't it? Changing colors can save a chameleon's life. Just as my friends walked right by me when I was hiding in a tree at night, a chameleon's enemies walk or fly right by because it blends into the scenery.

Even though changing colors to hide is a good thing for the chameleon, it isn't a good thing for you. Oh, it might be fun when playing hide-and-seek, but a Christian should always show his or her true colors wherever they might be. We ought to be the same kind and loving people whether we're at church, at home, or playing with our non-Christian friends down the street. Jesus was that way. He showed love to everyone He met, and He always stood up for what He believed, no matter who He was with.

That's pretty hard to do sometimes, isn't it? In fact, without Jesus it's impossible. But as you and I learn to trust in Him more, He'll give us the courage to stand strong. He'll teach us to always show our true colors.

Jim

Feb 23

God's Rope Swing

Let us strip off anything that slows us down or holds us back, and especially those sins that wrap themselves so tightly around our feet and trip us up. Hebrews 12:1, TLB.

The horses were going single file along a narrow trail running between a high mountain wall and a deep precipice. The bulging saddlebags bumped against the mountain wall. Realizing their danger, the riders finally unstrapped the excess baggage and watched their survival provisions roll over the edge of the precipice. When the trail became even narrower, the riders sorrowfully dismounted and continued on foot.

As the trail became little more than a skinny ledge, some flattened themselves against the wall, paralyzed with fear. Looking about her, Ellen White, a young woman dreaming she was a traveler in this group, noticed thin cords hanging down the smooth mountainside.

The travelers took hold of the cords, carefully testing their strength, and then began to rely somewhat on their individual cords—especially after abandoning their shoes, for the uneven ledge had become even narrower than the width of their shoes. When walking in their stocking feet caused them to slip too easily, they removed their socks as well.

Then their cords began to increase in diameter, becoming sturdy ropes.

At long last an exquisite green meadow appeared on the horizon. But separating the travelers from this paradise was a wide, dark chasm.

Then a comforting voice said, "God holds the cord." In that instant and without a word, Ellen's husband, next to her in the line of travelers, swung himself out over the deep pit into the beautiful fields beyond.

Ellen wrote about what happened next in her dream: "I immediately followed. . . . I was happy, perfectly happy."

In order to use God's "rope swing" (His strength and power), the travelers had to unload all their excess baggage. For some of us excess baggage might be pride, temper, or substance abuse. For others of us it's harmful TV, reading, music, or friendship habits. But whatever it is—and however sweet it seems—if we don't choose to let God help us unload it, it will make us too heavy to "swing" across to the other side. **Carolyn**

Between a Rock and a Hard Place

I am always amused by stories about "stupid" criminals. They always have some excuse for why they got caught. It never seems to occur to them that the most important thing to know is why they attempted the crime in the first place.

One such criminal was a burglar in New Haven, Connecticut, who brought along a tool to loosen the bolts from the bars of a first-floor apartment. Because he was in a hurry, and because he was small, he loosened the bolts of only two bars and held them open while pushing his shoulders through. That was where the trouble started. To his dismay, the bars snapped back into place around his waist and held him there, painfully tight.

He was indeed "between a rock and a hard place." Whatever happened next was going to be uncomfortable. He could either stay trapped and be in pain, or he could call for help and be arrested. Fortunately for him, a desk was within reach, and on that desk was a phone. He dialed 911 and asked them to come rescue him quickly. As he was led away by the police, he excused himself for getting caught by saying it was his first burglary. Does that explain why he decided to steal? No. And isn't it more important to know why he chose to be a burglar than why he got caught?

So many people cause so much unhappiness to themselves and to others because they don't have a good answer to the question Why am I doing this? Why do you go to school? Is it so you can learn how things work in your world and be prepared to go to college and use your talents in a job that will be enjoyable to you and a benefit to others? Why do you put God first in your life? Maybe it's because of the promise Jesus gave us in **Matthew 6:33: "Seek ye first the kingdom of God, and his righteousness, and all these things shall be added unto you."** You put God first because with Him as your leader, you won't get between a rock and a hard place. With God there is no entrapment; only good endings.

Nancy

Feb 25

New Toys

When I was a child, I talked like a child, I thought like a child, I reasoned like a child. When I became a man, I put childish ways behind me. I Corinthians 13:11, NIV.

I still remember it. It was red and shiny and had a white metal ladder attached to each side. I was 8, and it was a brand-new toy firetruck that I had saved my money for. I had a great time playing with it.

I can remember some of my other favorite toys too. I wanted to be a cowboy, so my grandma bought me a toy cowboy rifle. When I pulled the trigger, a little cork popped out of the end of the rifle. And then there was my monkey. It was so worn out that the feet and hands had to be attached to the rest of the body with safety pins.

I don't even know where my old, most favorite toys are now. Somehow they don't seem very important anymore. The toys that seem most important to you now won't seem important to you either when you get older. That's because as we get older we put away our toys. Other things become more important in our lives.

You are still a child, but the time will come when your toys won't be so important to you.

Jim

Garbage Pit Princess

Oh, the joys of those who do not follow evil men's advice, who do not hang around with sinners, scoffing at the things of God. Psalm 1:1, TLB.

Look at the little princess in a church dress!" taunted Sandra.

"You mean the little baby! Betcha can't jump over this," teased Connie, her brunette pigtails flying as she sailed through the air.

In the days before garbage trucks picked up trash, the six families living on our lane dumped lawn clippings and household trash into the neighborhood garbage pit on the adjoining vacant lot. Every two weeks or so one of the fathers would set the trash ablaze, reducing it to a layer of grimy ashes.

Though I was scrubbed, shampooed, and dressed in a clean pink dress for Friday evening worship and supper, the voices of neighborhood children drew me into the backyard. They were daring each other to jump over the garbage pit—and doing it.

No 4-year-old likes to be called a baby. And Connie had glided so effortlessly over the hole. Maybe that pit wasn't as wide as it had looked the afternoon Daddy had showed it to me and warned me to stay away from it.

Watching the excited children take turns sailing through the air, I suddenly found myself near the edge of the pit. I wrinkled my nose at the sight of the used bandage and moldy cantaloupe rinds lying beside the blackened banana peels.

"What about it, baby? Afraid to try?" Harold sneered.

"I think the little princess in the church dress could do it," cooed Connie in an uncharacteristically sweet voice. Her sudden smile encouraged me.

"Nah, she's a baby," someone else said.

That did it! Taking a giant step backward, I ran toward the pit and jumped as hard as I could. The next thing I knew my legs were burrowing through decomposing garbage into two feet of black, powdery ashes.

Satan once tempted Jesus to jump from the top of a temple, telling Him He wouldn't get hurt (Matthew 4:1-11). But Jesus, remembering His Father's words, chose not to "follow evil men's advice."

By not joining others who hung around garbage, our Saviour kept Himself "clean." With His help, we can too. **Carolyn**

A Shot in the Dark

A long time ago a man we'll call Mr. Smith lived in an old house with a very squeaky front door. There was no way anyone could go in or out of that door without everyone else in the house knowing about it.

One night Mr. Smith was awakened from a sound sleep by the squeaking of his front door. He slid his hand under his pillow for the pistol he kept there and stealthily made his way to the stairs. It was dark in the stairwell, but not so dark that Mr. Smith couldn't see the shape of someone making his way up the stairs toward him. Mr. Smith pulled the trigger—a shot in the dark—hoping he wouldn't miss. He heard a shout as the intruder tumbled down the stairs, where he lay silent and unmoving. Only then did Mr. Smith turn on the lights. To his horror, he found his son lying dead at the foot of the stairs. His shot in the dark had been tragic.

To take a shot in the dark means making a decision in spite of missing information. It's risky; just as risky as shooting at something in the dark.

Do you believe in evolution, or do you believe the Bible's explanation that God created our earth? Is it easier to believe an eyewitness, who sees and knows everything that happens, or someone who bases an opinion on hearsay—a shot in the dark?

Where was God when creation happened? You can find out in **John 1:1: In the beginning was the Word, . . . and the Word was God.** God was an eyewitness to Creation—a participant. He saw it happen right before His eyes!

Evolutionists, on the other hand, base their theories on what "might have been." They are missing information. They weren't there at Creation. They didn't see it happen, so they're just guessing. And they even change their minds on some things they once presented as "facts"!

Who are the fools? Those who believe someone who takes a shot in the dark, or those who believe the eyewitnesses? When the sun goes down tonight and the world gets dark, close your eyes for a moment and smile. You can smile because God sees you everywhere—even in the dark. He's been there from the beginning, and He'll be there forever.

Nancy

Choose Me, Choose Me!

We ought always to thank God for you, brothers loved by the Lord, because from the beginning God chose you to be saved. 2 Thessalonians 2:13, NIV.

When I was growing up, I played baseball, hockey, football, and other games with the guys in my neigborhood. The way we usually chose teams was to pick two captains who would take turns choosing players for the teams. If you were chosen first, that usually meant you were good. If you were chosen toward the end, it meant that the guys didn't think you were a very good player. It seemed like everyone was saying, "We don't really want you to play, but since you're hanging around, I guess you can." Nobody wanted to be chosen last. The guys who were chosen last would usually do one of two things: either they would practice until they were able to play better, or they quit showing up to play.

I still play sports. It doesn't bother me anymore if I'm chosen last. One reason is that I know there are more important things in life than playing sports. The other reason is that I know that I'm Jesus' first choice. Did you know that you're His first choice too? He chose you and me to be saved. What a great honor! But someone had to be chosen last, and that Person was Jesus. He took our sins and became the player who was chosen last when He died for our sins. What an amazing thing Jesus did for us!

It's hard to be chosen last for a baseball or football game. Sometimes people can be cruel and even make fun of those who are chosen last. Just remember, whether you're chosen first, last, or somewhere in between, Jesus has always made you His first choice.   **Jim**

Mar 1

Rowing the Extra Mile

He who did not withhold his own Son, but gave him up for all of us, will he not with him also give us everything else? Romans 8:32, NRSV.

Fourteen-year-old Bizimana dipped his hand-carved oar into the waters of Lake Kivu, powering his dugout canoe onto the Rwandan shore. His solo canoe venture at an end, he stretched wearily, then picked up the precious bundle and started the climb toward home.

Bizimana saw his father, a quarter of a mile downshore, painstakingly sorting the catch in his fishnet. The boy knew his father would gather the still-quivering slivers of silver into a damp cloth to carry home for the visitors' supper. Waving, Bizimana clutched his precious bundle closer, and resumed his upward trek.

Around another bend in the distant shoreline Bizimana spotted his mother and older sister machete-chopping piles of skinny green reeds. Tonight the visitors, sleeping on the family's only bedframe, would have a 15-inch thick layer of fresh reeds under their cornstalk-packed muslin mattress. Bizimana continued upward with his bundle.

Just before he got to the sagging doorway of his parents' thatched-roof house, Bizimana noticed his younger brother and sisters on the adjacent hillside, bent over at their waists, sweeping excess dust off the hard-dirt trail with makeshift twig brooms. *The visitors won't get dirtier than necessary on our trail,* Bizimana thought. Carefully clutching the costly bundle in both hands, he stooped to go through the low doorway.

Late that afternoon another brother, who'd spent the day posted at a distant road, guided the weary visitors—my husband, our 4-year-old son, and me—along the twig-swept trail to the home of Bizimana, one of our students. During supper his family presented us with the precious bundle that had taken all their money and an eight-hour canoe trip to obtain—a loaf of fresh bread.

I don't know if any other family has ever worked so closely together and so sacrificially to enable me to get to their home and have a comfortable stay. Except for God's family in heaven, of course. They continue pulling out all the stops in preparation for our upcoming stay in their home.   **Carolyn**

Peanut Gallery

In a "dinner theater" sandwiches and drinks are served during the concert or play. Traditionally, "real" food is served only to people on the ground floor, nearest the stage (the most expensive seats). Seats in the balcony, farthest from the stage, aren't set up around tables. They're bolted to the floor in rows, and the only food offered are peanuts and popcorn.

People who sit around the stage may display a sense of arrogance. Being wealthier and "more cultured," they consider their own opinions on the quality of the concerts to be of more importance than the opinions of the people who sit in the balcony. To hear from the "peanut gallery" is to hear from someone whose opinion isn't worth very much.

There's Someone who *does* want to hear from the peanut gallery, though. Actually, this Someone doesn't recognize a peanut gallery—everyone sits directly in front of the stage. Read about how much God cares about the details of your life in **Matthew 10:29-31: Not one sparrow can . . . fall to the ground without your Father knowing it. And the very hairs of your head are all numbered. So don't worry! You are more valuable to him than many sparrows (TLB).** God wants to know what's troubling you, whether it's a short-term problem (a test tomorrow), or a long-term problem (your folks are getting a divorce).

As with any problem, you'll feel better if you look for any part of it that *you* can control. Can you tell the teacher which questions to put on the test? No. But you can study for the test so you know most of the material. Can you prevent your folks from divorcing? No. But you can still love them and tell them gently how you feel. You won't always be dependent on them. Look ahead to a bright future for yourself as a grown-up, in spite of what your folks do with their lives. Life really does go on.

As you walk down the street or sit in class, let every person you see remind you of how big God's heart is. God knows everyone; everyone is special. Imagine God praying for you in this very room right now. Kneel down with Him and talk back to Him. He's listening.   **Nancy**

Mar 3

Good Color, Bad Color

"I now realize how true it is that God does not show favoritism but accepts men from every nation who fear him and do what is right." Acts 10:34, 35, NIV.

Take a look around. Notice what color each person is wearing. There are probably some blues, reds, and greens. Now, would you make fun of people because of the colors they're wearing? I'm sure you wouldn't think bad things about any person because he or she is wearing a certain color.

In 1968 there were riots in downtown Detroit, Michigan. After it was all over, my dad took me to see the ruins of the burned, and even bombed, buildings. I can still see the piles of rubble, the half-destroyed buildings, charred black with smoke, and the people—people wandering through what was left of their homes and businesses.

Had there been an enemy invasion in Detroit? Did terrorists from a foreign country invade the city and destroy a section of the downtown area? No, I'm sad to say, it was the people of Detroit who did this to themselves. When people are at war, they usually have a reason for fighting. The people of Detroit had their reason too. You see, there were people with black skin and people with white skin who didn't like each other just because the color of their skin was different. That's it! Some of them had it in their minds that if others had skin that was different from theirs then they weren't as valuable. In fact, they were the enemy.

When you think about it, disliking someone because their skin is different is about as silly as disliking someone because their clothes are different. But sometimes people do silly things. The color of skin, the country one is from, or how much money a person has makes no difference to Jesus. It shouldn't make any difference to us, either. Let's ask God to help us see past the outward appearance and into the heart, just as He does.

Jim

Driver Ant Attack!

Happy are all who perfectly follow the laws of God. Psalm 119:1, TLB.

"Coming immediately when you're called is still one of our family's safety rules—even if you *are* getting older," insisted Mom.

Silently Brandt sulked off to his room to put a Lego car together. Two days later Josh and Marc came from next door. As the boys played with Lego pieces in Brandt's room, Mother's kitchen helper, Mathilde, a student at the nearby African school, came rushing through the back door.

"Madamu!" she called quietly to Mother. "The driver ants have come!"

Mother hurried out to the back porch. There, along the sidewalk, below the last step, stretched a seemingly endless three-inch-wide ribbon of thousands upon thousands of shimmering red driver ants. Mother remembered reading that driver ants can strip a cow's carcass to its bare skeleton in minutes.

"Josh! Marc!" their mother called through the front door. "It's time to come home for lunch!"

The neighbor boys had a bad habit of running *away* from their mother when she called. They suddenly ran out the back door, laughing, with Brandt right behind them.

"Boys, stop!" Mother ordered sharply.

With a disgusted groan, Brandt stopped in his tracks. But Josh and Marc continued running—right into the line of driver ants. Screams of painful terror pierced the air. Soon the two mothers and Mathilde were yanking at the younger boys' clothes and pulling off the swarming ants, in whose pincers were tiny hunks of the boys' skin.

As they watched the sobbing Josh and Marc leaving with their mother, Mom hugged Brandt and said, "I am so proud of you for stopping when I asked you to!"

"Oh, Mom," said Brandt, "I *like* that family rule now!"

Our loving heavenly Father also established 10 safety rules (the Ten Commandments). Choosing to obey (as Brandt did, even when he didn't feel like it) will keep us safer and happier—and away from Satan's driver ants.

Carolyn

Mar 5

Fit to Be Tied

There is something that nurses sometimes do in hospitals that doesn't seem very kind, but often it has to happen—they have to tie patients to their beds (with the consent of their families, of course). There's a one-point tie, in which just one hand is tied to the bed. (This might be the hand that a confused patient uses to pull out their IV or their bandages.) There's also a two-point tie, in which two limbs—either both arms or both legs—are tied to the bed with soft fabric strips. Worst of all is the five-point tie: both legs and both arms are tied, and a vest with ties is fastened around the patient's chest and tied to the bed frame. The patient can't even turn over until the nurse comes in and releases him or her.

Five-point ties aren't used often—only for patients who are "fit to be tied." These are patients who are so angry or irrational that they might be dangerous to themselves or to others unless they are restrained.

Anger, the result of certain chemicals or hormones being released in the body, is a feeling, and feelings are chemical mixes that our bodies secrete in response to various events. You probably don't like salt in your lemonade; you probably don't really like the chemical mix you call anger, either.

But something good happens when you look out for others. Today's verse, **Proverbs 11:17,** promises that: **Your own soul is nourished when you are kind (TLB).** A much healthier mix of chemicals occurs when you are kind. You've felt it before; it's that good feeling you get when you do something nice for somebody without being asked to. If you experience kindness more often than anger, your body is actually healthier. So the next time you take a swallow of sweet fruit juice remember to nourish your heart, too, and try to do at least one kind thing before the day is over.

Nancy

The Compass Points the Way

You diligently study the Scriptures because you think that by them you possess eternal life. These are the Scriptures that testify about me. John 5:39, NIV.

You're lost in the woods, but you know it's not really a problem because you have your trusty compass. You know that the river is somewhere to the east, so all you have to do is find the river, because it leads to civilization. You pull out your compass and notice that the needle is lying at the bottom of the compass case, no longer connected to the pin that allows it to swing around and point north.

Do you know why a properly working compass points north? The earth, this big rock we live on, has its own magnetic field. All around us are magnetic waves floating by. A piece of material that is magnetized and can swing freely, such as a compass needle, will line itself up with the earth's magnetic field. If the compass is working correctly, that needle will always line up to north.

Hikers and mountaineers have learned to trust their compass. Even when it seems to them that they're heading the wrong direction, they trust their compass. It's pretty easy to get directions mixed up, but the compass always points to north.

The Bible is a lot like a compass. It always points us in the right direction. It shows us how to live our lives; it shows us the pitfalls of life we need to avoid. But more important, it shows us the way to Jesus, the Way, the Truth, and the Life. Without Him we are lost. Many people try to find their own way to Jesus, a way that seems right to them, but we need to look to the Bible, not our own way. Just as hikers can become confused without their compass, it's easy to become confused without the Bible. We can have confidence that the Bible will point us in the right direction to our precious Saviour. **Jim**

Mar 7

Good Dog, Turtle!

Many shall run to and fro. Daniel 12:4.

Although he was slow as a puppy, Turtle grew into doghood with boundless energy.

Occasionally a large flock of African crows would swoop down from the eucalyptus treetops nearby and light on the back lawn, which was situated 12 steps below the front yard at the base of a steep bank. When he spotted them, Turtle would take off barking and send them back into the treetops.

From our dining room window one day I saw the flock of crows descending on the picnic lunch I had started to lay out on the lower lawn. "Turtle!" I called. "Let's go chase the crows." He looked confused but excited as he ran at my heels out the front door.

Rounding the corner of the house, Turtle heard the cawing of two dozen crows. He paused only a moment, his muscles tightening. Then with his head thrown back in fierce barking, Turtle forgot about the stairs and ran straight for the bank. As he sailed the 12 feet down, the big birds rose up, squawking, in a flurry of black and white feathers.

"Good dog, Turtle!" I cried.

Something must have happened to Turtle's mind that day, for after that, whenever he heard the word "crow," Turtle was literally "outta there." More than one visitor, after innocently saying the C word in Turtle's presence, was startled by his sudden rush for the door, his struggle for traction on the slick linoleum floor before exploding through the front door in a barking frenzy. "Whatever is wrong with your dog?" they'd ask in great alarm.

Turtle would sometimes repeat this exhausting process endlessly, running to and fro, until he wore himself out—even when there wasn't a crow in sight!

The prophet Daniel predicted that in the last days "many shall run to and fro" with no purpose in their lives. If we invite Jesus to be the purpose—the center—of our lives, we will never be among those who exhaust all their energies chasing crows that aren't there. With Jesus, not only will we know *where* we are going, but more important, we'll also know *why*.

Carolyn

Look Through
Rose-colored Glasses

Pink fingernails are an indication that your body is well oxygenated and everything is going well with your respiratory system. One of the fastest ways we can assess that newborn babies are breathing well on their own is to look at their fingernails. They're not always pink in the beginning, but as the baby cries loudly and its circulation gets better, its fingernails pink up, and everyone else breathes a little easier.

We speak of people being "in the pink" when things are going well. There's an old story about a boy who felt his life wasn't going so well. Although everyone around him was cheerful, he wasn't. He'd been told not to tell a lie, but he was becoming rather uncomfortable having to say he wasn't "in the pink." He wanted to be like everyone else. One day he came up with a solution. He found a pair of old glasses and painted them pink. Then, when anyone asked how life was going, he could honestly say, "I'm in the pink!"

However, the people of his town were so used to hearing him say how awful life was that they pointed out he was just looking at things "through rose-colored glasses," as though his optimism wasn't worth believing in. No matter; the boy's outlook on life changed because he chose to believe that things were going well.

Proverbs 15:15 says, **When a man is gloomy, everything seems to go wrong; when he is cheerful, everything seems right! (TLB).** Sometimes it takes a lot of faith to believe that. If you can't believe things are going well, at least you can believe things can change for the better. God can use anything that happens in life to teach us a lesson, and once we learn that lesson we can make a change. Looking for what you can do to improve the way your life is going can make you feel good. Soon you won't need your rose-colored glasses anymore.

You have the power to label the events in your life any way you want to. You can look back and say your life is ruined, or you can look forward and say your life has just turned a corner. Then make new choices that keep you going straight. A poster I like says "The past is not your potential." Keep that in mind.
Nancy

Hey, You!

The wicked man flees though no one pursues. Proverbs 28:1, NIV.

Jack headed home from school. It was hot and humid, and he was thirsty. As he walked the dusty road toward home, he saw two girls at the side of the road who had set up a lemonade stand. Oh, a cold glass of lemonade sounded good! He reached into his pocket, only to discover he had no money. How would he be able to feel the tangy coolness of ice-cold lemonade flowing down his thirsty throat if he had no money?

As Jack neared the house, he heard the girls' mother call them in for a moment. As he walked up to the stand it was just he and the lemonade. Without any more thought, Jack grabbed a glass of lemonade and hurried down the road as fast as he could. After running no more than 40 or 50 steps he heard someone yell "Hey, you!"

Oh no! thought Jack. *"They're after me. I shouldn't have stolen the lemonade."* He began to run even faster, but as he picked up speed he forgot to look where he was stepping. His foot landed in a hole in the road, and his ankle twisted violently. The glass of lemonade fell, breaking into a thousand pieces and spilling lemonade into the dirt.

Ankle throbbing, Jack pulled himself up, thinking his pursuers would soon grab him by the collar and haul him back to the house. But when he turned around, no one was there. It seems that the man who had yelled had only been shouting to his neighbor across the road. Jack could see them talking by the house.

Your conscience is there to protect you. It's a combination of all the good things your parents and teachers have taught you, plus God's own Holy Spirit giving you guidance each day. Listen to it. Be honest with yourself and others, and keep your conscience clear. That way, you'll have nothing to run from. **Jim**

Mama Kitty

Men speak abusively against whatever they do not understand . . . these are the very things that destroy them. Jude 10, NIV.

Keenan named his Siamese cat Mama Kitty because she was always so protective of her many kittens. She especially distrusted dogs. One afternoon Keenan and Elisse, an African friend, were trying to help Dad push Daji, Keenan's dog, off the front porch and toward their truck for a trip to the vet. Terrified of vehicles *and* vets, Daji refused to budge and began howling.

To Mama Kitty's limited understanding, Daji's howling could mean only one thing—her babies were in danger. She headed straight for the front porch. At the door, Daji's loud yelping and three pair of human legs shuffling around confused Mama Kitty. Not understanding the situation, she blindly attacked. With a yowl of rage and terror, she leaped through the air, claws extended, and sank them into the backs of Elisse's plump legs! Immediately a human howl joined Daji's.

Keenan's mom, seeing the whole thing, sent Mama Kitty back to her babies and rushed Elisse up to the medical dispensary for first aid. Poor, gentle Elisse had been needlessly hurt because Mama Kitty hadn't understood that she wasn't an enemy.

Like Mama Kitty, many people needlessly attack and wound others because they just don't know or understand them. We say such people are "prejudiced." Yet the truth is that many prejudiced persons have probably never taken the opportunity even to get acquainted with one of the individuals they're so unfairly judging. Jude 10 states that people put down that which they don't understand—and this behavior eventually comes back to destroy them.

Jesus' disciple, Peter, was prejudiced. Through a dream God showed him—and us—that all racial groups are equally precious in His sight (Acts 10:1-35). Peter understood that he needed to treat everyone with respect.

Two ways we can be more like God are (1) by choosing not to participate in putdowns or even jokes that show disrespect for a particular racial group; and (2) by making the first move to befriend—and understand—someone not of our own ethnic background.

And guess what often follows understanding—love! **Carolyn**

Cork-brained

Almost everyone knows that cork comes from the bark of a tree. But even if they don't, almost everyone knows what cork looks like—brown, light, airy. Cork has air-filled spaces of nothing. That's why some big brothers may choose the word "cork-brained" to describe a younger brother's intelligence. It isn't at all kind. And yet, some kids do seem to have empty spaces in their brains when it comes to taking advice.

Two fathers were once discussing their philosophies of child rearing. Mr. Brown said, "I try not to influence my children too much because I want them to think for themselves and not be influenced by my beliefs."

The second father, Mr. Thurman, was appalled by that attitude. "If you don't give your children advice and lead them properly, they will make too many mistakes."

They argued a bit, and then Mr. Thurman suggested they go outside. "I want to show you my garden," he said. He showed his friend a plot of land completely covered in weeds.

"Why, this is no garden," Mr. Brown exclaimed. "There's nothing here but weeds!"

"I'm surprised you find it offensive," Mr. Thurman replied, "for this is the same haphazard way your children's beliefs are being allowed to be formed."

Do your parents give you a lot of advice? Does it sometimes make you bristle? Perhaps that's because you don't understand why they do it. I'll tell you why they give you advice: your parents want your life to be as beautiful as a well-tended garden. They want you to enjoy your life. When they say no, it's not because they're on a power trip. They give you advice for a good reason: they want the best for you.

Family rules are there to protect you. Don't be cork-brained about them. What does **Proverbs 15:5** say about corkbrains? **Only a fool despises his father's advice; a wise son considers each suggestion (TLB).** When you see weeds today, thank God for giving you parents who have been planting flowers in your life, not allowing weeds to have their way.

Nancy

Car Crash!

You did not receive a spirit that makes you a slave again to fear, but you received the Spirit of sonship. And by him we cry, *"Abba,* Father." Romans 8:15, NIV.

As I drove down the busy road I noticed that a line of cars was stopped up ahead. I stepped on the brake, but the brake pedal didn't budge. The car wasn't stopping, and I was coming closer to the cars that were stopped ahead.

If I continued straight ahead, I would run right into the cars. On the right side of the road was a line of trees, so I decided it was a bad idea to swerve right. I couldn't get over to the left, because traffic was coming toward me. So I did the only thing I could do: I drove straight ahead, put both feet on the brake pedal, and hoped something would happen.

It did. About 50 feet from the stopped cars something snapped and the brake pedal went to the floor. I heard skidding and then the worst crashing noise I'd ever heard as I plowed into the car in front of me, which plowed into the car in front of it, which plowed into the car in front of it.

A police officer, who was driving on the other side of the road, saw the whole thing. He got out of his patrol car and asked us to pull into a convenience store parking lot nearby. When I got out of my car, do you know what the first thing I did was? I didn't buy a candy bar, I didn't fill up with gas, and I didn't ask the police officer how his family was. The first thing I did was call my dad. You see, I knew my dad would help me.

That's how God is. Get to know Him as your Father. Soon you'll not only call on Him when you're in trouble; you'll begin to love Him so much you'll be talking with Him every day. **Jim**

Mar 13

No Excuses

Now there is in store for me the crown of righteousness, which the Lord, the righteous Judge, will award to me on that day. 2 Timothy 4:8, NIV.

After my accident Dad was down to help me in just a few minutes, as I knew he'd be. The officer thought I was only a 17-year-old kid who hadn't been paying attention. I tried to explain that I hadn't been careless, and that something was wrong with my brakes. My dad looked under the car, and sure enough, brake fluid was leaking all over the pavement. But it didn't make any difference to the police officer. He wrote me a ticket for careless driving and told me I could either pay it or go to court.

I was nervous as I entered the courtroom. Once again my dad was with me. Finally it was my turn. The judge ordered me to approach the bench. "What do you have to say?" he asked gruffly.

"Well," I said, "I was driving my car, and my brakes failed, and I ran into the back of another car."

"What do you want me to do about it?" the impatient judge shot back.

"I had a brake problem; it wasn't my fault."

The judge looked at me and said coldly, "You were driving a car. You were supposed to stop it, and you didn't. Go pay your fine."

That was it. It was over. He hadn't let me say much of anything. My dad and I went down the hall and paid the $60. I was angry at the judge, but as I think about it, he was right. It wasn't the fault of the woman whose car I hit, and it wasn't the fault of the guy who was buying groceries in the convenience store. It was obvious to see it was my fault.

All of us are guilty of sin before God, our Judge. The great thing is that this Judge wants to set us free. That's why He sent His own Son to pay sin's penalty of death on a cross. Think of it: we are guilty, but we can spend eternity with Jesus because the Judge loves us. **Jim**

Waiting for the Other Shoe to Drop

Has anyone ever told you that they're "waiting for the other shoe to drop"? Apparently the saying stems from the experience of a hotel clerk in the late 1800s.

Late one night a customer entered the hotel and asked for a room. There was only one room left, and the clerk had been asked to keep it empty, if possible. The clerk would be in trouble if he turned the man away. So the clerk opened the key cabinet, took the only key from its hook, and handed it across the counter to the late-night customer.

"I must ask that you be very quiet," the clerk said. "The occupant of the room one floor below yours is one of our regular customers. He's quite a light sleeper and has requested that we keep the room above his empty, if possible. But since it's so late, and I can see that you are tired, I'll let you have the room."

The customer thanked the clerk, then picked up his bags and headed for the elevator. Once in his room, this thoughtful customer walked softly on tiptoe before finally sitting on the side of his bed to take off his shoes. He accidentally dropped his first shoe on the floor. Feeling bad about that, he removed his other shoe more carefully and very quietly placed it on the floor beside the first shoe. Then he crawled into bed and was soon asleep.

Hours later he was awakened by loud knocking at his door. It was the man from the room below. "You woke me up when you dropped your shoe. And I have been waiting for hours for the other shoe to drop!" the irate man screamed at him. "Will you please drop it so I can get back to sleep?"

To "wait for the other shoe to drop" means you're waiting for more bad things to happen to you. Maybe you find yourself doing that with schoolwork. Maybe you think that just because you didn't do well on one test, you won't do well on any test. Or just because you had problems with school last year, you'll have trouble this year too. What does the Bible say about failure? Read **Proverbs 24:16: A just man falleth seven times, and riseth up again.** The important thing is that you keep trying. Don't wait for the other shoe to drop. Get on with doing your best from this point on. As the old saying goes: "Today is the first day of the rest of your life." **Nancy**

Mar 15

Dew Be, Dew Be, Dew

In your hands are strength and power to exalt and give strength to all. I Chronicles 29:12, NIV.

Quiz time! How does dew form? . . . All right, let's see if anyone guessed the correct answer: dew is formed at night when the earth becomes cooler than the air. Most of the time the air around us contains water, tiny particles of water in the air that are too small to see. When these water particles touch the cool earth at night, they condense, which means the particles collect together to form little water drops. When you've got all those little drops of water on the ground, you've got dew.

Do you remember the story of Gideon? God wanted to use Gideon to defeat Israel's enemies, the Midianites, but Gideon didn't understand why God would use him, so he asked for a sign. God used the dew to give Gideon a sign that He was with him. What God did with the dew could only be considered a miracle. He asked God to make a wool cloth that he put on the ground wet with dew, while keeping the ground dry. And God did it! Still doubting, Gideon then asked God to make the *ground* wet with dew and keep the *fleece* dry. God did that too. From what you know about how dew forms, there's no way that should have happened. If the ground was cool, the wool cloth should have been cool also. Dew should have formed on both.

Do you think God asked an angel to cover up the fleece to keep it dry one night, and then sprinkled water over the fleece to make it wet the next night? The fact is, we don't know how God did it. What we do know is that God is so much greater than we can imagine. An even greater thought is that we can call Him our Father. Aren't you glad you've got a Dad like that? **Jim**

Have I Got a Plan for You!

"I know the plans I have for you," declares the Lord, "plans to prosper you and not to harm you." Jeremiah 29:11, NIV.

The thief had plans! Finally the cold dark night he'd selected for his crime arrived. Around midnight the thief broke into the antique dealer's home. So far, so good. His plan was working. His mouth fairly watered at the sight of all those expensive antiques: vases, furniture, even coats of armor! Soon he'd cart off as much as he could carry. He was now ready to put the next part of his plan into action.

Fifteen minutes later a loud clanging awoke the sleeping antique dealer. Rushing to the landing at the top of the staircase, he beamed his flashlight on the most unusual—and fearsome—sight. One of his fifteenth-century suits of armor appeared to be making a clumsy attempt to climb the stairs! The thief had *planned* that the dealer would think he was a ghost and flee.

But this part of his plan failed. Not only did the antique dealer not believe in ghosts, he didn't believe in running away from problems. Flying down the stairs, the dealer pushed the thief off balance and sent him crashing to the floor. Next, he pushed a small wooden cabinet onto the thief's breastplate and notified the police.

Although the police responded promptly, it took them 24 hours to extract the thief from the suit of armor because the cabinet had dented his breastplate. During this time the thief had to be fed through the visor of the medieval helmet he was wearing.

"But I thought I could scare him!" the thief kept repeating. Serving a prison sentence gave the thief a lot more time to think about how his plans had failed

People make plans all the time. The thief had plans to diminish the antique dealer's prosperity and do him harm. But God's plans for us are exactly the opposite. "'I know the plans I have for you,' declares the Lord, 'plans to prosper you and not to harm you.'"

In the Bible God sounds excited about His plans for us! Knowing what kind of planner God is, we can be excited too! **Carolyn**

Mar 17

Get the Hang of It

When I was a little girl in Sri Lanka, most of what I wore didn't come from a department store. I wore thongs most of the time, but when I needed lace-up shoes, I had them made by the shoemaker, a Chinese man with a permanent smile. He could make nearly anything his customers wanted. All I had to do was take in a picture of the shoes I wanted and stand on a brown piece of paper while he drew around my foot. (It tickled.) I'll never forget the blue and white saddle oxfords he made for me.

But shoes weren't the only things I had made for me. Since there weren't any department stores in Ceylon, my clothes were made by a tailor. I took in the fabric and showed him a picture, and he made the dress or slacks for me. It was kind of fun to have that much choice! And the tailor was obviously very good at what he did to be able to make clothes without a pattern.

The phrase "get the hang of it" refers to tailors. When you can't seem to understand how something is done, you say you can't get the hang of it. A tailor, on the other hand, does get the hang of it. A tailor makes dresses and skirts and suits hang right.

Do you think good tailors are born knowing what they know? Of course not! They have to practice for years before they're considered an expert. One success leads to another; a mistake leads to learning; until at last the tailors can make anything their customers want and everything hangs right.

The Bible gives practical advice for how to get the hang of being a success. Read about it in **Ecclesiastes 9:10: Whatsoever thy hand findeth to do, do it with thy might.** Take the time to learn all of your spelling words. Don't just turn in a math paper, turn in a neat math paper. Remember that you don't go to school for your teacher or for your parents. You go to school for *you*. Your whole future depends on how well you learn the things your teachers explain to you. So do your best to get the hang of it. The better you learn it the first time, the easier it will be when you come back to it again.

Nancy

80

What's for Dinner?

To obey is better than sacrifice. I Samuel 15:22.

What if your mother told you she was going to cook your favorite meal for dinner? Admit it, you'd be excited. All day you'd think about the fragrant smells at home. You'd wait expectantly for that moment when you'd put the first morsels of delicious food into your mouth.

But wait; what's this? As you enter the front door a terrible odor confronts your nostrils. You rush to the kitchen, thinking something must be burning. Your mother smiles and hugs you. "I changed my mind, honey," she says. She tells you she didn't make your favorite meal after all. She decided to make a meal with all the foods you hate the most. She says she thinks it will build your character. Do you think you'd be disappointed? Maybe a little upset?

There was a man in the Bible who pulled a switch with his meal. Cain and Abel brought a sacrifice to the altar. Abel brought the best lamb he could find in his flock, but Cain brought the finest fruits and vegetables he had raised. Although they were Cain's best fruits, they weren't what God had asked him to bring. God accepted Abel's lamb; He did not accept Cain's fruits and vegetables.

What was the problem? Why was it such a big deal to God that a lamb be brought to the altar? There are at least two reasons. First, a lamb represented the death of Jesus, who would pay for Cain's and Abel's and everyone else's sins. The second reason is that when God asks us to do something, He wants to know if we will be loyal to Him.

You see, if God is worthy of our worship, we ought to worship Him in the way He desires. Cain wanted to do it his own way. He must have thought he knew better than God. We too should worship God in the way He's asked us. Fortunately, He's shown us exactly how He wants us to do it. It's in His Word, and how happy He is when we read it and obey. **Jim**

Mar 19

The Really Dumb Prayer

"As the heavens are higher than the earth, so are my ways higher than your ways and my thoughts than your thoughts." Isaiah 55:9, NIV.

I prayed a really dumb prayer once!" Janna confided to Samantha.

"Oh, tell me!" The two earliteen girls were "camping" out in Janna's fenced-in backyard under a starry sky during summer vacation.

"When I was 5, I stood under a tree holding out a banana and praying that God would make one of the blackbirds fly down and be my pet."

Samantha burst out laughing. "Did you really think He'd answer your prayer?"

"Yeah, I thought God automatically gave whatever you asked."

"What did you do when no bird flew down?"

"I decided God didn't hear my prayers and went back in the house and cried."

"Do you think He hears you now?" Samantha became serious.

"Yes," answered Janna, "because of what Grandma told me. She lived with us and was baking bread when I came in crying."

Samantha snuggled down in her sleeping bag. "So what did she tell you?"

"Well, as best I can remember, she explained that God loves me and wants what is best for me. Of course, that made sense. Then she explained that God also loves the animals He created and wants what's best for them too. Then she asked what I would have done with a bird."

"What *would* you have done?" Samantha wanted to know.

"I was planning to give it peanut butter sandwiches, dress it in doll clothes, and keep it warm in a shoebox left in front of the open oven door."

Samantha giggled. "It would have died for sure!"

"I know that now, and I'm glad God didn't answer my prayer. I guess His way was a whole lot better than mine!"

"Since He knows everything about what's best for us, I'm sure glad He's in control," commented Samantha.

"Me, too!" agreed Janna. "In fact, knowing that makes it feel even safer out here, doesn't it?"

Samantha yawned. "Yep, sure does. . . . Good night, best friend."

"G'night."

Carolyn

82

Mar 20

Bent out of Shape

If you've ever had an X-ray taken of your bones or your chest you know that X-rays don't hurt. They allow the doctor to see what's happening inside your body without doing surgery. There's another test doctors sometimes order that takes an even better look at your insides—an MRI that uses strong magnetic power.

The patient lies on a narrow bed while the bed slides slowly inside a long white tube—just like the toilet paper holder slides inside the toilet paper roll. I once asked the man who operates the machine if I could look at it more closely.

"As long as you don't have any metal on you," he said. "The magnet in that machine is so strong that if we get the wrong kind of wheelchair in the room, it is pulled right up against the machine, and we can hardly get the patient out of it."

The only metal I could see was the metal buttons on my sweater. But the man said those were OK. I forgot about the metal hair clip at the back of my head. When I was within about five feet of the machine I felt my hair beginning to lift, as though an invisible hand was back there. The man laughed. He said that sometimes women forget about their earrings. When they get close to the machine their ears bend out of shape as the machine pulls the earrings.

Things that are bent out of shape look odd. When someone is angry, we say they're "bent out of shape" because we know they aren't their usual self. What does **Ecclesiastes 7:9** say about being "bent out of shape"? **Be not hasty in thy spirit to be angry: for anger resteth in the bosom of fools.** Anger is a chemical response of your body to frustration. You may not be able to control the start of the feelings, but you can make the choice not to stay "bent out of shape" for too long.

The best thing to do is to categorize the cause of your anger. Is it something you need to talk to someone about so you can work it out? Or something that you can't control, that needs to be put behind you? Anger doesn't die because we talk about it; anger goes away when we *choose* to let it go. Isn't it nice to have a choice?   **Nancy**

83

Mar 21

Over the Speed Limit

We do not have a high priest who is unable to sympathize with our weaknesses. Hebrews 4:15, NIV.

It was the day I was going to get my driver's license, and I was pumped. I was nervous, but I'd studied the driver's manual and practiced driving around our country home. Yes, I had almost driven right through the chicken coop at first, but I had practiced and now was better.

I passed the written test; it actually seemed rather easy. It was the driver's test I was fearing. That's where one of the test people sits in the car with you and tells you where to drive and watches everything you do. This was going to be nerve-racking.

The tester asked me to make a right turn out of the parking lot. I drove a block and everything seemed to be going smoothly. "Turn left," he said. I turned, but as I did, I knew something was wrong. I pulled into the far lane. "You're supposed to turn into the closest lane, ya know."

"Oh," I said.

"Now turn right."

I did, but all I could think about was the goof I'd made on my turn.

"You're driving five miles over the speed limit."

I quickly looked at my speedometer. I couldn't believe it! I was speeding on my driving test! After what seemed like a two-day drive we arrived back at the county building. "Well, it wasn't too bad, but I can't pass you this time. If you speed on the test I'm forced to fail you."

How humiliating! I had failed my driver's test. How would I ever live it down? I went back one month later and passed my test. I was careful to watch the speedometer this time, and now that I have my driver's license, that failure doesn't seem quite so bad.

Did you know that Mrs. Fannie Turner failed the written portion of her driver's test 103 times? She didn't give up. She finally passed it on try number 104. Sometimes it feels as though we make one mistake after another. Aren't you glad we have God, who understands our weaknesses?

Jim

Light Up!

"The wise replied, 'No! there will not be enough for you and for us; you had better go to the dealers and buy some for yourselves.'" Matthew 25:9, NRSV.

D o you all have extra batteries and light sources?" Ms. Sutcliffe asked the four junior high girls standing outside Mason Cave.

Monica excitedly checked her pack while Darien, Corrie, and Kara nodded. "This is so cool!" bubbled Corrie as she switched on her headlamp. "I'll lead going in."

Ms. Sutcliffe let the girls "discover" the small subterranean lake beyond the twilight zone (the part of the cave beyond which entrance light no longer reaches).

"Hey, my headlamp just went off!" called Kara. "Oh, no! I forgot extra batteries." Then she moaned, "My backup flashlight is so dim I can't see a thing!"

"My headlamp just died too," exclaimed Corrie. "But I've got a candle. O-o-o-oh! A candle, but no matches!"

Monica unzipped her backpack. "Here are three matches, Corrie, but I may need the rest."

"Anyone have extra batteries?" pleaded Kara.

"Just my headlamp; sorry," answered Darien.

"Well, Monica and I can use the candle, and Corrie can walk in front of Darien's headlamp."

"No," Ms. Sutcliffe reluctantly disagreed. "That's not enough light to cave safely. We need to head back to the entrance before someone gets hurt."

"I was so dumb. All my extra stuff was right there on the kitchen table," groaned Corrie. "Why did I go off and leave it?"

Jesus once told a story about another group of girls whose lights went out. The 10 bridesmaids (Matthew 25:1-13) never expected their lights to go out either, but they did. Each girl was responsible for her own light source, but only those who'd brought enough backup supplies were allowed to go into the party.

Through this parable Jesus lets us know that our spiritual lamp is the Bible. If we read it, pray, and make choices according to its counsel, it will give us the necessary faith in Jesus, the heavenly Bridegroom. And He will keep our path well-lit—all the way to the door of the party. **Carolyn**

Stab in the Back

Do you know anybody named Judas? Why not? Did you say it's because Judas wasn't one of Jesus' friends? He sure pretended to be a friend! Judas ate and traveled with Jesus. It probably seemed that he was one of Jesus' friends. But Judas didn't act like a friend. Judas "stabbed Jesus in the back."

Well, he didn't actually stab Jesus with a knife. The expression means you pretend to be a friend, and then you betray that person. Maybe you say something really hurtful about him or her to somebody else. When your friend hears what you said, it's as surprising as an attack from behind—and sometimes more hurtful.

The North American Indians' word for friend is "one who carries my sorrows on their back." A friend cares about you and never hurts you intentionally. So what should you do when someone you thought was a friend stabs you in the back? What does **Proverbs 25:21, 22** recommend? **If your enemy is hungry, give him food to eat; if he is thirsty, give him water to drink. In doing this, you will heap burning coals on his head, and the Lord will reward you (NIV).**

I'm not sure exactly what it means to heap coals of fire on someone's head, but my understanding is that your enemy wants to make you hot and mad. But when you stay cool, it's as though you're dumping the coals right onto your enemy's head, and he or she becomes the one who gets burned. In contrast to your kindness your enemy's meanness is obvious to everyone.

It's not easy to be patient when someone is unkind to you. But God will reward you for your patience. If someone says something bad about the friend who hurt you, don't add your own insult. While admitting you were hurt, you might say, "Yeah, I was hurt, but I can't believe she did that on purpose. There must be something about it that I don't know yet." If you don't jump to conclusions, you can possibly salvage a friendship. Eventually you'll have lots of friends when people see how kind you are to others.

Nancy

Ear Today Gone Tomorrow

Do not repay anyone evil for evil. Romans 12:17, NIV.

People usually fight wars for very good reasons. You know, stuff really worth arguing about. But there are some exceptions. Take, for instance, the case of Captain Jenkins.

One day in 1739 Captain Robert Jenkins brought a jar to the British Parliament in which was a very unusual object—his ear. At least he said it was his ear. The captain definitely did not have an ear, and he apparently talked the members of the British Parliament into believing that the ear in that jar was his. He said that an enemy, a Spaniard, had cut it off with a sword. I guess that's all it took, because Great Britain went to war with Spain in the Battle of Jenkins' Ear.

It didn't take long for the British to realize that Captain Jenkins' ear wasn't really worth sending the country to war over. There were a few battles at sea that ended up in a tie, and then the war was over. How silly!

There was man in the Bible who lost his ear. Peter, one of Jesus' disciples, hacked off the high priest's servant's ear with his sword in the Garden of Gethsemane. After all, there were men trying to arrest his Master. Jesus could have made a run for it, but He didn't. He told Peter to put his sword away. He said that He could have called on His Father in heaven and instantly had thousands of angels coming to help Him. Then Jesus picked up the man's ear and put it back on his head. Healed instantly!

Jesus was mistreated many times, but He never hit anyone to get his point across. He simply trusted His Father and told people the truth. Sometimes that truth hurt, but it was always with the hope of leading people to His Father.

I know that I sure have felt like hitting someone a time or two when I've been mistreated. But I know that wouldn't have helped. Treat those who hurt you with love. Jesus did, and He can help you do the same.

Jim

Mar 25

Tongue Twisters

The tongue is a small thing, but what enormous damage it can do. James 3:5, TLB.

If you go down to the river, watch out for crocodiles!" Amoni's father warned.

"*Yego, Data,*" 11-year-old Amoni promised, his eyes following Mother and Father as they headed for market on the trail leading through the banana plantation.

By early afternoon the hot African sun seemed to burn through even the banana leaf shelter set up outside the family's kitchen hut. Shading his eyes with one hand, Amoni scanned the calm surface of the river for any sign of a crocodile. He saw no sign of the creatures.

Just a quick wade, the boy thought. A couple minutes later he let out a sigh of relief as the cool water enveloped his feet . . . and calves . . . and—

He still doesn't remember where it came from, but suddenly a green shiny beast flashed from out of nowhere, barely breaking the water's surface before clamping its jaws just below Amoni's right knee. Through the slightly parted jaws the boy could see its sharp teeth digging painfully into his freshly torn flesh.

Just then a bit of survival advice from his old grandfather flashed through Amoni's memory. Quickly he thrust his right arm through the croc's jaws and found its tongue. Grabbing the long, fleshy muscle, Amoni twisted it as hard as he could. The crocodile instantly loosened its grip long enough for Amoni to extract his wounded leg and hurry painfully toward the house. Saved by a tongue twister!

Like Amoni, we can sometimes get trapped by a pair of jaws—our own. We trap ourselves when we don't control our tongues. Jesus, who created humankind's ability to speak, sometimes held His own tongue when He knew answering back would make a situation worse (see Mark 15:1-5).

When we ask Him, God gives us the strength to get ahold of our tongue—like Amoni did to the crocodile's. Not only will a twist-hold on our tongues *get* us out of deep water, it will *keep* us out too.

Carolyn

What's a White Elephant, Anyway?

You may have heard about a white elephant gift exchange. The origin of that phrase goes way back to the years when kings ruled Siam (now called Thailand). A white elephant (what we would call an albino elephant today) was as rare then as it is now. Because they were rare, they were considered sacred, and no one was allowed to kill them. If anyone discovered a white elephant in the jungle, it was captured and given to the king as a special gift. But white elephants, being sacred, couldn't be used for work and couldn't be ridden. And they couldn't be sold. A white elephant was good for nothing; it was simply an expensive burden.

Now, the king could easily afford to feed an extra elephant. But whether or not he wanted another elephant was another matter. Usually he wanted usable elephants. Since he couldn't sell the elephant, it had to be given away—not to a friend, who would also find the elephant useless, but to an enemy. You see, the king knew that that elephant would be so expensive and useless to its new owner that soon the new owner would experience financial ruin and become a beggar. Giving away the white elephant was a way to get rid of something unwanted and appear generous at the same time.

The next time you go to a white elephant gift exchange, remember that it means you are giving away something that nobody else really wants.

What does **Matthew 7:12** say about what the king of Siam did? **Therefore all things whatsoever ye would that men should do to you, do ye even so to them.** A white elephant gift exchange is OK for entertainment, but to cause serious trouble for someone else is unkind. God treats us as He would like to be treated. When we practice being that way, we become more like God. And as we become more like God, we become more ready for heaven. **Nancy**

An Eclipse of the Heart

Now we see but a poor reflection as in a mirror; then we shall see face to face. I Corinthians 13:12, NIV.

A total eclipse of the sun is a beautiful and eerie sight. It doesn't happen very often that the moon moves directly between the sun and the earth, but that's exactly what happens during an eclipse of the sun. During this time all that can be seen are the exploding gases that leap from the surface of the sun. You are never to look directly at the sun, even during an eclipse. It takes special equipment to see just a reflection of this awesome sight.

When sin marred our world, we could see only a portion of God's glory. Before sin Adam and Eve walked and talked with God face-to-face in the Garden of Eden. When they chose to sin, they hid from God. Because God's full glory and sin cannot exist in the same place, God has had to hide Himself to keep us from being destroyed.

Throughout history God has revealed glimpses of His glory to us. For instance, when God asked Moses to come to Mount Sinai to receive the Ten Commandments, the Bible says that Moses' face shone with the glory of God. When Peter, James, and John were with Jesus on the Mount of Transfiguration, they saw some of the glory of God as Jesus shone with heavenly light.

God longs to bring us back without sin to heaven where we can behold His glory and the wonders of the earth made new. Like a full eclipse of the sun, the wonders and glory of God have been hidden from our sight because of sin. But we have the great hope of seeing the glory of all the angels returning to earth one day with our Saviour in all His brightness. Some will want to hide when Jesus comes because everything will be so bright. But we who have trusted in Jesus for our salvation will look at Him without protective lenses, and shout for joy as He comes to take us home.

Jim

Tattenai

It is an honour for a man to cease from strife: but every fool will be meddling. Proverbs 20:3.

In an ancient kingdom a group of people started rebuilding a temple. Tattenai, the kingdom's meddling governor, demanded, "So who said you guys could build here?" Then, although it was none of his business, he wrote a letter to the neighboring king of Persia that went something like this.

Yo, King! Tattenai the Cool here. What's up? Hey, there's a bunch of guys over on the next hill rebuilding a church. They say they have a building permit from your predecessor, King Cyrus, but I say they don't! So—be a pal, would ya, and check in your kingdom's old-timey records. Help me prove these builder people are a bunch of liars. Write back soon!

Yours truly,

Tattenai THE Great

PS: Self-addressed stamped envelope is included for Your Highness's convenience.

Imagine Tattenai's surprise upon reading King Darius's prompt reply, that went something like this:

Dear Governor Tattenai,

About that church being rebuilt? You stay away from there. Do not interfere with the work on this temple of God. Everything the Hebrew builders have told you is true. Cyrus, my predecessor, did give them a building permit—and a whole lot more!

Guess what else? Since you're such a "concerned" governor, any money these men need is to come out of your royal treasury. Oh, yes, and give them daily, without fail, anything else they need for worship and well-being. I've included a suggested list for Your Highness's convenience.

And by the way, Tattenai the Great, anyone who tries to change this order of mine will have to pay—big-time [see Ezra 6:11].

Sincerely yours,

Darius the GREATER. (See Ezra 6:3-12.)

Oops! So the Hebrews were able to rebuild their temple, much of it at the expense of Governor Tattenai.

The next time you're tempted to meddle in someone else's business, remember the nosy Tattenai. **Carolyn**

Mar 29

Gum Up the Works

L et's start today's time by reading **Ecclesiastes 7:20** right now. **There is not a single man in all the earth who is always good and never sins (TLB).** Does it make you feel good that you're "normal" if you don't do what's right all the time? Or does it make you wonder why anyone should try at all not to sin?

When we sin, we "gum up the works" of our relationship with God and sometimes even our friends. Just as having gum in your hair can result in your needing a haircut, having gum or something else sticky in machinery can result in ruining the machine.

Sin has a way of becoming stickier and stickier, uglier and uglier. The consequences of sin become more and more frightening. Perhaps one of the first sins anybody commits is to call someone a bad name on purpose, just to hurt their feelings. This gums up the works of that potential friendship, doesn't it? If you never repent, you become hardened, and it becomes more and more difficult to feel sorry for others.

Fortunately, God has a way out of that cold sin-hardened condition. It starts with one baby step at a time, putting yourself in the other person's place, asking yourself how you would feel if you were them.

A certain preacher was told that his sermons were too harsh. "Do you have to say 'sin' so often, Pastor?" his parishioners asked. "Can't you just say 'mistake,' or 'indiscretion'?"

The pastor nodded. "I could," he said. He went over to the cupboard and picked up a bottle of strychnine. "What does this label say?" He paused, and then answered his own question. "It says 'poison.' I could relabel it and call it 'cinnamon' and nobody would ever know how dangerous it really is."

Sometimes sin can "gum up" lives and even cost us a loving friendship with God unless we recognize it for what it is. What is sin? Something we do that makes us want to hide from God, from our parents, and from others. That's how sin separates us from God. It's not something others do to us; it's something we do, even though we know we shouldn't. Ask Jesus to help you the moment you're tempted. He can help you, but only if you move toward Him. **Nancy**

Excellence

Do you see a man skilled in his work? He will serve before kings; he will not serve before obscure men. Proverbs 22:29, NIV.

What do Esther, Nehemiah, and Daniel all have in common? Give up? They all served kings. Esther became the queen, Nehemiah was a king's cupbearer, and Daniel was the king's adviser. How did each of these people get to such high positions? They were faithful to God and excelled in what they did.

Esther was a most gracious queen who saved her people. Nehemiah held a position of trust. He brought the king's drinks to him, and the king had to know that his cupbearer wouldn't put poison into the royal beverage. Daniel was a wise man who interpreted the king's dreams. He knew what they meant because he talked often with God.

How about you? God has given you talents that He wants you to use to serve Him. In fact, He wants you to do your very best in all that He's given you to do. That means your schoolwork, your friendships, your relationship with your family, and your hobbies.

You might wonder why all these things are so important. I'll tell you why. God has already started to prepare you for a special work. You may not even know what it is now, but all the parts of your life will fit into place when the time comes. He wants you to work your hardest and do your best, because He'll use all these things to honor Him and bring others to Jesus.

Think of something you do well right now. It might be putting models together, or math, or speaking, or even getting along well with others. Not everybody can do these things well. God has put a special combination of gifts in your life that no one else has just exactly like you do.

Who knows? You could be a Daniel or an Esther. You might serve famous people. Wherever God places you, serve Him with all your might and be the tops in your field. **Jim**

The Case of the Disappearing Dishtowels

In the beginning was the Word, and the Word was with God, and the Word was God. John 1:1, NIV.

Mom, did another one disappear?" asked 10-year-old Bryce as his mother peered into the empty long-handled basket.

"Yes, dear, it looks as if it has," said Mother.

"And when you sent fresh bread to Mrs. Josiah in this basket and covered it with the pink striped towel, it disappeared too. Mom, do you think that Mrs. Zacharie just *stole* the blue dishtowel?"

"Five dishtowels have disappeared like this," said Mother, sinking into a chair near his home-schooling desk. "But Bryce, I just can't believe those women would intentionally steal from us."

Johnson, an older African student at the school where Bryce's parents taught, dropped by that afternoon to help Mother with her African language study. When Bryce and Mother explained about the disappearing dishtowels, Johnson laughed hard. "I can explain everything," he assured them. "It's a case of miscommunication. In our country when you lightly *cover* a gift with a cloth, the cloth is returned with the basket. But when you cover a gift with a cloth by *wrapping* the cloth *around* the gift, the cloth is considered part of the gift."

Both Mother and Bryce nodded in understanding—and relief.

"Your dishtowels are very safe anywhere around here, Madamu," concluded Johnson, "as long as you clearly communicate by their placement if they're part of the gift or not."

After that Bryce noticed that whenever Mother's gift-giving basket was returned, so were the dishtowels. The Case of the Disappearing Dishtowels was solved—by communicating clearly!

Our God is a wonderful communicator. The Bible clearly communicates everything we need to know about who He is. Another way to know what God is like is to read about the life of Jesus. Jesus said, "If you know Me, you know the Father" (see John 14:9).

Maybe that is why one name John used for our wonderful Communicator-Saviour was "the Word."   **Carolyn**

Instruments Don't Lie

P art of an airplane pilot's training involves some time spent "under the hood." When a student pilot is under the hood, it means they attach something to their head that limits their vision to only the dials and numbers in front of them; they can't see out of the plane.

The purpose is to train the pilots how to fly in foggy weather or at night when they can't see the ground or any landmarks. Some pilots who haven't trained under the hood and find themselves in bad weather become disoriented. They may think they're flying level, even though the instruments say they're heading down. If they believe their feelings rather than what the instruments tell them, they may fly the airplane right into the ground and be killed.

It takes practice to trust those instruments. And it takes practice to trust in God, too. Sometimes our feelings may be so strong that we want to trust them more than God. Our feelings may come between us and God. Maybe we want to be popular and do something that God has told us will actually hurt us. **Isaiah 59:2** warns us about what might happen then: **But your iniquities have separated between you and your God.** Because God says "Don't do that," we may be tempted to shut God out of our lives. That's very dangerous. Like the pilot in a fog, the safe thing to do is to fight the feeling that we don't need to obey God's commandments and choose to go with what God says is right. Then we get back on track. God's commandments aren't painful; they are rules of ethics that result in contented lives.

Why, then, do some people struggle so hard against them? Think about it. Do you think it hurts more to break a commandment—lie, steal, be disrespectful to parents, kill, obsess with wanting something that someone else has—and live with the consequences, or does it hurt more to follow the commandments? **Nancy**

Apr 2

Help Me Go to Buhanda!

If we ask anything according to his will he hears us. I John 5:14, RSV.

Now remember that we should pray for Baby Naomi across the road, who has malaria," Mom said to 10-year-old Brandt and the two younger neighbor boys they were baby-sitting that day. "Because of the gasoline shortage her parents haven't been able to drive her to the hospital."

Mother prayed, then Brandt, and then 6-year-old Josh. Then it was 2-year-old Marc's turn.

"Help me go ride in a car," he blurted out. "Help me go Buhanda. Help me go Kigali. Help me go Butare." As Marc continued to list towns in the African country where his missionary family lived, Josh, his 6-year-old brother, began to giggle.

"M-a-a-arc," said Brandt in an irritated whisper, "you're *supposed* to be praying for Baby *Naomi*."

"Oh, OK," said Marc, and he began praying again. "Help Baby Nomi go Buhanda. Help Baby Nomi go Kigali. Help Baby Nomi go Butare. And me too!"

How long would you like to be friends with someone whose entire conversation with you consisted of "I need a baseball glove—can I have yours?" "Cool purse—give it to me!" "Hey, there's a Taco Bell—buy me a seven-layer burrito and a large drink!" Forget it! You'd tire of all the begging and be searching for a new friend!

Praying is talking to God as to a friend. In conversation with friends it feels good to know they like you, that they think you're worth something, and that they appreciate you for occasionally helping them out with their problems. God enjoys these same things in our conversations with Him.

Fortunately, God doesn't dump us when our prayers become selfish, constantly asking for ourselves, as little Marc did. But it is His *will* that when we talk to Him in prayer we don't forget everything else that our friendship is about.

In the Bible, John reminds us that when we pray according to God's will, *that* is when things start happening! (First John 5:14 to the end of the chapter.)

By the way, Baby Naomi did get well, and Marc had *many* rides in a car.

Carolyn

Runnin' Scared

"Do not be afraid, little flock, for your Father has chosen gladly to give you the kingdom." Luke 12:32, NASB.

Harvey was the result of my ninth grade biology teacher's helping me skin, preserve, and stuff a little brown rabbit. (A neighbor had spotted it in his lettuce patch and, sadly, shot it.) I stuffed Harvey with his front and back legs extended, as if he were having a relaxing nap on his bulging tummy. I soon discovered Harvey's tummy bulge made him smoothly plane across a waxed linoleum floor when given a quick shove. Boy, Harvey could really travel!

My roommate, Nancy, and I had a friend whom we nicknamed Scaredy-cat Stacey. When I brought Harvey back to the girls' dormitory to show Nancy (always a willing partner in crime), we immediately hatched a plan.

Later that evening, after the dean had turned the room lights out, we sneaked into Stacey's dormitory room and started telling a made-up story about giant killer rats overrunning a farm. Over the side of Stacey's bed my dangling foot searched out the hidden Harvey and administered a swift kick. It sent him racing like an ice skater across the waxed floor.

"What was that?" gasped Stacey, hyperventilating.

"What was what?" I asked, trying to sound innocent but choking back a laugh.

"It looked like a giant killer rat!" she moaned.

"It must have been your imagination," said Nancy, sending Harvey back in my direction.

Then I screamed because suddenly Harvey did look like a giant killer rat. That did it! Stacey was out the door, screeching all the way to the dean's office. Of course, Nancy and I quickly made things right with Stacey—and the dean. And I felt extra stupid for getting scared of my own stuffed rabbit!

A characteristic of His that God wants to share with us is fearlessness. He told Moses, Joshua, Rahab, David, the 12 disciples—and us—to "fear not." He knew that in this life we would meet a lot of "Harveys"—both real and imagined. And if He's willing to give us His kingdom, don't you think He's also willing to give us His courage when we ask for it? **Carolyn**

I'm Not Dishonest; I'm Speechless!

When I was 16, I was fortunate to be able to tour Egypt on our way back to America from the mission field. We saw the mummies at the museum in Cairo, and I will never forget looking down at the brown, shriveled face of the king who ruled after Moses left Egypt. If Moses hadn't obeyed God by leaving Egypt and going into the desert, probably he'd have been one of Egypt's rulers. He might have been one of those mummies I looked at. Instead, where is Moses now? The Bible tells us he went to heaven. He's alive, enjoying heaven, instead of being a dry and shriveled mummy in a silent glass case.

The country of Egypt began before Jesus was born. According to my encyclopedia, sometime about 3100 B.C. a king named Menes began to rule the people who lived along the Nile River. For more than 3,000 years Egypt remained one of the richest and most civilized lands in the world. Because it is so dry in that area, many old treasures have been preserved, including old letters that people wrote on strips of the papyrus reed that grew along the river. One letter from a little boy-king asks his captain to bring back a dwarf dancer from Africa. A collection of wise sayings recommends "Think much, but keep thy mouth closed."

It made me wonder. . . . Does keeping your mouth closed prevent you from being dishonest? What if you see one last cookie on a plate in the kitchen. You take the cookie and eat it. About that time your mother comes in and asks, "Who took that cookie?"

You don't say anything. Are you lying?

Then she asks, "Did you see who took that cookie?"

You don't answer, but you raise your eyebrows innocently.

Without saying a word you are telling her "I don't know." Is that the truth?

Now read **2 Corinthians 13:7: Ye should do that which is honest.** Each time you choose to be honest, you take one more step toward heaven. God wants to help you get there, so just ask Him for help when you need it.

Nancy

Doctor Who?

He . . . healed those who needed healing. Luke 9:11, NIV.

Let me tell you about Dr. M. C. Modi. Dr. Modi is an eye surgeon in India, a country in which millions of people live. This means Dr. Modi has plenty of patients. He had so many that he decided to come up with methods that would allow him to operate on more eyes each day.

One of Dr. Modi's specialties is cataract surgery. Cataracts are like scales that form over the eyes and prevent a person from seeing clearly. Dr. Modi's record for the number of cataract surgeries in one day is 833. Dr. Modi must have missed his lunch that day! Even if all the people he operated on that day had two eyes with cataracts, that means he would have operated on more than 400 people.

What's more, Dr. Modi has visited 46,120 villages, worked with more than 1 million patients, and has performed over a half million operations. What a doctor! What dedication! Dr. Modi certainly has affected many lives for good.

As wonderful as Dr. Modi is, however, there's another doctor who has done even more. Jesus, the Great Physician, healed many people, visited numerous villages, and even raised people from the dead during the years He lived on our earth. But something else Dr. Jesus has done is even greater than that: He's discovered the cure for the worst disease of all—sin.

Sin infects everybody, and the only cure is death! That's right; someone has to die to bring about the cure for sin. Fortunately for us, our Great Physician has already done it. The cure is already available; all we have to do is accept it by faith. How do you do that? Simply ask Jesus to cleanse your life of sin, and He'll do the operation. He'll give you eternal life, and you'll be under the care of Dr. Jesus as long as you want. It doesn't mean that you won't slip and bruise yourself again, but Jesus will bandage your wounds and forgive you.

Call the Doctor today. Ask Jesus to give you the cure for sin.

Jim

$\mathbb{A}$pr 6

Tsunami

Let your light so shine before men, that they may see your good works, and glorify your Father which is in heaven. Matthew 5:16.

I heard the powerful motor of the Bass boat rev up. Sitting on a far shore, I caught a brief glimpse, through a small break in the fog, of that beautiful craft as it whizzed by. Nearly two minutes later the sound of the boat had all but disappeared in the distance. But strong little waves made by that boat suddenly rolled through the fog and broke at my feet. I jumped up in order not to get wet.

One kind of wave that results from a distant agitation (often an undersea earthquake) is called tsunami (tsoo-NAH-mee). Seismographs can pick up vibrations, known as seismic waves, when an undersea earthquake occurs. Since seismic waves travel faster than tsunamis (usually between 500 and 600 miles an hour on the open seas), scientists can estimate how soon a tsunami will hit land. They can then warn people, since a wave can form a water wall more than 100 feet high as it approaches shore. One of the most destructive tsunamis struck East Pakistan (now Bangladesh) in 1970 and killed 266,000 people.

The everyday choices we make are like little undersea earthquakes, or speedboats cutting through calm water. Everything we do or say sends out ripples that can become "waves," impacting the lives of others. A cruel taunt, carelessly hurled at someone, can be like a destructive tsunami that will tear that person down. And the kind word or deed you chose to send in someone's direction will bring happiness long after you—like that Bass boat—have "left the scene" of your choice.

After nearly 6,000 years the tsunamis of sin, caused by Adam and Eve's first wrong choice in the Garden of Eden, continue to flood more misery upon this earth than ever before. But the good news is that the choice Jesus made on Calvary will continue to send waves of peace and hope, even into eternity.

How will the choices we make today affect the lives of others?

Carolyn

Put Your Shoulder to the Wheel

A pioneer wagon train is making its slow, exhausting way across a dry and barren plain. Tumbleweeds blow by. The oxen are thirsty, foam dripping from their mouths. Skillets and other cooking utensils dangle from the sides of the covered wagons, clanking noisily together like an erratic wind chime. Perspiration drips off your forehead and burns in your eyes as you trudge beside the wagon.

Toward evening you realize that a cloud cover has formed quickly. A thunderstorm blows up, dumping cool rain in torrents. You stand near the wagon, grinning delightedly as you enjoy an unexpected refreshing shower.

Too soon the shower is over; time to get going again. But now you must make your way through deep mud. The oxen strain against their yokes as they try to pull the heavy wagons. Rolling their eyes at you, they complain loudly, flicking their tails and stamping their feet. You slap them to get them going. They're trying, but the wagon wheels are sunk too deep to budge.

This is when you "put your shoulder to the wheel" and push against the spokes to start it rolling out of the mud. The oxen suddenly scramble forward, their job made easier because of your help. You've helped the oxen, not to condemn them, but to assist them because you care about them.

In the same way, Jesus didn't come and die to make us feel guilty. He came to prove Satan wrong. Read about it in **John 3:17: For God sent not his Son into the world to condemn the world; but that the world through him might be saved.** Satan said God wouldn't care about us if we sinned; Jesus came to prove him wrong. And because He came and put His shoulder to the wheel, and got right in there and lived with us, you and I can choose to believe there is a good supernatural Force, a Force that cares about us and will someday take us to a perfect world.

Nancy

Apr 8

Out Cold

In the morning, O Lord, you hear my voice; in the morning I lay my requests before you and wait in expectation. Psalm 5:3, NIV.

Have you ever seen anyone faint? Maybe it was at a wedding. It seems as though a lot of people faint at weddings. They just fall right over. They don't even try to stop themselves.

Our bodies need oxygen. In fact, your body needs oxygen more than it needs food and water. If your body doesn't get enough oxygen, your brain becomes confused and your muscles don't work right. When you breathe in oxygen from the air, it goes right to your lungs; your lungs absorb it and put it into the blood. Your blood then carries it to all parts of your body—your brain, arms, legs, and everywhere else.

Sometimes a room may get stuffy. You might be wearing a shirt with a collar that's too tight. Or you may be sitting in a position that isn't allowing oxygen to flow freely to all parts of your body. If your brain doesn't get enough oxygen, it may even shut down temporarily, causing you to faint. It's clear that without oxygen our bodies won't work properly. If our whole body goes without oxygen for too long, we will die.

Our spiritual life is no different. If you and I go without talking and listening to God by reading His Word and praying, our spiritual life will die. Oh, everything may seem like it's going just fine, but God is the source of our spiritual strength and our salvation. If we get cut off from Him, the Source of our salvation, we will surely die.

God has so many great things planned for you and me. He wants to use us to give joy and love to others around us, but if we're not in contact with Him, He can't give us our spiritual oxygen. Take some time with God today. He'll give you a fresh supply of spiritual strength as you stay in contact with Him. **Jim**

"You Look Like Raggedy Ann!"

Be at peace among yourselves. I Thessalonians 5:13.

Wearing heavy makeup and clothes that were too baggy, Miss Roberts came down the little runway as one of the teacher-participants in a "reverse" fashion show teachers were presenting at the beginning of the school year. That way students would know what was—and wasn't—appropriate clothing to wear to school.

"Look, everyone!" called out fifth grader Melinda. "Miss Roberts looks like Raggedy Ann!"

After school that day Melinda approached Miss Roberts. "Uh, Miss Roberts—" she began. "I don't *really* think you look like Raggedy Ann. You just had pink circles on your cheeks."

"Oh, Melinda, I wasn't offended. Besides, you were just being honest."

The girl looking relieved. "Wanna know something else I *honestly* think?"

Miss Roberts nodded.

"I really think that, uh, in your *condition*—"

"What do you mean, 'in my *condition*'?" Miss Roberts asked.

"Well, a little something on your face might, uh, help your appearance . . . you know—"

Miss Roberts still looked puzzled.

"You know," Melinda said, stepping forward as one does when about to share a secret with a good friend, "with all those wrinkles under your chin now, and those circles under your eyes and stuff . . ." Suddenly Melinda turned and fled.

Knowing Melinda's intentions were sincere, Miss Roberts chose not to be offended and actually enjoyed a good laugh after her well-meaning student had left the room.

Most of us have tried, at one time or another, to make an uncomfortable situation better and instead we've made it worse. That seems to be part of life. But take courage—nobody's perfect! The apostle Paul knew that too and counseled us simply to do our best in getting along with each other.

If you blow it once in a while, well, a *good* friend will give you another chance like Jesus always does. And if you follow Paul's advice, you'll do the same for your friends.   **Carolyn**

Don't Miss the Boat

Do you believe in God? Sometimes people question the existence of God because they can't touch Him. They can touch their cars and homes. They can touch their parents and their dogs. But they can't touch God and begin to wonder if God is real. If they wonder too long and don't accept Him, they may eventually miss the boat—in the same way you would miss the boat if you arrived at the dock too late. Missing the boat means you understand something too late for it to be of any benefit to you.

Once upon a time a minister was called to go to a tavern and deliver a message to the husband of one of his parishioners, who was ill. When the minister entered the tavern, he easily spotted the man and made his way over to him. The man, now hopelessly drunk, tried to embarrass the minister by calling out, "There is no God! Cheers!"

The minister laid his hand on the man's shoulder and said, "Friend, what you have said is not new. The Bible said that more than 2,000 years ago."

The drunkard blinked his eyes in amazement. "Aw, c'mon! Show me!"

So the minister read **Psalm 14:1: "'The fool hath said in his heart, there is no God.'"** Then he added, "There's a difference between you and that fool, however. The fool in the Bible said it only in his heart; he didn't shout it out loud in a tavern."

G. K. Chesterton, a famous writer, once said, "It is often supposed that when people stop believing in God, they believe in nothing." Unfortunately, it's even worse than that—when they stop believing in God, they believe in anything.

I believe in God because I believe in Satan, and everything in life has an opposite. If Satan is real, then God is real, too. Satan just happens to be more open about his presence, but God is just as real and even more powerful.

Why should you believe in God? Because belief gives you direction to your life. It gives you peace and hope. And if you have these things, you will not miss the boat. **Nancy**

The Stolen Bible

They . . . examined the Scriptures every day. Acts 17:11, NIV.

There was something different about this housekeeper. Mrs. Rodale couldn't put her finger on it, but whatever it was, she liked it. At the end of the interview Mrs. Rodale told Mattie that she had the job and that she would see her tomorrow for work.

The next day Mattie came right on time to work at the Rodales' house. "Now, Mattie," Mrs. Rodale said, "this afternoon my friends are coming over for a Bible study. Would you please make us some sandwiches and lemonade?"

"Be happy to, Mrs. Rodale," Mattie said enthusiastically as she quickly went to work preparing for the guests.

Soon it was time for the guests to arrive, and Mrs. Rodale went to get her Bible where she always kept it, right beside her bed. But her Bible wasn't there! *Where could I have left it?* she thought. She searched around and under the bed. No Bible. By now she was getting a bit frantic. All her notes were in that Bible. She liked to be prepared, especially when it came to Bible study.

Running downstairs, she found Mattie setting out the sandwiches and lemonade. "Mattie, Mattie, have you seen my Bible?"

With a smile as big as her face Mattie exclaimed, "Well, praise the Lord, praise the Lord!"

"Mattie, what are you talking about?"

"Well," Mattie said, "the first thing I do when I go to work at a new house is to hide the Bible. I want to see how long it will take the people to miss it. You'll find your Bible in the linen closet under the sheets."

How long has it been since you've read your Bible? Would you miss it if someone hid it? God has so many things He wants you to know. There's so much He wants to say to you, and it's all in the Bible. Do you know where *your* Bible is right now? Better go check; someone might have hidden it!   **Jim**

Apr 12

Giant Beanstalks

No eye has seen, no ear has heard, no mind has conceived what God has prepared for those who love him. I Corinthians 2:9, NIV.

The beanstalk grew all the way up to the clouds so that Jack could climb up to another world," I overheard fifth-grader Rita say to Gregory. The three of us had just gotten "frozen" during a freeze tag game during recess and were talking until someone on our team could make it over to "unfreeze" us.

"What?" I interrupted. "That story sounds really dumb."

"Haven't you ever heard of 'Jack and the Beanstalk'?" Rita asked.

No, I hadn't, because my parents didn't allow me to read fairy tales. Neither did Gregory's parents. So Rita filled us in.

"Someone really had to work hard to think that story up," commented Gregory when Rita finished.

"Guess you're right," she agreed. "Nothing in this world really grows that big or that fast."

Rita was right, of course—but not by much. Although I didn't know it back then, God really *did* create some amazing plants for our world. Check these out:*

• The stinking corpse lily in Southeast Asia measures three feet across and weighs 15 pounds. (It really does smell bad, too!)

• In July 1978 a plant known as *Hesperoyucca whipplei* grew 12 feet in 14 days. (That's 10 inches a day.)

• The largest cactus, located near Gila Bend, Arizona, grew to a height of 57 feet, 11¾ inches.

Although these plants are pretty astounding, "we ain't seen nothin' yet." Not compared with what God's planning to create on this old world after He comes again. Why? Simply because He loves us. The Bible says we can't even *imagine* anything close to it!

In the earth made new I want to introduce you to my friends, Rita and Gregory. You'd really like them—they're a lot of fun. Why, Rita may even challenge you to a game of freeze tag on her own giant beanstalk! **Carolyn**

---

*Peter Matthews, editor, *Guinness Book of Records* (New York: Facts on File, Inc., 1992), p. 47.

Through the Mill

There's a charming old house in Volcano, Hawaii, known as "My Island Bed and Breakfast." Even though it's about 100 years old, it still has the original hearth, natural boughs for stair rails, and the original tub—rectangular, made completely of wood!

The windows, most of them still with original glass, have areas of distorted imperfections (as glass had 100 years ago when the thickness wasn't even). Through the years some of the windowpanes have cracked. Knowing that if the panes were replaced with modern glass the windows would look patched, the owners came up with a creative solution.

They called for the services of a local artist. This man, experienced in the art of stained glass, kept as much of the original glass in place as possible. He fashioned a stained glass design in the cracked windowpane, making the windows more interesting.

In one windowpane a brilliant red cardinal sits on a twisted bough. In another a vine of green leaves and soft pink blossoms winds its way across the window. No one would know there had ever been a blemish on any window. Because of the cracks and the artist's skill the windows are more beautiful than they would have been otherwise.

You could say those old windows have been "through the mill." There has been hardship, but the windows came through the hardship more beautiful than they were before. To go through the mill means to endure hardship with a positive attitude, confident that you'll be changed for the better after it's all over. Read what **Galatians 6:9** says about going through the mill: **Let us not become weary in doing good, for at the proper time we will reap a harvest if we do not give up (NIV).**

Sometimes the immediate results of doing what's right don't feel so good. Your friends may make fun of you; you might have to pay a penalty for confessing to a lie; you might temporarily miss something you've shared with someone who doesn't seem to appreciate it. But that's the short-term stuff of going through the mill. The long-term stuff—how you feel about yourself—is the great reward. You'll really like yourself for being honest. Or kind. Or generous. You'll become known as a person of integrity.

Nancy

A_{p}^{r} 14

"Forgiven," the Movie

In him we have redemption through his blood, the forgiveness of sins, in accordance with the riches of God's grace. Ephesians 1:7, NIV.

I gathered up the rented movies to return them to the video store. As I was picking them up, I noticed a movie that looked like it came from the video store, but I didn't recall renting it. Oh, well, I'd take it back and see if it belonged to them. I set the videos on the counter and looked around while the clerk checked them in. Since I was returning them on time, I didn't think about paying a late fee.

"Sir," the clerk said, "I think there's a problem with this video. It appears that you owe $287.46 in late fees."

I was shocked! "That can't be right! When was it checked out?"

The clerk punched a few buttons on the computer, and we discovered the movie had been checked out almost a year before. The strange thing was I'd never received any late notices.

"Sir, I'll call a manager and get this straightened out."

I tried to think of how I was going to come up with almost $300 to pay for the late video. My thoughts were interrupted as the manager asked what the problem was. The clerk explained the situation, and the manager started pressing computer keys and looking at the screen. As a puzzled look came over his face, thoughts of going without food for the month crossed my mind.

"Well, I don't know what the problem is, but I don't even see that movie in our system," said the manager.

"But it was there just a minute ago," said the clerk.

"Well, it's not now. We'll just keep this video, if you don't mind, and you're free to go."

I was free to go! I walked out of the video store not knowing what to think. In a few minutes I had gone from owing almost $300 to owing nothing. Talk about joy!

You know, Jesus did something far greater than that. He took our sins and said, "You're free to go." Actually, that makes us free to stay—with Him, for eternity.

Jim

Kim of the Concrete Jungle

When the enemy shall come in like a flood, the Spirit of the Lord shall lift up a standard against him. Isaiah 59:19.

Kent had heard how the school watchdog, Kim, tore both pant legs—and the flesh—of any student who risked a nighttime trip to the one restroom after 10:00 p.m. Kent also knew that Kim's presence at this small mission was necessary. Garden thieves and armed robbers in the city still had respect for big dogs with sharp teeth.

"Mommy, I feel sick!" 4-year-old Kent called out one night.

His mother rolled over and looked at her wristwatch: 1:00 a.m. That meant Kim would be out guarding the mission. "Are you sure you can't go back to sleep, sweetheart?" she pleaded.

"No-o-o-o, I'm gonna throw up!" he wailed.

Offering a quick prayer that Kim wouldn't hear them, Mother led Kent outside and down the breezeway. Her body suddenly went cold as the sound of large animal feet pounded across the dry lawn. Then deep ferocious barking filled the midnight air.

"It's Kim!" shrieked Kent in terror.

Acting almost from instinct, Mother scooped Kent into her left arm and whirled to meet the giant of a dog with foam flecks gathered about his mouth. "No!" she screamed, rushing at him.

Kent fell silent as the snarling Kim abruptly stopped and circled to the right, his wild eyes glowing red in the flashlight's beam.

"Bad dog!" roared Mother, keeping her flashlight shining steadily into the dog's unblinking eyes.

Kim stubbornly held his threatening preattack crouch.

Suddenly Kent's thin but courageous little voice pierced the air. "Go away!" he ordered authoritatively, pointing a finger at the big dog.

At the sound of Kent's voice Kim's snarl turned to a whimper, and Mother watched in amazement as the huge dog slunk off sheepishly into the shadows of the African night.

Like Mother sweeping Kent into her arms, God wants to carry us through all of Satan's attacks. And safe in our heavenly Father's arms, we—like little Kent—will find the courage to look the tempter in the eyes and say, "Go away!"   **Carolyn**

Life Is Just a Bowl of Cherries

Humorist Erma Bombeck has written a book entitled *If Life Is Just a Bowl of Cherries, What Am I Doing in the Pits?* To say that "life is just a bowl of cherries" is supposed to mean that life is wonderful and beautiful—like a bowl of cherries. But you need to be careful when you eat a bowl of cherries, remembering there is a seed inside that you don't want to swallow. And another thing, if you eat too many cherries, you may get a stomachache.

Personally, I think today's phrase makes sense. Cherries are beautiful by the bowlful, and life is mostly enjoyable. But with beauty comes caution. The most enjoyable life will have its moments of fear and anxiety. However, it is those moments of anxiety that make the good times so much sweeter. In those moments when you are most *uncertain* that life on this earth is sweet, the only thing you have left to look forward to is the next life—with Jesus, in heaven. Being in the "pits" contains the active ingredients for a new life in the same way that cherry pits contain future cherry trees.

It's like the bees that develop throughout the first stage of their lives in a honeycomb. When they are mature and have eaten up all the honey available to them, they must work hard to get through the waxy doors of their cradles to get out. It exhausts them, but struggling out of their tight quarters scrapes away the membrane that covers their tiny wings. And after the struggle they discover that they can fly!

Perhaps this is what Jesus was referring to when He said, **"My grace is sufficient for thee: for my strength is made perfect in weakness" (2 Corinthians 12:9).** Your struggles scrape away your satisfaction with this life. And when you're hungry enough for true happiness, you search for Jesus. Total dependence on Him moves you toward heaven. Remember that the next time you eat cherries! **Nancy**

What's in a Name?

A good name is more desirable than great riches; to be esteemed is better than silver or gold. Proverbs 22:1, NIV.

One of the many things I wanted to be when I grew up was a detective. Detectives look for clues left behind after a crime to see if they can figure out what happened. It's like a jigsaw puzzle. You take the pieces and fit them all together until you come up with a picture of what happened.

I think that's why I like fossil collecting so much. What does fossil collecting have to do with detective work? Well, for one thing, fossils are like clues that were left behind thousands of years ago. In Arizona there are huge fossilized trees. They aren't made of wood anymore—they are completely stone. Water, maybe at the time of the Flood, completely soaked those trees. When the trees dried out, the minerals in the water stayed behind, and after many years the wood rotted away. All that was left was the minerals that formed an exact replica of the tree. Every detail of those trees is preserved. You can see how big they were, how old they were, and what their bark looked like.

When detectives are looking for clues, they'll often look through people's garbage. Yuk! Why the garbage? By looking at what people throw away you discover many things—what a person eats, where they shop, and sometimes who they call on the telephone.

Everything we do leaves clues as to what kind of persons we are—the words we say, how we treat people, and the way we conduct ourselves. You may not think that anybody pays any attention to you, but that's not true. There are little boys and girls in every school who look up to older kids like you.

Fossils can show us something about life thousands of years ago. Garbage can tell us about a person. What kind of impression will your actions and words leave? It will be a good one if Jesus lives within your heart.

Jim

A Mouse in the House

I pommel [beat, discipline] my body and subdue it, lest after preaching to others I myself should be disqualified. I Corinthians 9:27, RSV.

Gross me out! But not at first. No, when I'd first spotted a few rodent droppings on the kitchen floor I suspected a mouse had passed through. But since my house was so clean, I did nothing about it. When I found droppings a few weeks later, I still did nothing. I didn't *really* have a mouse problem!

The next week I returned home to find a gaping hole in the rocking chair, the corner of a throw rug chewed up, and more droppings along the kitchen counter. *Now gross me out!* Rushing to the hardware store, I bought two mousetraps, the kind that look like little black coffins. You bait them, trap the mouse, and then throw the whole thing away—never having to get your hands dirty.

When I got home from school the next day, I found both traps sprung—but still empty. I looked about and saw *lots* of droppings, whole portions of carpet badly soiled, and *more* carpet chewed up! The horrible truth dawned on me—that mouse was expecting babies and was making a home for them!

How depressing! In a few short weeks *one little* mouse had taken over my house, my life, and was now preparing to reproduce itself at an unknown location under my roof. And all this because I hadn't gotten rid of it when I first suspected its presence.

I headed straight for the grocery store, bought a no-nonsense, show-all, spring-operated trap, and the smelliest cheese I could find. The next day when I came home there was the very expectant—but very dead—mouse in my trap.

One sinful habit, continually tolerated in our "house" (which Paul calls "the temple of God"), is like that cute little mouse taking over my house. If not resisted early on, that sin will chew away, soil, take over, and eventually destroy us.

With God's help, through prayer, Bible study, and the choice of positive friends, we can trap those mice early on—before they do any lasting damage to our "house."

Carolyn

Don't Turn Your Geese Into Swans

During the early seventeenth century there must have been someone who exaggerated and told big lies. Perhaps it was a young "swain" who tried to impress a certain maiden with glowing reports of how wonderfully well he was doing. Maybe he told her he had 50 horses on his property (he didn't mention they were toys). Maybe he exclaimed about one of his "teachers" who was certain he would someday become a knight (he didn't say the teacher was his mother). He might have even suggested that one day he would be king (of his own home).

Whatever the case, once upon a time someone exaggerated the truth and made everything seem better than it really was in order to impress someone. And the statement was made, "He has turned his geese into swans." Geese, being rather noisy, common birds, differ quite radically from elegant swans. Turning geese into swans might be something like telling people there's a Ferrari in the garage when really it's a VW bug.

Maybe such people don't think they're good enough. What really happens is that after their friends learn that they lie a lot they not only lose the trust of their friends, they may also lose those friends.

Sometimes it's fun to say "My maid didn't clean up my room today" when your friend drops in unexpectedly and your room is a mess. You both know there is no maid. But if you exaggerate all the time so that people can't trust you, you need to stop doing that.

King Solomon has some advice in **Proverbs 22:1** about the importance of your reputation: **A good name is rather to be chosen than great riches, and loving favour rather than silver and gold.** You don't have to have what everyone else has to be a good friend. In fact, if you have honesty and integrity (that sense that you have nothing to hide), you may already have more than a lot of other people.

So what do you do when someone begins bragging about how expensive their clothes are or about how wonderful their trip to Disneyland was? Begin to feel jealous? No! Just say "I'm happy for you." Say it nicely, and mean it. Later, make a list of the things you're happy *you* have. Your list will be different, and that's OK.

Nancy

Apr 20

Famous Friends

I no longer call you servants. . . . Instead, I have called you friends, for everything that I learned from my Father I have made known to you. John 15:15, NIV.

It's nice to know that when you tell a secret, it won't go anywhere. It's nice to have a friend with whom you can share your deepest thoughts. That's the difference between a friend and an acquaintance.

Is there someone famous you'd like to be friends with? Wouldn't your friends be envious if you brought your famous friend to school to meet them?

One day Jesus was having a very important discussion with His disciples, as you've probably had with some of your friends. By now the disciples knew that Jesus was God's Son. (How would you feel if you actually knew God's Son? I mean, you knew Him face-to-face. That would be something to impress your friends with!) As the disciples were wondering why He was telling them so many important things, Jesus said an amazing thing. He told the disciples they were His friends—not just followers, not just servants—but friends. How do you think that made the disciples feel? The reason Jesus said they were friends was that He was telling them things about His Father that He hadn't told anyone else. What great secrets to know! The disciples could really impress their friends now!

The most incredible thing about this is that you and I know *those same secrets!* They're all written down in the Bible. That means *we're* God's friends too. What an amazing thought! When your friends here on earth fail you and even treat you badly, just remember, Jesus knows all your secrets and your mistakes, and He still wants to call you His friend.

Now, *that's* something you can impress your friends with. Hey, why not invite them to be friends with Jesus too! **Jim**

Double Bubble Trouble!

He Himself gives life and breath to everything. Acts 17:25, TLB.

D o you like to blow bubbles with bubble gum? Susan Montgomery Williams of Fresno, California, does. In fact, in 1985 she set the record for the greatest reported diameter for a bubble gum bubble: 22 inches!*

I remember trying to set my own big bubble record in fifth grade. I both blew and made noises so that my younger brother would turn and see my huge impressive bubble.

When he finally turned around, his eyes got big. I thought he was coming over to have a closer look. Instead, with lightning speed, he play-fully jabbed his pointer finger right into my pale pink masterpiece! *Kafoom!* This quick action smacked the burst bubble back onto my face—and spread its rubbery remains from eyebrows to chin, from east ear to west ear. Not only was some of the guck nearly impossible to get off, but desperate facial scrubbing actually left raw patches on my chin for the next few days.

Getting control over a bad habit is something like bubble gum blow-ing. Just when we think we're getting along pretty well with something such as temper or foul language control, Satan comes along and bursts our fragile bubble. He does this by giving us a temptation in our weak areas, and we can't seem to resist.

The first Bible account of someone blowing air into something is found in Genesis 2:7. Do you know who it was? God, the Creator. He blew the first breath into the first man on the sixth day of Creation. What a miracle! And another miracle is that He still gently blows His Spirit into our lives so that in Him we can "live and move and have our being" (Acts 17:28).

By staying close to God every day through prayer in whatever we're doing—even chewing bubble gum—we'll be breathing His Spirit and learning to blow bigger, better, and eventually unburstable bubbles.

Carolyn

---

*Peter Matthews, editor, *Guinness Book of Records* (New York: Facts on File, Inc., 1992), p. 197.

Apr 22

How Do You Know You Don't Go to Heaven When You Die?

The September 1994 issue of *National Geographic* has a fascinating story entitled "Fantasy Coffins of Ghana." The first photograph is of a wooden Mercedes-Benz. "Pop the hood and a wooden Mercedes-Benz makes a final resting place for a man who drove the real thing around Ghana," the article begins (p. 121). Other coffins include a huge pink fish for a fisherman, a KLM jet chosen by a pilot, a huge outboard motor on its side for a mechanic, a leopard, a cow, and a green onion.

Why do Seventh-day Adventists believe that we don't go to heaven when we die? Because of **Ecclesiastes 9:5, 6: For the living know that they will die, but the dead know nothing; they have no further reward, and even the memory of them is forgotten. Their love, their hate and their jealousy have long since vanished; never again will they have a part in anything that happens under the sun (NIV).**

It's hard to understand why some people believe one of the most dangerous myths going around: when you die you go up to heaven to be with your "dead" relatives. It may sound like a good idea on the surface, making dying seem like something we should want to do so we won't be lonely anymore. But when you think about it, if you were up in heaven, looking down on your family as they grieve for you, wouldn't it be frustrating not to be able to comfort your family? Does that sound like Paradise?

How does it make you feel about God if you believe He "takes" people from their families on earth to be with Him in heaven? How many people does He need? It doesn't make Him seem very loving toward us.

That's why I believe Satan is behind that myth. Satan wants to play down the pain of loss and make death sound wonderful, while making God sound selfish. It could make those who don't know God hate Him.

The Bible says the dead don't know anything. They're fast asleep, unconscious. Someday they'll go to heaven, but not until Jesus comes to take us there. That's when the great reunion that we look forward to will happen.

Nancy

Flight Disaster

My son, do not forget my teaching, but keep my commands in your heart. Proverbs 3:1, NIV.

I could hardly wait. I had built my own remote-controlled model glider. It had a six-foot wingspan, little electric motors that controlled the rudders, and ailerons. And I had put it all together. I was proud. And now it was time to fly.

The man at the store where I bought it had told me, "Be sure you have an experienced glider pilot with you when you fly for the first time. If you don't, you will crash."

As I was driving to the soccer field those words kept ringing in my ears. I tried to drown them out by thinking, *I'm coordinated; I'm smart; I built the plane, didn't I? Surely I can fly it. How hard can it be?*

My heart was beating wildly as I pulled into the parking lot. Good, nobody here. When I landed, I didn't want anybody in my way. I carefully pulled my glider out of the car and headed for the soccer field. I pounded a stake into the ground that held a giant rubber band. I carefully hooked the rubber band to the bottom of my plane and slowly started walking backward to stretch out the line. Rubber band pulled tight, plane in my left hand, radio in my right hand, I was ready to fly.

With a heave I threw my plane skyward. It took off and started to loop above my head. Then it was flying over my head backward. Then it headed for the ground. And then, with a sickening splintering sound, it crashed nosefirst into the ground, destroyed. Why? Because I refused to listen to and obey the words of the store manager who told me not to fly alone.

Do you think God is even wiser than that store manager? I think so. No, I know so. When God gives us instructions in His Word, it's for a reason. The reason is that He loves us and wants what's best for us. Do I wish I had listened to that store manager? Definitely. Do I think you and I should listen to and obey God? Most definitely. **Jim**

Apr 24

Real-life Ski Bum

If anyone is going to boast, let him boast about what the Lord has done and not about himself. 2 Corinthians 10:17, TLB.

lam! Ouch! The icy metal chair on the ski lift slammed into my rib cage as another skier, coming out of nowhere, tried to lunge onto the chair beside me. Two lift operators pushed him securely back into the chair as his poles and skis waved about wildly.

Oh great! I thought. *I'm stuck with this guy—50 feet above ground—for the next 10 minutes.* In spite of the pain in my rib cage, I tried to make conversation. "So how long have you been skiing?" I asked.

"Never tried before," he answered, confidence coming into his face. "This will be my first run. My cousin's waiting for me at the top. I tried to get onto his chair but fell off."

I believed him. "But this is an intermediate to advanced run," I warned him.

"I know, but I can do anything I put my mind to. Always have. You might say I'm a real sports jock."

The frosty air and my chairlift chum's continual account of his athletic coolness made the last eight minutes of our ride seem like forever.

As we neared the top, he suddenly asked, "So how do you get off one of these things?"

"Very quickly," I answered. (That was certainly *my* plan.)

"Oh, I can do that!" he bragged.

The scrambling noises his skis, poles, and body made scraping down the icy exit ramp behind me quickly faded into the distance. The next time I saw this guy was when three members of the ski patrol were strapping him into a toboggan for downhill transport. The last thing I remember was his protesting screams, "But I really *can* ski! I *can!* I'm *awesome!*"

What do you like to boast about? Paul said, "When someone boasts about himself and how well he has done, it doesn't count for much. But when the Lord commends him, that's different!" (2 Corinthians 10:18, TLB).

Carolyn

As Close as the Bark to the Tree

If trees could talk, some of them would have tremendous stories to tell. Recently a 500-year-old tree that had stood majestically on a mountaintop in Colorado fell to the ground. It was just a sapling when Columbus landed in San Salvador, its roots just beginning to strengthen their grip on the earth. Pushing its head higher and higher into the sky, the tree had grown strong and proud for four centuries. Those who seemed to know said the tree had been struck by lightning 14 times, withstood windstorms, and even an earthquake. But one tiny thing brought it down: beetles had bored between the bark and the tree, chewing away its mighty fibers. Finally, its bond with the bark broken, the tree succumbed to the most recent storm.

The bond between a tree and its bark is essential. This bond describes the deepest bond between friends. You may have heard someone say that two friends are "as close as the bark to the tree." Take one away from the other and they both become scarred, because they mutually nourish each other. If you have a friend like this, you are fortunate.

Jesus is such a friend. If you're at a time in your life when you're in a new school or a new town, or you are struggling to make new friends because the old friends have different values than you do, start with Jesus. He's a friend who knows why you do what you do. He knows everything that has happened to you, and He still likes you and wants to take you to His house to meet His Father. It makes me feel strong to know Jesus is my friend. Read **Romans 8:31** and find out why: **If God be for us, who can be against us?**

The quickest friends to make are those who know someone you know. As you choose your new friends, you'll be happiest if you choose friends who also know Jesus. **Nancy**

Apr 26

Heavenly Gophers

Be patient, then, brothers, until the Lord's coming. See how the farmer waits for the land to yield its valuable crop and how patient he is for the autumn and spring rains. You too, be patient and stand firm, because the Lord's coming is near. James 5:7, 8, NIV.

I baled hay during the summers I was in academy. When the hay was ready to harvest, we'd drive through the field on a tractor with a big cutting blade and cut the hay. After the hay had dried for a few days, we baled it and loaded it on the wagons. It was then used to feed the animals.

I always thought we humans were the ones to figure out this thing about baling hay, but I was wrong. Long before we began doing it, God created animals that dried out "hay" for the winter. One of these animals is the tiny pika. Mountain climbers are usually the only ones ever to spot these little creatures. Pikas are fit-in-your-hand animals with large round ears and big eyes. These cute little guys are smart, too. They know when winter is coming, and our Creator has told them what to do to be ready for it. They go about gathering stalks of plants, twigs, and seeds, and lay them out on rocks to dry and preserve. After the drying process is complete, they hide the dried plants in their burrows for many healthy meals during the cold mountain winters.

The Bible says we should be farmers who harvest, just like the little pika. Jesus is coming again, and we need to be ready for Him. The farmer waters and cares for the crops so they can be harvested in the fall. We need to take care of the field of our hearts. Each day we need to spend time with Jesus so that He can care for us and grow us into healthy Christians, ready for the harvest at His second coming. Are you getting ready for the harvest? Water your heart by spending time with Jesus each day. You'll be amazed how His love can cause you to bloom into the person He wants you to be.   **Jim**

"Attack" of the Giant Cricket

God hath not given us the spirit of fear, but of power, and of love, and of a sound mind. 2 Timothy 1:7.

From my earliest years I'd been especially afraid of the dark. Although it felt a little scary when the electrical generator quit working that stormy African night, Matayo (the student night watchman), Dorcasi (another student who couldn't go home for vacation), and I had lit a kerosene lantern, drunk another cup of hot chocolate, and then said our evening prayer together.

When Matayo stepped outside to take up his night watch position, Dorcasi retired to her room. It was then, while walking away from the fireplace with my candle, that I first heard the "cricket." By the time I'd reached my bedroom at the end of the hall, a grating sound mixed in with the cricket's chirp. My stomach went cold.

But when I blew out my candle, the sudden symphony of terrifying sounds made it seem as if a monster cricket was lumbering down the dark hallway, giant pincers extended toward my open bedroom door.

Between my sheets and paralyzed by a nameless terror, I screamed a silent, *Jesus, help me!*

The next thing I knew, warm sunbeams were streaming through the bedroom window. Strangely, I didn't even *remember* about the previous night's horror until Matayo stopped by the house to tell Dorcasi and me that sorcerers (witch doctors) had been on the prowl the previous evening, raiding chicken coops.

"Their silly sounds just made me laugh," he added, "so I scared them away from your chickens, Madamu."

Wow, it was hard to believe! After my prayer God had not only given me instant peace and deep sleep, but had also taken away all my fear of the dark.

God wants His children not to be afraid. He wants us to be bold, powerful, and balanced—like He is. How wonderful it is that, for the asking, He will develop all these qualities in us.   **Carolyn**

121

Apr 28

Giving Pearls to Pigs

When I was a junior in Sabbath school, I had a collection of marbles that my brother and I played with. My favorite marble was creamy-white, like custard, and had a diamond-shaped center of ruby red. I loved that marble; I wish I still had it. It was probably the closest thing I had to a pearl.

I like pearly white things. Apparently pearls like people too. People who own pearls tell me that pearls become more luminous the more they are worn. They are treasured for many reasons, not just for their ability to catch the light and reflect a rainbow in their creamy whiteness, but because the people who harvest them do so at great risk to themselves, diving deep under the ocean. When something is hard to get, it becomes very valuable.

These days pearl farms keep oysters in enclosed areas and force sand into them so they'll make pearls. But in Jesus' time finding a pearl in an oyster was not so easy. Because of that, pearls were very valuable, and some people died while trying to find them. That's why Jesus is called the "Pearl of great price"—He died giving Himself to us. Perhaps that's why the gates of heaven are made out of pearl.

Jesus contrasted the pure and beautiful pearl with a pen of pigs—swine, grunting and bristling, shoving their fat noses into slime with ignorant abandon. You wouldn't want to set your feet in their pen, much less a precious pearl!

Judge Manuel Rocker of Shaker Heights, Ohio, once sentenced a 19-year-old boy to three hours in a pigsty because the boy had referred to a police officer as a "pig." After the boy had served his time, he told the judge he had learned his lesson and would never again call a police officer a pig.

Read **Matthew 7:6** to find out what Jesus has to say about pearls: **Do not give dogs what is sacred; do not throw your pearls to pigs (NIV).** We shouldn't offer something of value to those who can't appreciate its worth. Don't give a pearl to a pig; the pig can't appreciate it. If Jesus is the Pearl of great price and we don't appreciate what He did by living with us here, does that mean we're . . . somewhat like pigs? **Nancy**

Through Different Eyes

Everything that was written in the past was written to teach us, so that through endurance and the encouragement of the Scriptures we might have hope. Romans 15:4, NIV.

All right, everyone up! Stand in a circle with your backs to each other. You should now be forming a circle, facing outward. Now, one-by-one, describe what you see. After you finish describing what you see, sit back down and read the next paragraph.

How similar were all the descriptions? Chances are some of them were very different. Maybe some of you saw the same things. It could be that some of you saw things that the others did not see. If someone on the telephone was listening to you describe what you saw, they might think that you weren't all in the same place. How could everyone be in the same place and describe some things that were completely different? It's because you were all describing things from your own perspective. You were all very close to the same spot, but you were facing different directions and seeing different things.

Did you ever wonder why Matthew, Mark, Luke, and John all wrote books about the life of Jesus? Yes, it's because they too saw things from different perspectives. Matthew was a disciple and a tax collector. He saw and understood things differently from John, who was also a disciple, but was part of Jesus' inner circle of friends. Mark and Luke weren't even disciples. Mark probably wrote down the stories of Jesus he heard from Peter, and Luke probably wrote down stories of Jesus that the other disciples had told to Paul.

They were all different, and they wrote for different kinds of people. Everyone listening to this reading has different likes and dislikes. We're all different, and God wouldn't have it any other way. In fact, He made us that way.

Aren't you glad God wants you to be different? Aren't you glad He wrote His Word so you could find something in it especially for you? I sure am. **Jim**

Apr 30

No Big Deal

If the Lord delights in a man's way, he makes his steps firm; though he stumble, he will not fall, for the Lord upholds him with his hand. Psalm 37:23, 24, NIV.

Whew! In my new satin high heels (1½ inches high) I'd negotiated the nonhandrailed, uncarpeted platform stairs twice—without falling—during the eighth grade graduation program.

Now, following Rosie in the line of graduates leaving the stage, I thought, *Just one more trip down those stairs, and I'm home free!*

But as I neared the top step, the long full skirt of my dress suddenly swept forward, coming between my vision and my white heels. Still pretty certain of the first step's location, I confidently took . . . the plunge.

I had overstepped! Immediately I landed on my rear as momentum from who-knows-where propelled my out-of-control bounces down each of the polished wooden steps. My high heels clattered loudly against the side retaining wall. Somehow I managed to grab at the little wall and swing myself onto my feet. More amazingly, I found myself in step behind Rosie!

In the lobby my six classmates began waving their diplomas, screaming and hugging each other. When Rosie turned to me, she gasped, "Why are you crying?"

"Because I ruined our whole graduation with the stupid fall!" I blurted out.

"What? You fell?" asked Lowell.

"No way!" protested Nancy. "I didn't hear a thing."

"Well, I heard a little noise behind me," admitted Rosie, "but it was no big deal."

Only two people who'd been in the audience mentioned seeing me trip. Wow! What a relief when I realized that to most people present at graduation my fall had been no big deal.

Some of the embarrassing things we do—and come down hard on ourselves for—really aren't that big of a deal to others. Let's face it—*everybody* messes up now and then. And as for our mess-ups in the graduation walk toward heaven? At the bottom of any staircase we tumble down, Jesus is always there, holding out a strong hand, which, if we take it, will pull us onto our feet again—*every* time we fall.   **Carolyn**

Happy as a Clam at High Tide

Let's start today's worship by reading **Psalm 107:23, 24: They that go down to the sea in ships, that do business in great waters; these see the works of the Lord, and his wonders in the deep.** I wish I knew for sure what King David was talking about in today's verse, but I can only guess that perhaps he had heard stories about schools of porpoises that jumped into the air; whales so huge they could overturn a ship; and beautiful coral in pinks and greens, a home for shimmering blue and lemon-yellow fish.

A man I know who fishes commercially mentions patience and humility as qualities that those who fish must develop. Patience, because they must wait for the fish to come to them, and humility as they realize how very vulnerable they are to the sometimes unpredictable freak waves that can come out of nowhere and overturn a boat. He thinks that's why fishermen exaggerate their stories—because they feel so small.

Clam-digging is a popular pastime on the Pacific Coast. Serious clamdiggers study the tidal timetables and slog through the mud flats at low tide to dig up clams. They don't go out when the tide is high. And that's why clams are happy at high tide—because they're safe from clamdiggers.

Do you sometimes feel like a clam at low tide—helpless, vulnerable to what somebody else may decide for you? Sometimes a child is helpless when it comes to decisions his or her parents have to make, whether it's a decision to move to another town, get a divorce, or something equally painful. But take a lesson from the clams: nothing in life lasts forever—even the pain and the fear. When bad things happen to you, pretend you're in the ocean. Breathe evenly, put your feet up, and float over the top of this wave. It will go away.

Remind yourself "No pain lasts forever." In time the tides will roll in, and you'll feel comfortable again with a new "normal." You'll be "happy as a clam at high tide."   **Nancy**

May 2

You Are Here

"When he, the Spirit of truth, comes, he will guide you into all truth." John 16:13, NIV.

O rienteering is the ability of finding your way around the wilderness with a map and compass. The best kind of map to use is a topographical map. A topo map shows you where things are located and how far they are from each other, as does any map, but it has other features too. Every little detail is marked, including foot trails and small buildings. You'll also find lines that show the elevation and how steep hills and valleys are.

If you trust your map and compass, you have a very good chance of staying on course. But if you really want to know where you are, you need to have a handheld GPS device. It looks a little like a pocket calculator and receives signals from satellites circling around the earth. These satellites have the ability to tell you exactly where you are. With a map and compass you can tell pretty close, but with the GPS you can pinpoint your exact location. As long as you've got a map, and the batteries don't quit, there's no chance of getting lost.

God has given us the HS navigator (Holy Spirit navigator). It can be pretty confusing at times to know which direction to turn. Our friends say one thing, the TV and newspapers another. There's really only one way to know where you are, only one way to know the truth. It's through the Holy Spirit. The Holy Spirit inspired the prophets to write God's Word, the place to look if you want to know the difference between right and wrong.

Getting lost on a trip in the wilderness is a scary thing. Getting lost in Satan's territory is an even more dangerous thing. But just like a GPS device, the Holy Spirit will always guide you in the right direction, and you'll never have to worry about the batteries running out. **Jim**

May 3

Wild Dog Pack

The Lord will rescue me . . . and will bring me safely to his heavenly kingdom. 2 Timothy 4:18, NIV.

The snarling and howling of the wild dog pack awakened Kent from a deep slumber.

He heard the distant terrified cry of a cat. Then he noticed his little Persian cat was not on the pillow next to his—and that the screen door had been left ajar.

"Oh, no!" he exclaimed under his breath. "Sha-Chat!"* Barefoot and dressed only in pajama bottoms this warm summer night, Kent rushed through the door and across the pine needle underbrush. As he moved toward the frenzied yapping of the dog pack, Kent remembered first seeing Sha-Chat in the pet store and then buying her—using every bit of the money he'd been saving for a motorcycle. Now he was her best friend.

In the distance, up a gentle slope, Kent made out Sha-Chat's silver coat as she clung to the lowest branch of a skinny tree. *Hang on, girl!* his mind pleaded. Five dogs of varied sizes were repeatedly leaping at her. He could see their drooling jowls and sharp teeth as he shoved his way into their midst, knocking the largest dog off balance. Snatching Sha-Chat from the tree, Kent raced through the pack as they now turned their snarling attention on him.

Across the forest floor Kent ran as he'd never run before. The terrified Sha-Chat, her paws around Kent's neck, dug long red stripes into his bare shoulders and upper back as they made their flying escape.

The next day, after seeing the deep claw marks on Kent's shoulders, Mother cried, "Oh, sweetheart, taking on a wild dog pack was a very dangerous things to do. How that must have hurt you!"

"I won't do it again," Kent promised solemnly as Sha-Chat brushed up against his leg. "Mom, it's funny, but I don't remember the pain that much because all I could think about was saving her."

Like Kent, Jesus didn't let the pain—or anything else—stop Him from saving us when He died on the cross in our place.   **Carolyn**

_____
*Pronounced "shaw-shaw."

May 4

Nice Guys Finish Last

Sometimes it seems like nice guys really do finish last. But do they really?

I remember helping with a community project when I was in high school. We went into town and raked leaves for some of the townfolk who were too ill or weak to do it for themselves. The sense of camaraderie was lots of fun, and one little old woman even gave us cookies on her porch after we had finished.

When we got back to the school, we had to wait while a spaghetti dinner was being prepared for us. There we were, tired teenagers sprawled on chairs and tables, trying to amuse ourselves with throwing wadded-up napkins at each other and snitching combs out of back pockets.

And then they announced that supper was ready. Sudden pandemonium as we jockeyed for first place in the line. Being a person who loved to eat, I felt particularly fortunate that my roommate, who was near the front of the line, had saved me a place. I didn't hesitate for a moment, feeling so lucky that I wasn't one of the quieter types waiting at the end of the line, allowing the rest of us to crowd forward.

The meal was delicious, although the sauce was a canned watery type. As I left the cafeteria I was surprised to see that those at the very end of the line were feasting on fresh homemade fettucini with a creamy Parmesan sauce. When I commented on their premium menu, the cook said something about running out of the spaghetti and sauce, so she had had to whip up the fettucini instead. The "nice guys" had finished first, in my opinion.

That very same thing is going to happen when Jesus comes. Christians, who have spent their lifetimes in service and caring for others, may have been misunderstood all their lives because of their unselfishness. But they will be rewarded—big-time. You can read about that promise in **Psalm 37:7: Rest in the Lord and wait patiently for Him; Do not fret because of him who prospers in his way, because of the man who carries out wicked schemes (NASB).** Sometimes God's time seems to take a long time, but it will happen. One of these days the nice guys are going to be rewarded so delightfully it will make the people with "wicked schemes" want to be dead. Just keep on showing kindness and enjoy the sense of self-esteem that is the current reward for doing good.

Nancy

Now, That's Loud!

The Lord himself will come down from heaven, with a loud command, with the voice of the archangel and with the trumpet call of God, and the dead in Christ will rise first. I Thessalonians 4:16, NIV.

I'm a ham radio operator. I can cut a piece of wire to the right size, hook it up to my radio, and talk to people all over the world. I can talk in Morse code or use my voice. I can even make telephone calls from the radio I have in the car.

Ham radios can't do everything, though. I can talk to another person only if he or she is using the radio at the same time. Most of the time I can talk to people all over the United States, but it's difficult to talk to people in other countries at times. There are so many people who want to talk with foreign hams all at the same time that my voice doesn't always get through the crowd. When atmospheric conditions are good, I can talk to people all over the world very easily, but when the atmosphere is doing funny things, there are times when I can't reach anyone. Try as I might, I speak, but no one hears me.

Ham radio is a fascinating hobby, but there's an event coming to Planet Earth that you won't believe until you see it. One day, no matter what the atmospheric conditions, all will hear a voice and the sound of a trumpet that will be heard around the world. It won't matter if you've got a television set or a ham radio. It won't even matter if you're alive! The Bible says that even the dead in Christ will hear it and come to life. What a great day that will be. You can be a part of the most exciting telecommunication event in the history of the universe, the second coming of Jesus Christ.

Take some time each day to get to know Jesus. When He comes again you'll want to know His voice as the voice of your Best Friend.

Jim

May 6

Gotcha Covered, Soldier!

Put on the full armor of God so that you can take your stand against the devil's schemes. Ephesians 6:11, NIV.

Throughout history soldiers have worn special protective clothing known as armor.* Some of it was pretty weird, too. Chinese and Mongol warriors protected themselves by wearing five to seven layers of rhinoceros skin and ox hide "armor." Greek foot soldiers wore multilayered linen breastplates. Soldiers in India quilted their layered linen and used this protection until 100 years ago.

The most famous suits of armor, of course, were used in the European Crusades. Soldiers covered themselves with so many plates of steel that their only contact with the outside world was through a slit in their visors for seeing and small holes in their forged-metal helmets for taking quick gulps of air.

Fully armored cavalrymen weighed so much that they had to be lifted into their horses' saddles by mechanical hoists. The only true piece of old-time armor still being used in our century is the helmet.

Recently a small group of Christians in my church had to make doubly sure their armor was in place before they went into a dangerous skirmish. Someone who'd been involved with a Ouija board now wanted to be a Christian. But evil spirits had taken over her house.

Before the pastor and other church members went to pray with her, they spent several hours confessing their sins (so Satan wouldn't have a foothold in *their* lives) and making sure they had on God's protective armor. From helmet to *sabatons* (foot protection), from sword to shield, they made sure everything was in place. (Read about each piece of armor they wore in Ephesians 6:11-18.) Even on the road this group of warriors for God stayed in close contact with their Commander. They did this by singing spiritual songs and praying all the way to the possessed person's house and all the way home again. The enemy had fled.

God's armor is ours just for the asking. When each piece is in place, how safe we are. For He's got us covered!   **Carolyn**

---

*Facts taken from "Armour," *Encyclopedia Britannica,* fifteenth edition.

May 7

Down to Bedrock

I t was a house that everyone in the neighborhood eyed skeptically as
the foundation was going in. Concrete pillars, 30 feet high, straddled
a creek we knew flooded its banks every spring. Only the front 10 feet
of the house rested on solid ground. The builder had to fill in the concrete walls under the garage with fill dirt to support it.

When the owners moved in, they bragged to all of us about how
wonderful it was to hear the creek gurgling directly underneath their
kitchen windows. They felt as though they were living in a tree house!

And then the first winter came. And the water began to rise on the
posts. And underneath the posts, the soft earth began to sink. The house
started sinking; the plaster cracked. And the owners had a real estate
agent come to see about selling the house, but there was so much damage done to the sheetrock they were advised to wait until summer to sell.
By summer the creek would go back down, the earth would harden up,
and they could fix up the cracks. Nobody would know how much damage the house had sustained, the agent told them. Nobody would know
it was not built on solid rock, or even solid earth.

The best kind of rock is bedrock—the original rock created by God.
"Getting down to bedrock" means scraping away all the earth and soil
and anything else that gets in the way of our construction, and fastening
ourselves to something solid.

God's promises are solid. He is real, and heaven is a real place that
all of us can enjoy someday, if we choose to be God's child. What does
Joshua 24:22 say about finding bedrock? **"You have heard yourselves
say it,"** Joshua said—**"you have chosen to obey the Lord" (TLB).** The
most important decision you will ever make is to anchor yourself to God.
That means you will look for reasons to believe in Him and will make
choices that you don't have to be ashamed of when you see Him. Why
not choose to obey God, to put yourself in the picture He has for your future and practice a life of honesty and integrity? When you do that, you
take another step toward heaven. **Nancy**

May 8

Hate

There are six things the Lord hates. Proverbs 6:16, NIV.

When I was growing up, my parents taught me that I shouldn't hate anyone. They were right to teach me that, of course, but for a long time I thought it was wrong to hate anything. Imagine my surprise when I discovered that even God hates some things. You can find out what they are in Proverbs 6:16-19. They include things such as a lying tongue, hands that shed innocent blood, feet that are quick to rush into evil, and troublemaking. Why does God use such strong language? Why does He hate these things so much? I know He loves all people. These things bothered me for a long time, but I think I know the answer now.

Take lying, for example. When a person tells a lie they have to start remembering all the people they lied to. Why? Because, if they forget and tell a different story, people will begin to wonder what's going on. After a while it's easy to forget which story you told to which person.

Most people know when someone is lying with their tongue, because their body gives them away. The person lying often can't look others in the eye, or seems very nervous. The person being lied to can usually tell that something isn't right. It's also very hard to pray when you've lied. God knows, and unless you're asking for forgiveness, facing Him and pretending like nothing is wrong is miserable.

You see, God hates these things because they take us away from Him and hurt other people, people He's created. He loves us so much that He wants to spend eternity with us. When things such as lying take us away from Him, or a heart devises wicked schemes, He hates it. As we become more like Him, we'll hate those things too. We'll hate them because they take us away from God. So I guess we can say it's OK to hate. Just make sure you hate the same things God hates. **Jim**

May 9

Coconut Harry

"You will seek me and find me when you seek me with all your heart." Jeremiah 29:13, NIV.

Coconut Harry loved to sail. Something about those white sails snapping in a stiff salt breeze set his pulse to racing. How he loved to brace himself for secure footing as the small vessel leaped through the foamy whitecaps! He'd stand looking over the small rail, sniffing the air and . . . barking in excitement. Yes, Coconut Harry was a golden retriever.

Then one day a terrible thing happened. While sailing choppy seas with Coconut Harry near Key West, Florida, his owner, Naomi Simonelli, watched a large wave sweep Harry off of the boat's deck. In horror and helplessness Naomi watched the golden head of her beloved pet diminish quickly in the distance, and then disappear completely in the high seas.

"Where's Harry?" her friends wanted to know when she docked. Naomi told them.

"That's too bad," they said. "But he was a good dog."

"What do you mean *was?*" she answered. "I think that somehow I will get Harry back again." Naomi knew that Harry was a *very* persistent pup.

Sure enough, eight days later someone on Monkey Island, five miles from where Harry had been swept overboard, encountered a very tired, very skinny golden-haired retriever on the beach. Coconut Harry had managed to swim the five long miles through waves and strong currents until he reached land.

The quality that got Coconut Harry to land is the same quality Jesus told us to exercise in prayer. That quality is persistence. He once told a parable about a poor widow who kept bothering a judge until he finally ruled in her favor against her enemy (Luke 18:1-8). Instead of being bothered by our persistent prayers, God welcomes them, for they keep us in touch with Him.

Just as persistence was the quality that saved Coconut Harry's earthly life, persistence is the main ingredient necessary for a healthy prayer life.   **Carolyn**

May 10

Give It a Wide Berth

Many years ago we stood at the Ballard Locks near Seattle, Washington, watching the boats ride through on their journey up the river. They lined up, several at a time, waiting to enter the lower lock and tie up to the floatable sides of the lock. The massive doors of the lock swung shut slowly and the green water foamed at the edges. Slowly, almost imperceptibly, the boats and yachts rose to meet us. First the flags and sails reached eye level, and then the cabins themselves arrived, and we could see inside. Again the massive gates opened, and the boats continued their journeys upriver. They were replaced by another group of vessels wanting to be lowered downstream.

Everything seemed to be going smoothly until an unusually large yacht approached the entrance at the downside of the lock. It came to within a few hundred feet of the entrance before sirens and whistles and bells began to go off. The captain of the yacht reversed the engines, let down his anchor, and came to a stop.

There was much running around by the crew working the locks, and I heard them shout, "There's not enough room! It's too tight. Not worth the risk!"

After several minutes the yacht raised its anchor and slowly turned away from the lock, heading back downstream.

Giving a "wide berth" means to allow enough room for something. It may mean avoiding something, keeping clear of it, or changing the plan entirely. Now read **Proverbs 14:12: There is a way that seems right to a man, but in the end it leads to death (NIV).** We Christians must give a wide berth to anything that might ruin our integrity. What are some things that might make you not like yourself? Cheating? Spreading rumors? If it makes you uncomfortable, give it a wide berth and leave it alone. When we love Jesus, we make a move away from hurtful things.

Nancy

Heart Transplant

Create in me a pure heart, O God, and renew a steadfast spirit within me. Psalm 51:10, NIV.

God gave animals amazing ways of protecting themselves. Lions are just plain strong, and nothing much will challenge them. Some snakes bite and release poison into their victims' bodies. Cheetahs can run faster than any animal on earth. And no bird wants to eat a stinkbug; they taste terrible!

All of these are incredible, but have you heard about the broken tail trick? If an animal is chasing a lizard and grabs its tail, the predator will end up with only the lizard's tail in its claws. The lizard just runs off down the trail. It would seem as though this would be a problem for the lizard, but not so. It simply grows a new tail!

God does that for us, too. (No, I don't mean we can grow new limbs.) He gives us new hearts. The Bible says in Jeremiah 17:9 that our hearts are evil. It would be nice if we could clean them up somehow, but that can't be done. The only way to take care of the sin problem is to get a new heart. Not a transplant on an operating table, but a transplant from heaven. Only God can do it.

How does this amazing process happen? Well, David asked for it, and God gave it to him. It's that easy. It doesn't mean we'll never make mistakes again or there won't be difficult times. It does mean that when we stay close to God, He will begin to change the desires of our heart. Lizards can grow new tails. That's pretty amazing. But we can get new hearts. Now, that's a miracle! **Jim**

May 12

Beautiful Feet

How beautiful on the mountains are the feet of those who bring good news. Isaiah 52:7, NIV.

Years ago a fierce battle raged. The king anxiously awaited news from the battlefield. The battle commander sent a runner—we'll call him Messenger A—to give the king a report. Another soldier rushed up to the commander. "Let me run too."

"Why?" asked the commander. "You don't have any news to tell the king."

"I don't care—just let me run."

The commander threw up his hands and said, "All right, then, run!"

So Messenger B took off in a cloud of dust.

"Whoa! I see someone running!" a watchman called down to the king, who was sitting near the city gate.

"Whoa!" exclaimed the watchman again. "Here comes someone else, and he's gaining on the first man."

Panting heavily, Messenger B arrived first and happily blurted out "All is well!" before bowing at the feet of the king.

"Well, what happened?" asked the king anxiously.

"Well, uh, actually, I'm not too sure," answered Messenger B. "I did see a lot of confusion and—"

"Step aside!" ordered the king, who probably thought, *He looks like a messenger, but he has no message!*

When Messenger A arrived, he was able to tell the king *exactly* what had taken place on the battlefield. (You can read the whole story in 2 Samuel 18:19-33.)

When heaven's Messenger, Jesus, came to this earth, He brought good news about God's battle with Satan. God has won the war! And through Jesus' death on the cross we have won too. Now God invites us to be messengers running to others with this wonderful news.

Now, both of the men in our story *looked* like messengers, but only one of them had taken the time to learn enough about the battle so that he had something to say. Which of the two messengers are you like? Do you know enough about God's battle to share the news with others? **Carolyn**

Sock It Away

In the early American days, when banks were more at risk of being wiped out by holdups, people had to be very clever about where they kept the money they wanted to save. Apparently hiding the money in a sock was fairly common, because from that practice we get the expression "sock something away," meaning to put it in savings.

Late one night a fire destroyed a stately Victorian home that had stood proudly for many years on a quiet Portland, Oregon, street. When the firefighters combed through the wreckage, they found a wonderful treasure in the attic: a huge jar of early American coins, with a still-legible note inside. Hastily they plucked the paper from the jar and straightened it out. It was dated 1917 and said, "In the event of my demise these coins are to be delivered to my niece." It gave her name, but how would they find her? Miraculously, they did find her, now an elderly woman in her 70s, living in Georgia. She received a small fortune, but it would have been much more had her uncle kept his money in the bank.

There are some people in every church who think they can "sock something away" simply by showing up at church and following a set of rules. Like putting money in a jar, their focus is rather limited and will not pay long-term dividends. There's nothing wrong with regular church attendance and following your conscience by being there, but more valuable is being in love with Jesus and going to church to learn more about Him and receive encouragement from others who love Him. Going to church is something like taking a time-out from a basketball game and getting encouragement and advice from the coach. God is the coach, and the Bible contains His encouragement and advice. The friends you make there give you even more support.

What does **Hebrews 10:25** say about going to church? **Not forsaking the assembling of ourselves together, . . . and so much the more, as ye see the day approaching.** We don't go to church to get something out of it. Rather, we go to church to put something into it. And as we make churchgoing a habit, we get encouragement from God's Word.

Nancy

May 14

Hey, Where Did They Go?

You are the light of the world. A city on a hill cannot be hidden.
Matthew 5:14, NIV.

Everyone knows that in war you need good hiding places. Whether you're using squirt guns in the backyard or the U.S. Army is at war in a foreign country, places to hide are important. Throughout history armies have hidden in foxholes, caves, jungles, mountains, and anywhere else they could find.

In northern Africa you'll find mostly desert. When invading armies come, the local people don't have very many places to hide. There are very few trees in most deserts, and certainly no jungles, so in the town of Matmata, Tunisia, in northern Africa, all 5,000 villagers decided the best way to hide was to go underground. They got right to work digging tunnels, houses, and stores 10 to 40 feet under the hot desert sand.

They even built some hotels for guests to stay in. The Marhala, one of these hotels, has more than 40 rooms and 150 beds. That means that if you stay there, you might have four or five roommates. But even though you might be crowded, you can get a hot shower, read under electric lights, and use your American Express card to pay for your stay.

Jesus said, "You and I are the light of the world. A city on a hill cannot be hidden." But what about a city under the ground? The people of Matmata are safe from their enemies, but they'll never win any wars underground.

The Bible says we're fighting a spiritual battle. Satan is our enemy. We could hide, never letting anyone know that we are Christians, but God wants us to take a chance. He wants us to fight the war right out where everyone can see. We might run into some trouble that way, but remember that Jesus, our Commander, is already the winner of this war that will end with His coming in the clouds of heaven. That's when we'll see the true Light of the world.
Jim

Known by Your Name

Do not they blaspheme that worthy name by the which ye are called? James 2:7.

A friend of mine told this story and gave me permission to pass it on to you.*

Alexander the Great, one of the most renowned military generals who ever lived, conquered almost the entire known world with his vast army. One night during a campaign he was restless and left his tent to walk around the campground. While he was walking he came across a soldier asleep on guard duty—a serious offense. The penalty for falling asleep on guard duty was in most cases death . . .

The soldier began to awaken as Alexander approached him. Noticing who was standing before him, the young man feared for his life.

"Are you aware of the penalty for falling asleep on guard duty?" Alexander asked.

"Yes, sir," the young soldier responded with quivering voice.

"Soldier, what's your name?" demanded Alexander.

"Alexander, sir."

"What is your name?" Alexander asked again.

"My name is Alexander, sir," the soldier repeated.

A third time, and more loudly, Alexander asked, "What is your name?"

A third time the soldier meekly replied, "My name is Alexander, sir."

Alexander the Great then looked the young man straight in the eye. "Soldier," he said with intensity, "either change your name or change your conduct."

As soldiers in God's army each of us bears the name of our Commander—*Christian*. Non-Christians judge us by our actions. But even more important, they judge *Christ* too! By *our* actions, others can be led to believe that Jesus is unreasonable, rude, intolerant, impure, or short-tempered. Scary thought, isn't it!

With God's help let's determine that our actions will reveal us—and the One whose name we carry—to be fair, kind, accepting, pure-minded, and, above all, loving.

Carolyn

---

*Stephen P. Ruff, "Name Dropping," *Message*, November/December 1996.

May 16

Don't Put the Cart Before the Horse

There's a very good reason you go to school. Now that I'm a grown-up I understand that school is where we find out what other people have discovered through trial and error so we don't have to struggle with the same problems.

One of the first important things people figured out on their own was how useful a wheel could be. We may never know who really invented the wheel, but obviously somebody had to, and it's been a real hit.

I wonder who invented the first cart? And did hitching something to a horse happen right from the beginning? I wonder if there was any discussion about where that cart should go—at the front for the horse to push, or at the back for the horse to pull. It seems obvious to us that putting a cart in front of a horse doesn't make any sense. And if you've heard the phrase "He's got the cart before the horse," you understand it means someone is doing things backward.

In school you learn that everything has certain steps that must be taken in order. As a baby you crawled before you walked, and you walked before you ran. You ran before you could ride a bike, and even then you probably used training wheels before you went off on two wheels. Everything happens in some order or another, and for good reason.

What does the Bible tell us will happen if we choose to sin, or separate ourselves from God? Read **Romans 6:23** to find out: **For the wages of sin is death; but the gift of God is eternal life through Jesus Christ our Lord.** If we disobey God, we die. It's an orderly progression of downward events unless we say we're sorry and get ourselves back on track and hold on to Jesus. When Jesus comes, those who have chosen not to repent will choose to die because of a guilty conscience. But if we choose to turn around and accept God's gift of love and forgiveness, a new orderly progression can happen: we go up—to heaven! How do you choose Jesus? By believing that He is real and by treating others with kindness and respect, as He did.

Nancy

Watch Out!

"Watch and pray so that you will not fall into temptation." Matthew 26:41, NIV.

It was the beginning of rush hour in Denver, Colorado. I was waiting at the exit of a restaurant parking lot to make a right turn. I looked to the right and then to the left. There were still a few cars coming from the left, and then I could pull out. The last one passed by. I immediately turned my head back to look through the front windshield so I could make my right turn into traffic. I took my foot off the brake, and *thump!* I saw the head of a little girl disappear in front of my van.

I opened the door and ran around to the front of my car. I was hoping the little girl would still be alive. Where had she come from? She hadn't been there a minute before. Why was she moving in front of my car just as I was pulling into traffic?

A man who had seen the accident from across the street ran up to help. There on the street in front of my minivan was a little girl on a bicycle. She was getting up and saying, "I'm OK, I'm OK." The other man helped me walk her into the restaurant. We discovered that she had scraped her hand when she stuck out her arm to break her fall. That was it! She tried to sneak around the front of my car before I pulled out. Fortunately, she got only her front tire in front of the bumper and I knocked her bicycle down. We called her mother at home; she was a little upset, but just glad her little girl was OK.

Temptation is all around us. The Bible says that we're fighting a spiritual battle. That means Satan is out to get us. We need to watch and pray to make sure that we're out of the way when Satan tries to hit us with his tricks.

Jim

May 18

Davey's Dilemma

"I tell you the truth, this poor widow has put more into the treasury than all the others." Mark 12:43, NIV.

Davey's father was in jail. His mother, three siblings, and two dogs stayed in someone's spare bedroom part of the time and camped in the woods the rest of the time. A teacher at the school Davey attended stuck up for him when the other fifth graders (whose fathers all seemed to be doctors and business executives) picked on him.

What can I give Mrs. Morse for being so good to me? Davey wondered. On the way to their temporary living quarters one afternoon Mother stopped their rickety car at the supermarket to get food with her welfare check. "Meet me back at the cash register in 10 minutes," she told Davey.

Spotting something glittery on the floor, Davey walked over and picked it up. It was a large dented flower-shaped pin with a chipped green stone in the center.

"May I have this pin?" Davey asked a clerk.

"I don't know why anyone would want this ugly thing," laughed the clerk sarcastically, "but if no one claims it in the next 10 minutes, it's yours."

At the end of school the next day Davey handed Mrs. Morse a long smudged envelope. *Will she laugh at it too?* he wondered. *But it's all I have.*

As Mrs. Morse silently gazed at the badly chipped pin, Davey wanted to melt into the floor. "Davey," said Mrs. Morse after taking a deep breath, "did you know it was my birthday today? I find this gift very, *very* special."

Davey's heart swelled with joy.

Jesus and His disciples once watched a poor widow sneak into the Temple and timidly place her only two coins into the offering plate while rich people all around her showed off by tossing large amounts into the same container (Mark 12:41-43). Jesus told His disciples that, in His opinion, the embarrassed widow woman gave the biggest offering of anybody, because she'd given all she had.

Mrs. Morse must have felt the same way about Davey's gift pin, because she wore it at least once every week for the rest of the school year.

Carolyn

Pulling Your Strings

When I was little, I had a marionette that just sat on my bed. (A marionette, you know, is a puppet with strings attached to a T-shaped board that gives the illusion that the puppet is moving.) But my puppet just sat there, because I didn't know how to pull his strings. I didn't know how to move him the right way. Today when people say they can "pull your strings," they mean they can make you do something they want you to do.

Advertisers try to pull our strings a lot. You might have clothes in your closet that you never wear because someone pulled your strings. Someone said those clothes were just what you needed. Are you still playing with all your Christmas gifts? Did you get anything that seemed interesting in the advertisements, but didn't turn out to be as fun as you thought it would be? It's disappointing when that happens, and it happens to almost everyone. But just because you were disappointed one time doesn't mean you can never trust advertising again. Some advertising is actually honest.

The idea of advertising is very old. The first people to advertise lived more than 500 years ago. If a man who made pottery wanted to sell his wares, he would hire someone to go out into the streets with some of the pots. This person was paid to shout out suggested uses for the pottery and make people want to buy it. He had to give a reason the pots he was selling were better than anyone else's. "Our pots are thicker," he might say. Or "Our pots are sturdier." Or "Our pots are more beautiful."

How would people know he was telling the truth? Maybe they asked a trusted friend who had bought one of the pots. In the same way, your parents are raising you to be a Christian. They are advertising the fact that God loves you. Because you trust them, you believe them, and that's good. They trust the Bible because they trust the people who wrote the Bible. And the people who wrote the Bible knew God.

Read **Psalm 111:7: All his commandments are sure.** The whole Bible tells us over and over that God loves us. Jesus trusted the Bible, and that's a good enough reason for me to trust it too. God wants to pull our strings and have us know that He loves us. That is an advertisement that is true and good for us to know.

Nancy

May 20

The Upside-down Ride

"The thief comes only to steal and kill and destroy; I have come that they may have life, and have it to the full." John 10:10, NIV.

We entered the barn, and I'll admit I was intimidated by the horses. They were big; they weighed a lot more than I did, and I wondered how I could make them do what I wanted. Scott told me to grab the saddle that was resting on the fence. I put it on my horse's back. Next we had to cinch up the saddles. That means you take the leather strap hanging from the saddle, pull it under the horse's belly, and knot it to a ring on the other side of the saddle. *No problem,* I thought. Scott told me it had to be tied a certain way, but I was sure there were probably lots of ways to cinch a saddle. So I tied what seemed to be a good knot, and we led the horses out of the barn.

Once on my horse, I began to feel pretty confident. I thought of all those cowboy stories I had read, and I didn't want just to trot; I wanted to gallop. I snapped the reins and began to run the horse across the field. All of a sudden I noticed that my saddle began to slide, and before I could yell "My saddle is slipping," I was hanging on for dear life as it dropped to the side of the horse, and then under my horse, where I landed on the ground with a sickening thud. Blackie stopped and looked at me as if to say, "I could have told you that was the wrong knot to tie my cinch."

God gives us His laws to help us, to keep us from getting hurt, not to keep us from having fun. Sometimes we may be tempted to think we know better. I figured I could tie a good cinch knot without help. Trust me, God knows what's best. Listen to Him, just as I should have listened to Scott the day I rode Blackie upside down. **Jim**

Silly Races

Do you not know that in a race all the runners run, but only one gets the prize? Run in such a way as to get the prize. I Corinthians 9:24, NIV.

Do you like to race? Have you heard of these unusual ones?
- Bathtub racing. The greatest distance anyone paddled a bathtub in a 24-hour period was 90.5 miles (1983).
- Bed pushing. In 1976 a nine-member British team of hospital employees pushed a wheeled hospital bed 3,233 miles in 36 days.
- Stone skipping. A video camera captured the world record set by a 69-year-old California man in 1984: 29 skips ("14 plinkers and 15 pitty-pats").
- Hackysack kicking. The world hackysack-kicking record is 48,825 continuous kicks.
- Grape catching. In 1991 James Deady threw a grape 327 feet 6 inches. His teammate, Paul Tavilla, caught the grape in his mouth.
- Leapfrogging. Fourteen students from Stanford University leapfrogged for 10 days in 1991 and set the record distance of 999.2 miles.
- Now here's a challenge for you Pathfinders: The world record for consecutively tying six knots (square knot, sheet bend, sheepshank, clove hitch, bowline, and round turn and two half hitches) was set by a man in 1977. He tied all six on six different ropes in 8.1 seconds!
- Pogo stick jumping. It took two days in 1992 for a Los Angeles man to set the all-time record of pogo stick jumps at 177,737 jumps.*

Although competitions and races are exciting, not all of them are important. The apostle Paul said that athletes he'd seen compete ran in order to win a prize that would soon perish. Then he mentioned the most important race of all—the race for eternal life.

"Run in such a way as to get the prize," he counsels us. And our prize won't be just to have our name recorded in some record book. Oh, no! With Jesus as our racing coach, our prize will be to have our name written in God's book of life—forever and ever. **Carolyn**

---

*Peter Matthews, editor, *The Guinness Book of Records* (New York: Facts on File, 1992), pp. 197-200.

May 22

Are You "Wet Behind the Ears"?

Perhaps you've heard someone say, "He's still wet behind the ears!" I used to wonder what that odd expression meant until the doctors I worked with in the hospital became younger and younger. By and by some of them were almost young enough to be my children! Like the newborn babies they delivered, they were still "wet behind the ears." Now you can guess what that statement means, can't you?

Almost everyone knows that babies are born wet because they float in a clear fluid before they are born. One of the first things a doctor or nurse must do in the first minutes after the birth is dry the baby off so it doesn't become cold—like when you get out of the swimming pool. One of the places that we rarely dry is the warm place behind a baby's ears. It's not worth the bother. So if someone is still "wet behind the ears," it means he or she is still very new and innocent like a newborn baby.

Everyone is innocent at one time. Criminals, presidents, mothers and fathers—every one of us starts out innocent—so innocent that we make mistakes and often are afraid of what's going to happen to us because of it. We may try to tell a lie when we're afraid of punishment. But we rarely get away with it, especially when we're "wet behind the ears." Have you ever eaten a cookie and lied about it, only to have your mother point out the chocolate cookie crumbs around your mouth? Mothers are good at knowing when we lie.

Lying takes practice, and criminals often become very good at it. After a while they lie automatically, often without realizing it. If you're not careful, you may get very good at it too. But lying only creates more lies, and it never makes you happy. Let's see what the Bible says happens to liars in **1 Timothy 4:1, 2: In later times some will abandon the faith and follow deceiving spirits and things taught by demons. Such teachings come through hypocritical liars, whose consciences have been seared as with a hot iron (NIV).** It's best to take care of your conscience and not burn it by lying. A good conscience keeps you safe. **Nancy**

May 23

Munchausen Syndrome

There is no one righteous, not even one. Romans 3:10, NIV.

It's tough to say and even harder to believe: Munchausen syndrome. It's a rare and incurable condition that causes a person to want constant medical attention. Sometimes we call people hypochondriacs if they always seem to be sick or going to the doctor, but Munchausen syndrome goes way beyond that.

The most unbelievable case was that of William McMoy. William spent 50 years in and out of 100 hospitals. He had 400 major and minor operations, and the longest he was ever out of the hospital was six months. I don't know about you, but I just don't like hospitals that much. I'm glad to be there when I need one, but if I don't have to be there I stay out.

You might wonder how William could afford staying in the hospital all that time. Well, in England, where William lived, the government pays for your hospital stays, and they put out about $4 million for William to be sick. Did William ever get over wanting to stay in the hospital? Yes, he finally did. After 50 years he finally said, "I'm sick of hospitals," and moved into a retirement home.

Why would anyone want to be sick? It's so much better to be healthy and enjoying life. At least that's what most people think. We might ask the same question about sin. Why would anyone want to stay in sin? And yet the Bible says only a few will choose to be in heaven. Some get so wrapped up in their work and their houses and possessions that they don't want to be distracted with what God wants them to do. They choose to reject God.

The real answer lies in the fact that you and I have sinful hearts, and unless we ask God to change our desires, sin seems very attractive. Ask God to change your heart today. Ask Him to help you to want to choose Him instead of sin. Ask Him to heal you of sinful-heart syndrome.

Jim

May 24

H-e-l-p!

"Don't you think that God will surely give justice to his people who plead with him day and night? Yes! He will answer them quickly!" Luke 18:7, 8, TLB.

ook at Joey!" said Natasha to Sondra, her best friend from junior Sabbath school. Sondra had gotten permission from her parents to sit with Natasha's family in church.

"What's he *doing?*" Sondra whispered back.

Entwining his arms about his mother's neck, Joey whispered loud enough for the girls to hear a whiney "But I want to go to—"

Joey's mother firmly shook her head. Joey's father reached over and placed the small boy on his lap.

"Daddy—"

"Sh-h-h-h!"

"I'll bet Joey wants to go to the restroom," Natasha whispered.

"Yeah, but since church is almost over his parents are making him wait," added Sondra.

The pastor kept raising his arms dramatically to emphasize the final points of his sermon. Then Joey slid from his father's arms and quietly stood up in the pew between his parents. Turning around, the little boy faced the congregation, a sort of desperate look on his face. He looked warily first at his mother, and then at his father. Both were intently focused on the thrilling conclusion of the sermon. Then Joey raised his arms toward the congregation as he'd been watching the pastor do, threw back his little head, and called out a frantic "He-e-e-e-lp!"

Joey's father quickly scooped him up and hurried toward the back door of the sanctuary. Natasha and Sondra tried to control their giggles as they heard Joey say, "But I *told* you I had to—"

Sometimes we, like little Joey, feel anxious about something and pray frantic prayers to our heavenly Father. But perhaps, for reasons only He knows are best, He doesn't seem to grant our requests right away. Yet He still wants us—like Joey—to continue being faithful in telling Him what we need and want. And when the timing is right, God will answer our prayers according to His wisdom.   **Carolyn**

Show Your True Colors

I have always been a little envious of families in Europe whose ancestors have a coat of arms, an insignia that represents them. If you have ever worn a Pathfinder badge on your sleeve, you have worn a coat of arms. Perhaps you've seen an anchor on sailor suits in the store. That's a type of insignia too.

In Europe, when armies were ordered to show their colors, it meant they were to show their insignia, to show to whom they belonged. Navies showed their colors by flying the flag of their country aboard ship so everyone could know where they came from. For a while people could trust what they saw. But then someone came along and took advantage of the faith that people had in showing their colors. No one knows whose original idea it was, but all it took was one pirate to think up a game of flying false colors to obtain passage into waters where he would not otherwise be welcome. Under the guise of friendship the pirate ships would moor beside, and then plunder, the unsuspecting trade ships.

In time showing one's true colors involved lowering the false colors and raising the true flag—in the pirates' case, the skull and crossbones—so other ships would know who they really were.

It's my belief that juniors have only true colors to fly. The Bible supports this. Read **1 John 3:7: If you are constantly doing what is good, it is because you *are* good, even as he is (TLB).** I think Jesus advised grown-ups to be like juniors because of the kindness and gentleness that they feel most of the time, and their desire to please others. If you are a person who doesn't take advantage of other people and doesn't like to see anyone hurt, but who tries to make life happier for others, it's obvious you're flying the true colors as one of God's own. You're walking toward heaven. **Nancy**

May 26

Tom the Terrific

Remind the people . . . to be ready to do whatever is good, to slander no one, to be peaceable and considerate, and to show true humility toward all men. Titus 3:1, 2, NIV.

Tom was the best at everything he did. At least that's what he told everyone. When two people were talking about something they did, Tom would interrupt to let them know that he could do it better. Tom seemed to have no problem letting everyone know just how good he was. I'm afraid he didn't have many friends. Oh, if you were to ask Tom how many friends he had, he'd say hundreds. He figured that since he could do everything so well almost everyone he knew probably wanted to be just like him.

But Tom was actually very lonely. In his heart he knew that he didn't have any close friends. When Tom asked some of the guys to come to his house, they would always find a reason they couldn't come. Tom hadn't missed the fact either that whenever he would tell the kids at school how much he knew or how well he could do this or that, they would roll their eyes and say, "Yeah, right." It seemed that no one ever gave Tom the respect he longed for.

The saddest thing was that no one ever told Tom how they felt. They talked behind his back, and they dreamed of how someday they'd get even with him, but no one ever tried to help him. Tom only wanted people to respect him, but no one ever talked to him about his problem.

Maybe you know someone like Tom. The Bible says we always need "to be ready to do whatever is good." Tom needed some humility, but he needed someone to show him the way kindly, someone like you. Sometimes it's hard to tell people the truth. Someone may get their feelings hurt, but if you do it as Jesus did, with love, it makes it much easier.

Jim

May 27

Duh!

Be not wise in thine own eyes: fear the Lord, and depart from evil. Proverbs 3:7.

The young uniformed skycap, straight yellow hair poking out from underneath his cap's bill, looked down at me with bright blue eyes. "I'm flying to Baltimore," I told him.

"Cool!" he exclaimed, snatching my ticket. "You gonna fly under your own power or take one of our planes? Ha-ha-ha! Du-u-uh! I know the answer to my own question because you just handed me an airline ticket! Doo-ba-doo-ba-doo!" he sang, turning the pages of my ticket. "Hey!" he yelled suddenly, "what're you doing here already?"

Before I could open my mouth to answer, he cut in again.

"You're checkin' in 12 hours earlier than necessary. Du-u-uh, lady! Your ticket says 6:00 *p.m.*"

"But I thought that's when I'm scheduled to *arrive* in Baltimore," I answered nervously.

He looked at the ticket again, stuck a finger into the side of his face and exclaimed, "Du-u-uh! Why didn't I see that? Ha-ha-ha!" He keyed more information into his computer. "Doo-ba-doo-ba-doo," he sang self-confidently. "Okeydokey," he said, popping a Tic-Tac into his mouth, "your bags are checked to Baltimore, and you leave from Gate 6—Du-u-uh! I mean Gate 14."

I couldn't leave his presence fast enough. At Gate 14 not one person was around—and no plane was parked outside either. An airline attendant at Gate 10 checked his schedule and exclaimed, "Ma'am, your plane is boarding right now—at Gate 22. Ru-u-un!"

Dodging oncoming foot traffic in my frantic race for Gate 22, all I could think was *That full-of-himself skycap outside should have to wear a big lapel pin that reads: "Warning! Using me as your skycap could be hazardous to your traveling plans!"*

God cautions us, "Be not wise in thine own eyes: fear the Lord." God counsels us, instead of focusing on what we think is so great about ourselves, to keep our eyes on Him. That will keep us out of trouble. And it will also keep us from making trouble for others as well.

Oh, and I did make my plane—barely. **Carolyn**

May 28

How to Use Your Conscience

I was weeding the thick undergrowth in what I called my garden one quiet summer evening when a sudden rustling under the tomato bushes startled me. My trowel dropped to the ground. I suddenly became aware of a mother robin flying in desperation back and forth along the fence, cheeping loudly. Peering back under the tomato bushes, I discovered a brown, sorry-looking little chick that had evidently bailed out of the nest before passing its flying test.

I called for my husband to come. He pulled on heavy gloves and picked up the little bird and placed it in a paper sack. Then he climbed a very tall rickety ladder with the paper sack fastened to his belt. After using a bungee cord to fasten the ladder to the tree and himself to the ladder, he reached way, way out and gently dumped the little bird back into its nest on a precariously high branch of a mulberry tree. We called my husband a hero. But the real heroes were the mother robin and the little chick who listened to their instincts that they were in danger.

You have instincts too. You have that same sense of "safe" and "unsafe" that the birds did. It's called your conscience, and as long as you keep listening to it, it will get stronger. Some grown-ups have argued with their consciences for so long that theirs don't work anymore. They aren't as smart as you can be. Read **Matthew 11:25** to find out what Jesus said about children being wiser than adults: **At that time Jesus said, "I praise you, Father, Lord of heaven and earth, because you have hidden these things from the wise and learned, and revealed them to little children" (NIV).**

Anyone who tries to get you to do something against your instincts—your conscience—is dangerous. If you aren't strong enough to fight someone like this, flee from them. And certainly do what the birds told us to do—call on your parents (both human and divine) to help you. Get God on your side.
Nancy

Supper's Ready!

Then Jesus declared, "I am the bread of life. He who comes to me will never go hungry." John 6:35, NIV.

Diamond Jim's real name was Jim Brady, a rich man who lived about 100 years ago. And could he eat! After he died, it was discovered that Diamond Jim's stomach was six times larger than a normal man's stomach. Now you know where he put all that food.

I hope you haven't eaten yet, because you're going to get full just listening to what Jim ate on an average day. For breakfast Mr. Brady ate large amounts of hominy, eggs, corn bread, muffins, flapjacks, chops, fried potatoes, and beefsteak. He would then drink one full gallon of orange juice. And that was just breakfast.

About 11:30 Diamond Jim would then have a morning snack, consisting of two or three dozen clams. For lunch there would be more clams, two or three deviled crabs, several boiled lobsters, a large hunk of beef, and a mammoth salad. Big Jim would then top his meal off with a few pieces of homemade pie.

Are you full yet? Well, loosen your belts; we haven't even made it to afternoon tea.

For afternoon tea another plate of oysters or clams and two or three bottles of lemon soda would usually tide Jim over until supper, the biggest meal of the day. Supper was serious business for Big Jim. Two or three dozen oysters, six crabs, and two bowls of green turtle soup started things off. The main course was made up of six lobsters, two ducks, a sirloin steak, vegetables, and a platter of French pastries and two pounds of chocolate candy for dessert.

I don't know about you, but I feel sick. While it's true that Diamond Jim had an appetite that has probably never been matched, I can tell you about a hunger that is even stronger. God has created us with a hunger for Him. We need Him so badly, because without Him you and I have no hope of spending eternity in heaven with Jesus. Won't you take a healthy portion of the Bread of Life? It's the only way to satisfy your spiritual appetite.   **Jim**

May 30

Thinkin' of Ya!

While we were still sinners, Christ died for us. Romans 5:8, NIV.

Carolyn sat alone on the merry-go-round. *It's hard enough having to move and never see my friends again. But they act like they won't even miss me!* She could hear Audrey, Edra, and Marilyn laughing as they joked with Audrey's mother at the picnic table.

"Hey, Carolyn!" called Edra after a while. "Wanna sandwich?"

Eyes on her sandals, Carolyn shuffled off in their direction.

"Surprise!" they suddenly screamed in joyful hysterics.

Carolyn froze in place. On the table was the most beautiful white cake she'd ever seen. Beside the cake was a pile of presents.

"You were surprised, huh!" exclaimed Audrey.

Smiling from ear to ear, all Carolyn could do was nod her head.

"We've been planning this party since forever!" added Edra. "And we're *always* gonna be thinkin' of ya!"

Amazed, Carolyn thought, *I wasn't alone after all—they were thinking about me all along!*

You might be tempted to believe that you're alone—in your sins and bad habits. But like Carolyn's friends, Somebody has been thinking about you all along. Here's what seventh grader Melissa McGinnis wrote about that:

When God made the earth, speaking it into existence, He thought of you. The colorful trees, delicate flowers, and fuzzy animals were made with special thought of you.

Then one day the thought of you seemed almost to shatter—
Sin had entered the home you would live in someday.
But God had a plan to save you, because He cares for you.
On a hill near Jerusalem, atop a cross 2,000 years ago,
hung God's only Son, Jesus.
The price for your sins had been paid because God cares for you.

Now Jesus has risen from the dead and is waiting for you to ask Him to help you through all your problems, your heartaches, and your sorrows. Very soon He is coming in clouds of glory to take you to live with Him. He thought of you, died for you, cried for you, because He cares for you.

Isn't it nice to know that even when you feel alone, your Best Friend is always thinking about you? **Carolyn**

How God Feels About Lying

It was supposed to be the start of a wonderful vacation for the Jones family. Everyone was feeling good as they drove to the airport that morning. They parked by the curb and unloaded their suitcases, and then, while Father parked the car, Mother and the kids lugged the suitcases to the check-in counter. By the time Father returned, they were all checked in and ready to go through the security checkpoints and get on the plane.

That's when their vacation was ruined. Everyone put their carry-on luggage on the conveyor belt except Father. He walked through the little archway with his camera case around his neck, and the security guard said, "Sir, I'll need you to open that camera case, please."

Dad laughed and said, "Yeah, like you'd better make sure I don't have a gun in here or something!"

No sooner had the words left his lips than the police standing there took him by the arms and hauled him in for questioning. They explained that it is a crime even to joke about carrying a concealed weapon or explosives onto a plane. Father could have been charged with a year in jail and a $100,000 fine. He got off easy; he was allowed to go on the trip with his family, but he had to pay $5,000 in fines once he returned home. You can guess that the kids didn't get to buy many souvenirs on that trip, and nobody enjoyed themselves as much as they might have.

People who joke about serious things often get themselves in trouble. Don't joke in school about cheating from someone else's paper; don't suggest that you turned in your older sister's paper and just put your name on it. People take those things seriously, and you'll ruin your reputation. Even worse, you might begin to believe that cheating is OK.

What does the Bible say about lying lips? You can find out by reading **Proverbs 12:22: Lying lips are abomination to the Lord: but they that deal truly are his delight.** God says He hates lying lips, but notice the verse doesn't say He hates liars. Since you're planning on going to heaven, you want to develop a character like God's, and that means you want to be honest. The end of the verse says, "But they that deal truly are his delight."

Nancy

Don't Fall Through!

The prudent see danger and take refuge, but the simple keep going and suffer for it. Proverbs 27:12, NIV.

When I was a kid there was a stream near our house that would freeze during winter, perfect for skating. I knew it wasn't very deep, so I wasn't afraid of falling through the ice and drowning.

One day my next-door neighbor, who would sometimes skate with us on the stream, took me ice fishing. As we pulled up to the lake, I saw 50 or more little ice shanties on the frozen lake with cars parked next to them.

"Are we going to drive on the ice?" I asked my friend's dad.

"Yep," he said.

"Aren't you afraid we might fall through the ice?"

"Nope," he answered.

I looked at the cracks in the ice. I was nervous. This lake was much deeper than the little stream we skated on. But everyone seemed to be enjoying themselves as they fished. Nobody seemed to be worried about falling through.

Still nervous, I asked my friend's dad, "What do you do if someone falls through?" I wanted to see if he knew how to save me in case I fell through the ice into the frigid water.

"Well, what you do is to lie down on the ice and form a human chain. One person grabs the next one's feet, and so on. You don't want to just walk up to the edge of the hole and stick out your arm. The person in the water would pull you right in."

I guess I felt a little better. I could see the sense in being very careful when you helped the person in the water. It wouldn't do any good if you both ended up in it.

Sometimes we see our friends in trouble. They might be experimenting with tobacco or alcohol. If they are true friends, we will probably want to help them, but we need to be careful. Ask your parents, or another adult you trust, for some help. Being cautious when you help friends is very important. It won't do either one of you any good if you both end up in the icy waters of sin.   **Jim**

Jun 2

Tonsillectomy!

The eternal God is thy refuge, and underneath are the everlasting arms. Deuteronomy 33:27.

It'll just feel like a really bad sore throat," the nurse reassured me. She was trying to calm my nerves before the tonsillectomy. But nothing she—or the doctor or my parents—had said prepared me for the pain of that first swallow after the operation. I thought I would never live to see fifth grade!

Awaking from a troubled sleep that first night home from the hospital, I forgot—and swallowed! With raw pain overwhelming me and mucous in my sinuses making breathing nearly impossible, I thought, once again, that I might die. In spite of my fiery throat, I made a desperate attempt to call for help. But all that came from my voicebox was a raspy, helpless groan.

Even so, my father heard. (I knew he would.) Suddenly he was there by my side with a big warm hand over mine. I wanted so much to tell him to get Mother, my brother, and Skippy, the Boston terrier puppy, so I could tell them all goodbye. I did try to tell him, but somehow it all got mixed up because of the pain in my throat. Instead, what finally came out was this croaking plea: "Daddy, put your arms around me."

In an instant he was scooping me up in his strong arms and telling me how much he was hurting along with me. Somehow, with him holding me like that, it didn't matter so much that I tell him anything else.

The next thing I knew, the morning sun was slicing through the crack in my curtains, and I was feeling better already.

Through Moses, God made a special promise to Asher, one of Israel's 12 tribes. Moses told the people of Asher that God had promised to keep His arms around them, especially when the going got tough. Moses called God's arms "everlasting" arms. That means God would always keep His arms around Asher—and around us, unless we ask Him to take them away.

As my earthly father put his comforting, protective arms around me when I asked him to, our heavenly Father will do the same for us.

Carolyn

Have the World on a String

A curious thing happens to tenderhearted people when life is going well for them. They feel guilty. Guilty because *they* aren't suffering when they watch the news and see starving or war-scarred people in other countries. Guilty because they have a good job when they hear of other people standing in long unemployment lines. Guilty for whatever is going right in their lives while things are going so dreadfully wrong for others.

What does **3 John 2** say about having a good life and being healthy? **Beloved, I wish above all things that thou mayest prosper and be in health.** The Bible tells us that we shouldn't feel guilty when things are going well. A Christian life doesn't have to be solemn and serious. God's wish for us is that we do prosper and be healthy, both in mind and spirit. It's OK to feel that we "have the world on a string."

To have the world on a string means that you're managing your life very well, and you're in charge of where it's going. Like puppeteers who control their marionettes with strings, it's OK for us to feel that we have control of our lives. It's OK to feel exhilarated with how well things are going. It's OK to prosper—even to be rich—as long as we realize that wealth is only temporary and is given to us so that we can share it with others.

If things are going well with you right now, enjoy the peace and security you feel. Let it bubble out and touch somebody else, whether your sharing takes the form of material gifts, or just a smile and an encouraging word. Happy people who care about others are like a burst of fresh air in a stuffy room. Where will you take your happiness today? Try to find someone who isn't so happy today and show them you care. Often just having someone to be with for a while means more than anything else. That's what people on their way to heaven do. **Nancy**

Jun 4

It Was Just a Joke

A cheerful heart is a good medicine. Proverbs 17:22, NIV.

Brad was angry. He flung open the door, threw down his books, and yelled, "I'm never going back to that school again! My own friends made fun of me."

"What did they say?" asked his father.

"That I was nothin' but a . . . You know—they used that word that talks about the country we came from."

"Oh," Dad sighed. "Have you ever done the same thing?"

"No!" Brad sounded disgusted.

"Well, I thought I heard you telling a joke the other day. How do you think a person feels when you tell a joke that makes his whole nation sound ridiculous?"

"Not too good, I guess. I really never thought about it that way," Brad said slowly.

"Actually, aren't most of the jokes you tell intended to cut someone down?" Dad asked. There was silence as Brad thought about all the people he'd ridiculed with jokes.

So what's wrong with telling a few jokes? Well, if the jokes cut someone down, there's plenty wrong. You might wonder if God wants us to have any fun. Sure He does, but not at someone else's expense. It doesn't mean that when funny things happen to you or your friends you can't all have a good laugh about it. But be careful. Your friend may really be embarrassed. It might be better to wait a little while until your friend can look at the situation and laugh too.

Contrary to what many people believe, God isn't a grumpy old man, sitting up in heaven, trying to find something wrong with us. God *wants* us to have a good time. He *wants* us to enjoy life. He just doesn't want us to make other people miserable. Laugh at the funny things of life, and do whatever you can to make others happy too. **Jim**

159

The Real Thing

"Watch out that you are not deceived." Luke 21:8, NIV.

Designer labels have become a big deal in this country for many teens. Some people will pay big bucks to be able to wear a pair of jeans with a designer label stitched onto the waistband.

Observers in other countries have noticed our fascination with designer labels, and do you know what? They've figured out a way to make a fast buck off of you and me if we're into designer clothes. In fact, this foreign scam is such big business that the Public Broadcasting System recently ran a special on how we're getting ripped off.

It seems that certain clothing stores in Mexico are selling jeans with Levi and Guess labels. But they are jeans that neither the Levi Strauss or Guess factories ever produced. Stores south of the border are selling fake designer clothes that are being passed off as the real thing! And the United States clothing industry is losing billions of dollars every year. Phony marketers in Asia are doing the same thing with CDs and videos.

The PBS commentator stated that because of fakes being substituted for the real thing, the United States is being pushed out of the world market.

The first sad story in the Bible tells about Eve being deceived by the devil, who was disguised as a serpent. He led her to believe that his fake "label" was real. She was deceived into believing a fake was the real thing.

"You won't die if you eat of this tree's fruit," he promised her, even though God had told her just the opposite. Satan would have succeeded in squeezing God out of the "market" if Jesus hadn't come to this earth to show us how to tell the fake from the real.

You can read how our Lord met each of the devil's counterfeit offers with the real thing—truth from God's Word (see Matthew 4:1-11).

What's really scary about being deceived is that people often don't know they have a fake until it's too late. And fake things—whether it's fake designer jeans or fake friendships—just don't last too long.

God's "real thing," however, lasts—forever.   **Carolyn**

Put This Town on the Map

People who lived near Mount St. Helens, in Washington State, will forever remember May 18, 1980. I remember. It was a Sunday. I happened to be dusting the living room, listening to music and the chatter of my little boy, David.

All at once the music stopped, and an emergency message came over the radio: "Mount St. Helens has erupted. It is not known at this time if there were any casualties. We'll give continuing reports as they come in. Again, Mount St. Helens has erupted. And now, back to the music."

Neighbors poured out of their houses to talk to each other and to stare at the sky. Even though we lived a couple hours away from the volcano, we could see the gray clouds in the distance.

The next morning everything was smothered in gray dust—the front lawn, the flowers, the cars, and the houses. Nothing but gray. It was like living on the moon. And it was frightening.

News reports were coming out of Amboy, Washington, a town I had never heard of before, but a town that was suddenly "put on the map." Now everyone knew where it was.

When something newsworthy happens to a person or to a town, they are "put on the map." Suddenly everyone wants to know where they are. People want to "read all about it."

Salt was once something that people wanted to learn more about. It made food special, just as when you find someone you can trust, your life seems much safer and more enjoyable than before. Jesus calls that special feeling "saltiness." Read **Matthew 5:13** and imagine Jesus saying it directly to you. **"You are the salt of the earth. But if the salt loses its saltiness, how can it be made salty again? It is no longer good for anything, except to be thrown out and trampled by men" (NIV).**

You can bring a delightful change into many peoples' lives—and even into your own—by being trustworthy and reliable. Put yourself on the map. **Nancy**

The Wrong Key

"O my God, I am too ashamed and disgraced to lift up my face to you, my God." Ezra 9:6, NIV.

John and I worked on the maintenance crew at the academy we attended. Mr. Breyer, our boss, would give us a master key so that we could get where we needed to go. Mr. Breyer's trusting us with that key made us feel pretty important.

One day we had a job to do in one of the boys' dorm rooms. As we entered the dorm, I reached into my pocket to get the master key. It wasn't there! I had forgotten to get the key from Mr. Breyer, but neither John nor I wanted to go all the way back. That's when we had a not-so-brilliant idea.

We knew a guy in the dorm who had a stolen master key. He could get anywhere he wanted. We could go borrow his key, let ourselves into the room, do our work, and head back to the shop. So that's what we did.

As we were leaving the room, Mr. Wahlen, the boys' dean, met us at the door and held up a key. "Mr. Breyer called over and said you forgot the master key. I came up to bring you one, but I see you've already let yourselves in. How did you do that?"

At that moment I think we looked pretty guilty. I held up the stolen key and said, "With this."

"Where did you get that?" the dean wanted to know.

We explained and waited for the worst.

Dean Wahlen looked at us. "I'm really disappointed in you guys. I thought I could trust you." He walked away, and we hung our heads in shame. It hurt. What the dean said in those two sentences hurt more than any suspension we could have served. He could have held it against us, but he didn't. We asked forgiveness, and Dean Wahlen gave it.

We have even more reason to hang our heads before God. We are sinners, and sometimes we make pretty bad choices. Thankfully, though, we serve a God who forgives and allows us to lift up our heads and come boldly before His throne of grace. **Jim**

Sheriff Wannabe

"By their fruit you will recognize them." Matthew 7:20, NIV.

All nine contestants sat on the platform of the local high school gym so voters could interview them before election day. All nine were sheriff "wannabes."

Fish and Game Warden Norton wore a tailored Western jacket. Officer Crandall came in uniform. The rest wore business suits—except for the candidate at the far end, who was dressed in faded jeans and an orange-striped T-shirt stretched over his paunchy stomach.

This last candidate looked off into the distance, wiping at his nose and scratching his shoulder as the first candidate, a businessman, rose to tell about his community accomplishments and why he should be elected sheriff. Next, when the police officer outlined his proposed plan for county safety, the T-shirt man reached for an itch on the top of his head.

During the following presentations, the sniffling T-shirt man continued his scratching. Left knee, right shin, upper back, lower stomach.

During Warden Norton's impressive speech about his own accomplishments, the T-shirt man suddenly put one finger inside his right ear and gave it an energetic massage before reaching in the direction of his left armpit. The two women seated in front of me gasped.

By now I was dying of curiosity to learn what accomplishments the T-shirt man had done that would qualify him to run for county sheriff. He approached the podium—scratching the side of his nose. The audience fell silent.

"Well," he began after a long pause, "I ain't *got* no list of stuff I already done for this here county cuz—*heh, heh*—I ain't got the chance to *do* it yet. But make me yer sheriff and ya'll jes' gonna know what I *kin* do! Thanks kindly for yer votes." And he sat down.

"Are you kidding?" a man behind me quietly exploded. "Like I'm going to vote for Scratch-and-Sniff to be *my* sheriff?"

Jesus was talking about more than gardening when He said you can tell what quality of "trees" people are by the kind of "fruit" they bear. How true that is! And that's why we voters elected Warden Norton as our new sheriff. For you see, unlike the T-shirt man, Mr. Norton's "fruit" indicated he had the track record of a leader.

What kind of "fruit" do others see you bearing? **Carolyn**

Jun 9

House of Cards

Have you ever tried to make a house out of cards? If so, you know how unstable they can be. Sometimes people say that others are building a "house of cards"—putting their trust in something flimsy that won't hold up, something impermanent and untrustworthy.

How about you? Ever thought that being good-looking brings happiness? Or that being "popular" is more important than doing well in school? Worse, have you ever thought it was more important to follow your friends' values than God's?

Be careful whom you trust! When you trust God, you can be like the dogs who refused to worry. These dogs were owned by a scientist who had chosen to study what causes stomach ulcers. He had a theory that tension and worry caused the stomach to secrete more acid which then caused open sores in the stomach, called ulcers. So he tried to make the dogs feel stressful. He fed them erratically. He shouted at them. He didn't show them any approval. But those loyal dogs absolutely refused to worry or get tense—two primary causes of ulcers.

What the researcher found was that because these dogs had learned previously to trust their owner, they weren't worried by his strange behavior. They just lay down trustingly and waited for him to come back to normal.

You can decide today to trust God in the same way. God doesn't do research on us as this dog owner did, but sometimes you may think He's being mean when He doesn't perform more miracles in your life. Be patient. As the end of time nears, more and more miracles will happen. Today's verse, **1 John 2:28**, tells us something about those who have made a habit of trusting God. **And now, my little children, stay in happy fellowship with the Lord so that when he comes you will be sure that all is well, and will not have to be ashamed and shrink back from meeting him (TLB).** To trust God is a decision, not a feeling.

Nancy

Man Overboard!

The truly righteous man attains life, but he who pursues evil goes to his death. Proverbs 11:19, NIV.

Diving from high places frightens me, but it apparently doesn't frighten the lemming. Listen closely as I tell you about an unusual and sad dive that this furry little creature takes.

The lemming is a mammal that resembles a large mouse. It likes to live in cooler areas of the world, such as Alaska, northwest Canada, and Scandinavia. No one is sure why, but every once in a while the lemmings that live in Scandinavia will start heading toward the sea. They seem simply to panic and run over each other in an effort to get to the water. Do they want a drink? I don't think so, especially because it's salt water. Do they want to spend a little time on the beach? No, because there is no beach—only cliffs that drop abruptly to the water below. After stampeding many miles, the lemmings simply run right to the cliff and jump over the edge. They swim until they're exhausted, and then they drown. And no one knows for sure why they do it.

There's a story in the Bible that's something like that. When Jesus cast demons from two men on the shores of the Sea of Galilee, the demons asked to be cast into the nearby pigs. Jesus agreed, and as soon as the demons were in the pigs, the pigs headed right for the cliffs and jumped into the sea. If you'd been walking by at the time, you wouldn't have known why those pigs jumped in.

It's a sad reminder that sin leads to destruction. Satan is up to no good, but don't worry, you're safe as long as you trust in Jesus. Get to know Him better each day. Study His Word and talk to Him in prayer. As long as you stick with Him, you'll be safe from the cliffs of sin. **Jim**

Jun 11

Chicken Little

And my God will meet all your needs according to his glorious riches in Christ Jesus. Philippians 4:19, NIV.

I don't know if we'll be able to have a regular birthday cake for you next week," said Mother to Brandt. "It takes two eggs to make the kind you like. You know it's dry season in this part of Africa, and chickens—including your own Chicken Little—just aren't laying eggs right now."

Seeing Brandt's disappointed face, Mother quickly added, "Don't worry, we'll still have something good that doesn't require eggs—like cinnamon rolls."

"They're good," said Brandt slowly, trying to be cheerful, "but it just won't be the same."

"I know," answered Mother sympathetically. "When we visit Grandma and Grandpa in America on furlough next year, we'll go to a big bakery and you can choose any cake you want!"

"Dear God," prayed Mother, after Brandt left to go play with his friends next door, "please show me what to do for Brandt's birthday. He's so sweet and patient about going without a lot of things as a missionary kid."

The next morning when Mother went into the pantry and reached for the cooking oil, her hand stopped in midair. For on the top shelf, right by the tiny open window, lay a white egg. Mother reached for it and closely examined its moist shell. It was newly laid.

"Brandt!" she called. "Come see how God answered my prayer! We have an egg—enough for a very small birthday cake next week!"

The next morning Mother, shaking her head in disbelief, found another white egg—in the exact same place. And the following morning, a third egg—and Chicken Little, going out the window.

Mother had so many eggs that not only did she make a *big* birthday cake (so that Brandt could have a party with his friends), but Brandt's father made a big frosty container of homemade ice cream to go along with it. God has promised to supply our essential needs. But how often His great heart of love also supplies some of our wants as well.

By the way, when Mother went to the pantry the morning *after* Brandt's birthday, she found no egg. Chicken Little didn't start laying again until it was "egg season."

Carolyn

Make Hay While the Sun Shines

A farmer's life is often one of "living on the edge," doing as much as you can while the weather is favorable. To make hay a farmer must cut the grass and let it lie in the field to dry before he binds it together and stacks it in the barn for later use. The farmer does not cut the grass or lay it out to dry unless the sun is shining. Because the farmer always must work with the threat of a summer storm at his back, he can't waste one sunny day. If he's going to make hay, it must be now—while the sun shines.

When we say we "make hay while the sun shines," we mean we're taking advantage of an opportunity the moment it arrives.

The Bible says we should find something to be happy about every day of our lives. A good place to start counting your blessings is at home. To borrow the words of a James Taylor song, why not "shower the people you love with love"? Take advantage of every opportunity you can find to tell your mother or father, your sister or brother, that you love them. (Even if you're a little upset with them right now, you can tell them that you usually love them, but right now that isn't the strongest emotion you're feeling.) You can count your blessings as you look around your room and see the things you've been given by people who care about you. Call them up; tell them you were just thinking about how lucky you are to have them in your life. Tell something particular that you like about them. "Make hay while the sun shines."

What does **Psalm 118:24** say about our approach to life? **This is the day the Lord has made; let us rejoice and be glad in it (NIV).** Right now, stop reading this book and say out loud one thing you're looking forward to enjoying today. It may be a book you plan to finish, a favorite food you plan to eat, or a friend you plan to spend time with. Start a list of everything that's going right in your life. And you know what will happen? By focusing on good things, you'll feel the warmth of the sun inside your heart! Try it and see!   **Nancy**

Jun 13

Letters

I write these things to you . . . so that you may know that you have eternal life. I John 5:13, NIV.

OK, listen closely. First, go find a clean sheet of paper and something to write with. Now, I want you to write a letter to a friend or favorite relative.

Start off your letter by telling them something you appreciate them for. It might say something like "Grandma, thanks for always telling me that you love me. I love you, too." Or you might say to your friend, "Thanks for always being someone I can talk to."

Next, I want you to tell them how much God loves them. Tell them how glad you are that God sent His Son to die for you and them. Tell them it makes you very happy to think that you'll be able to spend the rest of eternity together with Jesus.

How do you think your friend will feel when they get your letter? If you haven't written in a while, they'll probably be surprised! I imagine that they might even read your letter more than once. Have you ever done that? I have. If they sent a picture, I looked at it very carefully, many times. Getting letters is great. I check my mail every day with excitement to see if a letter from a friend is in the stack.

You know, God's given us a letter. It's His Word, and He's just as excited for us to read it as you will be for your friend or relative to read the letter you sent. He wants us to read it again and again, so we'll understand exactly what He has to say to us. The thing that makes His letter different is that it can change our lives and tell us what we need to know and do to spend eternity with our best friend. Try reading some of God's letter every day and see how good it is to get a letter from a friend. **Jim**

Marisa's Secret

I have learned the secret of being content in any and every situation, . . . whether living in plenty or in want. Philippians 4:12, NIV.

Little kids who don't yet have the "big picture" about life sure give funny answers to questions sometimes. That's why they're so much fun to talk to. That's one of the reasons 3-year-old Marisa's parents loved to talk to her.

They lived on an isolated mission station, so Marisa didn't have very many toys. And often they had mostly rice and beans to eat. When Marisa was about to turn 4, Father said, "Risa, I'm going to the city to buy your birthday presents. Whatever you want, I will get for you—if I can find it in the stores."

Marisa's eyes sparkled as she thought. "I know. I want four presents—a blue one . . . a red one . . . a yellow one . . . and a purple one!"

"Sweetheart, you don't understand," said Mother. "Can you tell us what you want to be *inside* those pretty presents?"

Marisa thought some more and then nodded her head. "I want a can of peaches . . . and a balloon."

"Is that *all?*" questioned Mother. "What else? Surely there must be something else."

"OK!" agreed Marisa joyfully. "Then I want, uh, *three* balloons!"

The apostle Paul, like Marisa, seems to have learned the secret of being happy with what he already had. In fact, he said so in a letter he wrote to some friends: "I have learned the secret of being content in any and every situation" (Philippians 4:12, NIV).

What was this secret? Paul told the Philippians in the next verse: "I can do everything through him who gives me strength" (verse 13, NIV). In other words, Paul knew that God—his heavenly Parent—would *give* him everything *necessary* for a good life. So he just didn't worry about the extras he didn't have.

Because she had everyday evidence that her parents loved her and would provide for her needs, little Marisa had discovered Paul's secret too.

Carolyn

Diamond in the Rough

Have you ever looked in the mirror and made faces at yourself? One pimple can seem like it has flashing lights on it so that no one could possibly miss seeing it.

Life isn't fair, but misery is optional. What's God's response to us when we are unhappy? You'll find it in **Psalm 34:18, 19: The Lord is close to those whose hearts are breaking; he rescues those who are humbly sorry for their sins. The good man does not escape all troubles—he has them too. But the Lord helps him in each and every one (TLB).**

The truth is, everyone else is probably so preoccupied with their own pimples they don't really notice yours. (They may even like you because you *have* pimples and aren't more perfect than they are!)

Your friends see things in you that your parents and teachers may see differently. While you and your friends may keep track of your pimple farm, your parents and teachers see you as a "diamond in the rough." A diamond isn't much to look at until it's been polished—one may not even recognize that the stone has potential. But experts know better. And your parents and teachers see what you may grow up to be when life has polished you with education and experience. They see your talent, your potential.

Why not ask your parents what they think one of your strengths is? What do they most admire about you? What kind of work do they think you might enjoy? If they suggest that one of your friendships isn't likely to take you in the best direction, listen to them. Sometimes you have to hurt someone else's feelings and part company if the relationship isn't what's best for you.

Visualize yourself as a grown-up. Where do you want to be five years from now? What will you be doing in 10 years? Carefully make choices that will take you where you want to go. Someday you'll be polished, and your attitude of cheerfulness will make you sparkle.　　　**Nancy**

Love Is a Verb

If you love me, you will obey what I command. John 14:15, NIV.

Jesus said, "If you love me, you will obey what I command," not "If you love me, tell me so." In other words, Jesus wants us to put our love for Him into action. I think He wants us to do the same thing for each other, too. The best time to start is right now, so here are some ideas for acting out your love.

Do these to show your parents how much you love them: wash the dishes without being asked; buy a card, write a long loving note in it, and put it on your parents' bed; dust the top of the refrigerator and those other places that sometimes get missed; or organize the garage.

Try these ideas on your brother or sister: do their chores for them; call up their friends and plan a surprise party for no particular reason; draw them a picture; or buy a card, write a loving note in it, and put it on their bed too.

Watch your friends' faces when you try these ideas on them: go over to their house and help them do their chores; bake them cookies, get a gallon of milk, and have a little surprise party; or buy them a book you know they'd like.

These are actually pretty simple ideas, aren't they? Anyone can do them, and yet very few people ever take the time.

Jesus was always doing things for other people. He didn't say "I'll get back with you later and heal you then." He did it right away. When He saw someone in trouble, He took the time to go to their rescue.

So take a little time to plan something special for your parents, your brother or sister, and your friends. No one will be more surprised than they will, and no one will be more pleased than you. **Jim**

Jun 17

Death Trap at the Border

For he rescues you from every trap. Psalm 91:3, TLB.

Halt!" The soldier in camouflage clothing stepped from the Congolese underbrush onto the dirt road, the bayonet of his gun pointed toward our windshield. "What's your business?" he asked gruffly, fingering the trigger.

"My daughter and I are on our way to Kampala to purchase supplies for our mission station," my dad answered calmly.

"I wish we'd made this trip 24 hours ago like we'd planned!" I said fearfully, after the soldier finally let us continue.

"Well," answered my dad, "if only this car hadn't had battery trouble we would have been through here yesterday."

After being allowed through the Congo side of the border without much problem, we drove the two miles through "no man's land" before reaching the Ugandan border barrier.

A very astonished guard exclaimed, "Are you coming from the Congo? How did you get through? Wasn't the place over there crawling with rebel soldiers?"

Other border guards quickly gathered around, obviously expecting us to relate an exciting story. We told them about the one soldier who'd stopped us at gunpoint.

"That's all? Just one?" asked the guard. "That's amazing, considering what happened yesterday."

"What happened yesterday?" Dad asked.

"Why, a whole band of renegade Congolese soldiers came out of the jungle and took over these border stations. There was a lot of looting, a lot of shooting, and at least one person was killed. Anyone driving through during that time would have been robbed, at the very least."

"And," added another, "very likely killed!"

Whoa, I thought, and shuddered. *Although the car battery's going dead made it seem as if our trip was being ruined, God knew what was happening here at the border. By allowing that dead battery problem to arise, He probably saved our lives.*

King David wrote that God rescues us from traps (Psalm 91:3, TLB). A dead car battery was evidently God's way of providing for our safety the day He "rescued" us from a death trap at the border. **Carolyn**

Throw Straws Against the Wind

In a land where the king had to honor every request, two men requested the hand of a princess in marriage. She was a beautiful maiden, and old enough for marriage, but her wise father asked what her wishes were regarding these men.

"I don't wish to marry either one of them," the princess replied.

"Very well. Then I will give them an impossible task to do before they can win your hand in marriage."

On the appointed day of the challenge the entire town turned out to see if either man would win the hand of the princess. "Hear ye, hear ye!" the crier called out. "To the man who can throw straws against the wind will go the hand of the princess."

"But that's impossible!" the men objected.

"Then forfeit the challenge and accept the inevitable," the king replied. "You can no more have my daughter than you can sweep back the ocean with a broom or throw straws into the wind."

What are some straws you find yourself throwing into the wind, maybe some impossible things you try to make yourself believe? A common straw is the mistaken belief that you can please everybody and that nobody will ever disagree with you if you're "nice" enough. If you believe that, then you'll believe you can throw straws against the wind. Never to offend someone is the most hopeless job there is. Even Jesus offended some people sometimes just because He differed with them. Can you expect to be any different? It helps if you "agree to disagree," but it still may make somebody take offense. If it's a moral decision, however, the person who gets angry over your decision to be a moral person is not a true friend. Don't let them make you stumble. What does **Psalm 119:165** say about living by God's rules? **Those who love your laws have great peace of heart and mind and do not stumble (TLB).** Put God first.

Nancy

Jun 19

Abracadabra!

Everyone who has this hope in him purifies himself, just as he is pure. I John 3:3, NIV.

I was always fascinated by magic tricks. Actually, I should say illusions. True magic is Satan's territory; illusions just involve a person moving their hands so you don't see what they're doing. It's not really magic at all. I've watched many illusions as closely as I could, keeping my eyes glued on the illusionist's hands, only to end up wondering "How did he do that?"

There are times in life when we all wish we could use a little magic, times when we're really tired and have a really big job to do. I've heard people wish they could just wave their hands and the lawn would be mowed or the laundry would be done or their homework would be finished.

If faith can move mountains, then why doesn't God let us get things over with easily? Why are some things so hard? I think it's because God wants our characters to be strong. Our character is the part of us that helps you and me to be strong in tough times and to stand up for what is right. Jesus had a rough road to travel to His crucifixion. Why didn't God just get it over quickly? Because Jesus, our example, also had to build His character while He was here on this earth. The only thing you and I will take to heaven that we have here on earth is our character. It needs to be growing stronger every day.

It would be nice if all we had to do to overcome a bad habit was to ask Jesus to take it away and it would immediately disappear. But Jesus knows that you and I must build our character. It isn't by magic; it's by relying on Him each and every day and by making good decisions. It may be difficult at times, but God has all the power we need to build characters that will stand strong for Him.   **Jim**

The Ambassador's Stinky Car

A man's pride brings him low, but a man of lowly spirit gains honor.
Proverbs 29:23, NIV.

No way am I going to ride in this run-down Mercedes!" declared the new European ambassador to a small African country. "I will order myself a shiny customized Lincoln Continental limousine from the United States. Why? Because *I* am the ambassador!"

So when the proud young ambassador received word that his new limousine had been unloaded in Mombasa, Kenya, he quickly ordered a newly hired chauffeur and the chauffeur's brother to go pick it up. Soon the brothers were heading out of Kenya in the ambassador's Continental. They stopped at a huge outdoor market to buy food.

"Hey, brother, look how cheap chickens are here compared to back home," exclaimed the chauffeur. "My wife would love a few!"

"So would mine! Let's get some! But where would we put them?"

"Well, duh!" answered the chauffeur. "There's plenty of room for us *and* a few chickens. We'll just sprinkle some dried corn in the passengers' back seat compartment, close the partition, and forget about them."

Arriving at the European embassy four days later, the chauffeur and his brother left the car keys with the night watchman, collected their chickens, and went home.

"Hands off my new car!" called the ambassador to the curious onlookers gathered outside the embassy the following morning. Then he stuck his head in the passengers' compartment. "Peeee-yew! What happened to my car?" he roared, quickly backing out, holding his nose. As the people started to laugh, all the proud young ambassador could do was express his feelings in some very strong language.

And you know what? God used some very strong language too in expressing His feelings about the sin of pride. He said, "I hate pride" (Proverbs 8:13, NIV).

Maybe our loving Father in heaven hates pride because He knows how much damage it can do. Because of pride Saul lost his throne. David lost four sons. And Samson lost his eyesight. Know what happens when we harbor pride in our hearts and minds? We end up with an attitude that stinks. If you don't believe it, just ask the ambassador!   **Carolyn**

Windfall

In old times English landowners were called owners of the land. Literally. They owned just the land, and not anything *on* the land—not the trees, the grass, or anything else that grew there. The people couldn't cut down trees on their land for any use—firewood or an addition to the house—because the king owned the trees, and all trees were earmarked for use by the Royal Navy.

There was one exception to this rule, however. If a tree was blown over in a windstorm, the Royal Navy lost its claim to the lumber and the landowner could use the tree—it was a "windfall," a welcome discovery after a fearful storm.

Right now our troubled world seems to be in a self-destruct mode. We're in the middle of a frightening storm. Today's verse, **Joshua 1:9,** contains a wonderful promise to repeat when the events in our world seem to be more evil than good: **Have I not commanded you? Be strong and courageous. Do not be terrified; do not be discouraged, for the Lord your God will be with you wherever you go (NIV).**

We have a King who still owns everything on earth (even though Satan thinks *he's* the owner). Satan may think that whenever we fall he can have us as his windfall, but he's wrong! Our God picks us up and helps us stand again and learn a lesson from our fall. And if we use our mistakes to learn lessons about how to avoid falling again, we become very strong. Each time we're tempted to slip backward, we can choose to pray and run from the temptation. It's fun to make the welcome discovery that our life is controlled not by whims, but by convictions!

Nancy

Only Words

The hearts of the people cry out to the Lord. Lamentations 2:18, NIV.

The praying mantis. The name sounds nice—if you've never seen one. Prayer is good, right? But of course, praying mantises don't actually pray, they only look like they do. For one thing, they're insects, and even if mantises *could* pray, you'd wonder what they were praying about. Why? Because the praying mantis is a ferocious killer. It hides among the leaves of plants, waiting for an unsuspecting insect to come along. Then it strikes out with its lightning-fast claws and captures and eats its victim. Praying mantises will eat anything, including poisonous insects and other mantises.

Why do people pray? The writer C. S. Lewis once said that prayer didn't change God; it changed *him*. I think he was right. When we come to God in prayer and ask Him to show us His will, we need to accept it. For instance, God wants us to forgive our enemies and love the unlovable. We can do that only if God changes us.

If we pray without any intention of allowing God to change us and show us what He wants us to do, our prayers are only words. They really don't mean anything. When David asked God to create a clean heart in him and to renew his spirit, he really meant it. That's why David was called a man after God's own heart.

Do you want to be someone after God's own heart? If so, it means you've got to allow God to change you. You and I can't be like the praying mantis. We can't act as if we're praying, and then go and tear people apart. We can't pray without any intention of allowing God to change us. Being a follower of God means He's going to really make a difference in our behavior and our attitudes. Let's not be praying mantises. Let's be people who really mean what we pray. **Jim**

"Didn't Use My Head"

Blessings are upon the head of the just: but violence covereth the mouth of the wicked. Proverbs 10:6.

B rad, what are you doing climbing through my bedroom window?" asked Mother.

Brad swung his last muddy foot through the window bars and dropped to the bedroom floor. "I didn't use my head! I didn't use my head!" he panted.

"How didn't you use your head?" asked Mother, suddenly remembering that in family worship that morning they'd talked about the importance of thinking before making choices. "What happened?"

"Well," said Brad, almost trembling with fear, "I didn't use my head because Nick and I climbed into the guava tree and started throwing guavas at people down on the road."

"Brad!" exclaimed Mother.

"And," Brad continued hurriedly, "someone else's head is hurting now too. I kinda hit a big African man on the nose, and it's bleeding . . . and he's real mad . . . and coming this way!"

Just then someone knocked loudly on the front door.

"Oh, no! There he is now!" exclaimed Brad, dissolving into frightened sobs.

Much to Brad's relief, the person at the front door was Nick's mother. "Nick told me what happened," she reported. "I intercepted the angry man, treated his nosebleed, and sent him on his way with a big loaf of fresh bread."

"Oh, thank you," exclaimed Brad. "But I'm so sorry! I just didn't use my head!"

Some people in the Bible didn't use their heads either. People like Aaron (see Exodus 32). Like Brad, Aaron's choice desperately hurt those around him.

God has promised to be with those who use their heads. In fact, another way of saying Proverbs 10:6 is "God's blessings will be upon the heads of those who use their heads."

Hey, between your two ears God gave you something very special. Use it!

Carolyn

Roll With the Punches

They were tearing up the sidewalk outside one of New York's old hotels. As the workers cracked up the concrete, their sledgehammers slammed into something beneath the first layer that seemed to move. It was a 14-pound turtle.

When the sidewalk was first built outside that old New York hotel, the proprietor reported that one of his snapping turtles (which then weighed only five pounds) had disappeared. No trace of it was ever found, and it was generally supposed that the turtle had walked off somewhere. But here it was, 32 years later, not only as alive as ever, but nine pounds heavier. The mystery is, what did that turtle feed on all those years?

I suppose all of us sometimes feel trapped by life, as that turtle was. When we're young, we think we'll always feel helpless. But things are continually in the process of change. Our freedoms and philosophies change so slowly we may not know it's happening, just as when we grow. There was never a big moment when you could say it happened. Disappointments pass in the same way. You don't know it's happened until you find yourself happily looking forward to something else.

To "roll with the punches" means to do the best with what comes, to roll like a ball instead of being deflated when hit with disappointment or discouragement. If you feel as though someone has thrown cement all around and there's no way out, just wait. Disappointment has a life span. The basketball gets thrown down to the court, but it bounces back for a new beginning. Our God is a God of new beginnings. As time passes, eventually you'll see new opportunities. Today's Bible verse, **Psalm 27:14,** speaks about patience. **Wait for the Lord; be strong, and let your heart take courage; yea, wait for the Lord! (RSV).** Roll with the punches. Bounce back with faith in God. And very soon God will take His turn. He will make the final, winning basket, and we will be taken home.   **Nancy**

What Gift Did You Get?

There are different kinds of gifts, but the same Spirit. I Corinthians 12:4, NIV.

All right, are you ready for a math quiz? What's 8 + 6? Right, 14. Now a tougher one: What's 45 + 62? If you figured 107, you were right again. All right, now multiplication. What's 15 x 7? If you calculated 105, you really are a math whiz.

Before you think you've conquered the world, try this one. How far would a pendulum travel in 7 years, 14 days, 2 hours, 1 minute, and 56 seconds if it swings 9.5 inches in one second?

Someone once asked George Bidder that same question back in 1822 while he was competing for a mathematics prize. It took George less than one minute to figure it out. No paper, no calculator; all in his head!

Now, George was definitely a smart guy, but he wasn't the smartest. That honor goes to Solomon. The Bible says that Solomon's wisdom excelled the wisdom of all the men of the East and all the wisdom of Egypt. According to 1 Kings 4:32-34 he spoke 3,000 proverbs, wrote more than 1,000 songs, knew all about trees and birds and fish and anything else that crawled, ran, or flew. He was so wise that the leaders of nations from all over the earth came to learn from him.

Yes, Solomon was one smart guy. Why was Solomon so smart? By the sounds of it he studied an awful lot. But I think the real reason was that he asked God for wisdom to rule his people in the best way.

God has great plans for you too. You and I may never be as wise as Solomon was, but God does have a special job for each of us that will bless others. Thank Him for the talents He's given you, and ask Him how He wants you to use them. You'll be amazed where He leads you!   **Jim**

Hannibal

I have fought the good fight, I have finished the race, I have kept the faith. 2 Timothy 4:7, NIV.

I f someone told you in 218 B.C. that General Hannibal was taking a lot of trunks across the Alps from Spain to Italy, it wouldn't mean he was taking a fresh change of clothes for every day of the war. No, this Carthaginian general, an enemy of Rome for 15 years, decided he'd have a lot more military muscle if his armed forces rode on elephants—not horses!*

Now, common sense should have told Hannibal that elephant bodies are made for hot weather and lumbering through deserts. But no! Hannibal would have it his way and started toward the high Italian Alps during the summer months. However, unexpected problems with the enemy and a severe early winter left most of the elephants dead before they ever reached the St. Bernard Pass area on what is now the Swiss-Italian border.

It's easy for us to say, "How stupid! European horses, used to cold winters, would have lasted much longer in mountain blizzards than African elephants! Dumb move, Hannibal!"

Wait a minute! Maybe there are times *we* use elephants instead of horses to wage *our* "wars." When struggling to win battles over bad grades, low self-esteem, and family problems, some of us retreat on elephants—video games, excess TV viewing, destructive music, and drugs. These elephants slow us down mentally, physically, and spiritually.

But we can battleproof ourselves against Satan with the powerful war horses of prayer, self-control, caring friends, the Bible, and advice from wise adults who love us.

Hannibal's soldiers never reached their destination or won their war because their general outfitted them with elephants that only got in the way of success. If we choose to ride into battle on the horses provided by God, our commanding general, He will guarantee our victory

Carolyn

---

*"Hannibal," *Encyclopedia Americana* (1994).

Right as a Trivet

Maybe your mother uses a trivet, that wrought iron thing used to put hot casserole dishes on to protect the table. Because a trivet has three legs, it stands firmly on nearly any surface. This stability is probably where the old saying that someone was "right as a trivet" came from. This meant that person was solid and stable, not in danger of falling.

There are some people who don't think it's possible to be right as a trivet, never to fall. What do you think? Read **1 Corinthians 10:13: Remember this—the wrong desires that come into your life aren't anything new and different. Many others have faced exactly the same problems before you. And no temptation is irresistible. You can trust God to keep the temptation from becoming so strong that you can't stand up against it (TLB).**

Temptations call for action. Usually a temptation involves something that can hurt us. It may have a negative effect on our health (too much ice cream or candy). Or it may have a negative effect on our conscience when we have the choice to do something that damages our integrity (the sense of everything being right). The beauty of today's text is God's promise that He won't allow Satan to tempt us too much. There will always be a way of escape if we just look for it and leave.

The next time you are tempted to do something wrong, take the first step by recognizing you are being tempted. Take a second step to choose the right action. And as a third step, physically move away from the situation.

Just for today, live a life that's as right as a trivet. You always have a choice when you're tempted to do wrong. Tell yourself, "I will run away from temptation."   **Nancy**

Lunch in the Dark

There will be no more night . . . for the Lord God will give them light. Revelation 22:5, NIV.

How many 12 o'clocks are there in each day? Right, there are two—one about the time you eat lunch, and one when you should be sleeping. Noon is the nickname for the 12 o'clock when you eat lunch, and midnight is the nickname for the 12 o'clock when you're sleeping. (Most of you have also noticed that it's daylight when you eat lunch, and if you've ever been up at midnight, you've probably seen the darkness of the night sky.)

So why are we talking about such obvious things? Well, they aren't so obvious to everyone on our planet. For instance, there's a place called the "land of the midnight sun." Yes, the sun is actually shining at midnight in the summer. What's even stranger is that for a couple months the people who live in the northernmost part of this country have *no* sun in the wintertime. They have to eat their lunches in the dark.

This "land of the midnight sun" is Norway. Norway is so far toward the top of the globe that when it's summer, they always see the sun. When it's winter, there are times they never see the sun. That would be hard for many people to get used to.

Just in case you think you couldn't get used to the sun never going down, let me remind you of what the Bible says. The book of Revelation says in heaven we won't even need the sun. That's because the Son of God will be all the light we need. It sounds as though we won't even need to sleep. Think of all the things you could do if you didn't need to sleep!

Heaven will have so many great things we can't even imagine, and if we trust in Jesus, our Saviour, we will be there someday. All the amazing things we'll see there will be nice, but being with Jesus, our light and our life, will be the best of all. **Jim**

Jun 29

Jimmy and the Copperhead

And he [an angel from heaven, understood to be Jesus] laid hold on . . . that old serpent, which is the Devil, and Satan, and bound him a thousand years. Revelation 20:2.

"Watch out for copperheads today," Mother cautioned Jimmy as he headed outdoors to play.

"I will," he answered.

Later that afternoon he called through the front door, "I wanna go see Aunt Robbie."

"All right," answered Mother. "But just be on the lookout for any—"

"I know, snakes," Jimmy finished the sentence for her.

Happily, Jimmy ran off in the direction of the draw that separated his aunt's property from his own family's land. A little stream ran through the gully. A long plank had been laid across the stream as a sort of footbridge. Jimmy always felt a little uneasy crossing the narrow plank bridge with all the water swiftly gurgling underneath.

Why is Mom so worried about snakes today? he wondered, as he carefully worked his way across the plank. Just as Jimmy was about to step onto solid ground he saw something that made his insides freeze. A copperhead! It was way too late to turn back. Almost automatically the young boy leaped as high into the air as he could, at the same time screaming, "Copperhead!"

Aunt Robbie came running with her trusty hoe, and in a matter of seconds the copperhead lay in several motionless pieces.

Like that copperhead hiding on the other side of the bridge, Satan lies in wait for us to get within striking distance so that he can attack us with deadly poisonous temptations. We bring ourselves within that serpent's striking distance or stay away from it by certain choices we make. Read for yourself what some of them are in 1 Timothy 3:7; 2 Timothy 2:24-26; James 4:7; and Ephesians 4:25-27 and 6:11-18.

Jesus has warned us to be on the lookout. If we keep these warnings in mind, we'll automatically know how to get away from the enemy when we see him. Like Jimmy, we'll be smart enough to call for help. If Jesus is strong enough to imprison the serpent, who is Satan (Revelation 20:2), He is certainly strong enough to help us escape that serpent every time it tries to ambush us.

Carolyn

From the Horse's Mouth

Horse traders have a rather nasty reputation for being dishonest. Among other dishonest practices, horse traders have been known to lie about the age of a horse. And inexperienced horse traders might be inclined to believe these crooks. Experts say the best way to find out the age and health of a horse is to look in its mouth and count its teeth. To get something "straight from the horse's mouth" means to get to the source and find out something directly, instead of going by what someone else says.

We believe the Bible's accounts about Jesus because those accounts were written by people who talked directly to Him. Others didn't believe until they saw something special about Jesus for themselves. Read today's verse, **Mark 15:39: When the Roman officer standing beside his cross saw how he dismissed his spirit, he exclaimed, "Truly, this was the Son of God!" (TLB).** If you are a person who needs to see Jesus for yourself before you believe Him, you'd better be careful. You may never believe until it's too late. It doesn't have to be hard to believe.

Why do we struggle to believe historical accounts about Jesus, while we don't struggle to believe historical accounts about George Washington or pioneers or World War I? With anything historical, you have to make a decision to believe. It doesn't have to be difficult. The information in the Bible about Jesus comes "straight from the horse's mouth"—from eyewitness accounts. Those stories are supported by other historians, too. The next time you see a horse, remember that the stories about Jesus come "straight from the horse's mouth." They're all true. **Nancy**

Ju^l 1

They Just Don't Mix

What fellowship can light have with darkness? 2 Corinthians 6:14, NIV.

It's chemistry experiment time. Take this book with you and go to the kitchen. If you're not near a kitchen, you'll just have to use your imagination. Now, fill a glass about half full with water. Get some cooking oil and pour a small amount into the glass. What happens? Yes, the oil floats on top of the water. Why? Because the molecules that water and oil are made of are so different they prefer to stay apart. It's as if they don't want anything to do with each other, and because water has what is known as surface tension, the oil molecules just float on top as if there was a skin on the top of the water. That's why oil is a main ingredient in some paint—it pushes away water. That would be good in a rainstorm on the side of your house, wouldn't it?

There are many other things that are so different they don't want to have anything to do with each other. For instance, try putting the south poles of two magnets together. They repel each other. Try putting bug spray on your arm. If it works right, the bugs don't want anything to do with your arm. Or what about moms and dirt? Moms, it seems, don't like their kids to get their clothes dirty.

There are two other things that shouldn't have anything to do with each other—sin and righteousness. When Jesus comes into our lives, He wants to cleanse us from everything impure and unclean. He wants us to live a life free from the chains of sin. But Jesus is patient with us, and when we fall, He forgives us and continues His work of change.

If you ask Jesus to come into your life today, remember that He wants to make your life different. He wants you to live like a child of the King. So ask Him, and see the difference between light and darkness in your life.

Jim

Double Exposure

Purify your hearts, you double-minded. James 4:8, NIV.

"I'll erase the chalkboard, Ms. Carter."

"Oh, let me empty the wastebasket, Ms. Carter."

"Ms. Carter, I can run those papers down to the office for you."

Krista seemed to be the sweetest, most thoughtful junior high student that Ms. Carter had ever met. Krista was certainly being helpful to Ms. Carter during her first year of teaching in this new school.

One day at lunch break a younger student approached the table where Ms. Carter was eating with some students. "Are you the new teacher?" she asked.

"Yes, I am," answered Ms. Carter. "Who are you?"

"I'm Aimee, and I'm in the second grade."

"Well, it's nice to meet you, Aimee."

"You teach my big sister in seventh grade," said Aimee.

"Who's your big sister?" Ms. Carter wanted to know.

"She's Krista."

"Krista?" Ms. Carter could see the resemblance between the two sisters. "Oh, I just love Krista. She is *so* sweet."

The smile on Aimee's face turned to a look of confusion. She paused before saying, "Well, I've *heard* that Krista is sweet."

Suddenly Ms. Carter knew that Aimee must see a far different side of Krista at home than Ms. Carter saw at school.

The person who wrote the book of James in the Bible knew there were people like Krista in the world. People who are double-minded. People who have two sides to their characters and personalities. The person they seem to be to some is not the same person they appear to be to others.

Have you known Christians like this? Of course we have. In fact, we may (at times) be double-minded too: talking the Christian "talk," as they say, but not walking the Christian "walk." James has some special advice for those of us who have this problem. (See James 4:8 above.)

If you allow Jesus to help you follow that counsel, you'll be a happier person. And so will those who know you. For all your friends and acquaintances will be loving and trusting the *same* you—not the two sides of a double-minded you.

Carolyn

Jul 3

Don't Flog a Dead Horse

Once upon a time some peasants who were wandering between towns came upon a horse lying in the road. "A horse!" they exclaimed gleefully to each other. "A horse to ride. This will make getting around much easier. How could we be so lucky to find it just lying here!"

"Get up!" one of the peasants shouted to the horse.

The horse didn't budge.

"I said, get up!" the peasant shouted again.

The horse didn't even blink an eye.

Another peasant suggested, "You'll have to beat him. Here, fetch a stick. That ought to get the old beast up."

They beat the horse. But still it didn't budge.

Now, it happened that some villagers came by from the opposite direction and saw what the peasants were doing. "Stop that!" they demanded. "You stop that right now. That horse will never get up for you. He's dead. Don't flog a dead horse. Let him be and pass on by as we do."

Don't flog a dead horse. Don't engage in futile activities. Our verse for today, **Proverbs 20:24,** supports that: **Since the Lord is directing our steps, why try to understand everything that happens along the way? (TLB).** Notice that it doesn't say God throws trouble our direction. It says God directs our steps—over, under, around, and through—the troubles Satan has scattered on this earth. Someday, when we look back over our lives, we'll have new information. We'll see how one roadblock may have led us in another direction, under God's guidance, bringing different opportunities to us. I expect to be very excited when I see how everything fits together. And I also expect my love for God to burst out even stronger when I see how He used trouble to bind me closer to Him. At last, everything will make sense.　　　　　**Nancy**

The Man on the Moon

"Take my yoke upon you and learn from me, for I am gentle and humble in heart, and you will find rest for your souls. For my yoke is easy and my burden is light." Matthew 11:29, 30, NIV.

When I was 11 years old, I watched on television as the first man walked on the moon. One of the most interesting things about that walk on the moon was the way the astronauts floated when they moved. I learned that they could bounce and float because the moon's gravitational pull is one sixth that of earth. That means that if you weigh 100 pounds on earth, you weigh only about 17 pounds on the moon.

On the moon you can carry heavy objects with ease. You would be able to pick up your brother or sister or best friend and throw them up into the air, catching them in your arms. What great fun it would be to play on the moon!

Did you know that being a follower of Jesus is something like being on the moon? Some people think that being a Christian means you can't do this and you can't do that. They think that following Jesus will be boring. Actually, the opposite is true. Jesus doesn't burden us—He frees us from sin. Oh, He doesn't promise to take away all our problems, but He does promise to be with us every step of the way.

Best of all, life with Jesus is exciting! It's great fun to see what He's going to do for you next. Accept Jesus into your heart. Let Him take sin's weight from your shoulders, and bounce with the joy that only God can give you.   **Jim**

Jul 5

Don't Be Stupid!

The way of the Lord is strength to the upright. Proverbs 10:29.

I hope we're not lost!" moaned Kari in the dead-end cavern chamber. Since it was just a tiny cave, we'd neglected to tell the leader of the Pathfinder Teen Caving Invitational our destination. Now here we were, realizing we'd gotten off on a phony path.

"How could we have gotten off the *only* path in the cave?" I asked, feeling embarrassed. "That was really stupid."

"I know," said Kari. "And not saying where we were going was stupid too."

"Is this the right path?" a voice suddenly called out in the darkness behind us.

"We're not sure," I answered, not wanting to admit our being lost.

"We were just planning to try to find our way back," added Kari.

"Great," I whispered to Kari. "Now someone else is following the trail *we* made."

"Now I *really* feel stupid!" she snickered.

Back at the campsite Kari said, "I can't believe we got lost in a tiny cave because we weren't smart enough to stay on the only real path."

"Besides that," I added, "we made the wrong path more distinct and could have gotten hypothermia."

"Let's add a new rule to our list of cave safety rules," Kari suggested. "It's Don't be stupid!"

Although I laughed, I had to admit it was a great suggestion! Even in everyday life it *is* stupid to follow the path made by someone who doesn't really know where they're going, rather than following the "way of the Lord" (Proverbs 10:29) that would lead us straight to heaven.

Writer Ellen White said, "Let no one follow a crooked path that someone else has made, for thus you would not only go astray yourself, but would make this crooked path plainer for someone else to follow. Determine that as for yourself, you will walk in the path of obedience" (*Sons and Daughters of God*, p. 192).

Not making stupid choices will help keep our feet on the right path. And, just as good, it will probably help others keep from getting lost too.

Carolyn

In Fine Fettle

To be in "fine fettle" is an old expression that means someone feels splendid! "Fettle" comes from an old English word that means "girdle." With a fettle firmly in place under one's clothes, a person couldn't help but look splendid because there was no flab to jiggle and distort the shape of their clothes.

Although the phrase originally was used to describe how a person looked, it eventually came to describe how a person felt inside, for the English learned that how you look really can affect how you feel.

These days when we say someone is "in fine fettle," we mean they're in a jubilant state of mind. Read today's verse, **Romans 1:16: For I am not ashamed of this Good News about Christ. It is God's powerful method of bringing all who believe it to heaven. This message was preached first to the Jews alone, but now everyone is invited to come to God in this same way (TLB).** I think Paul was saying that he was "in fine fettle" concerning the gospel of Christ. He was jubilant about it and excited about sharing it. He invites all of us to feel the same way about the gospel.

What's so great about the fact that Jesus loves us and we love Him? Well, besides the warm fuzzy feelings it brings you to know that you're special, to be loved by someone means that you get to share whatever they've got. Just around the corner you've got a second chance at life, and that's good news. It should make you jubilant—especially if life has got you down right now. Your next life is going to be perfect, with everything going your way. So hold on, Jesus is coming! And when we're with Him, all our dreams will come true.   **Nancy**

Jul 7

Nicknames

God . . . gave him the name that is above every name, that at the name of Jesus every knee should bow, in heaven and on earth. Philippians 2:9, 10, NIV.

Did you ever wonder why people use nicknames? Sometimes it shows they like another person, and unfortunately, people sometimes give others nicknames to show how much they don't like another person. Sometimes people have nicknames that describe something about themselves, such as calling someone Red who has red hair.

Did you know that Jesus had nicknames? He actually had quite a few. Jesus was given nicknames that described all His wonderful qualities. Here are some of them: Adam, Advocate, Alpha and Omega, Apostle of our Profession, Arm of the Lord, Author and Perfecter of our Faith, Source of Eternal Salvation, Ruler of God's Creation, Beloved Son, Branch, Bread of Life, Author of Salvation, Chief Shepherd, Christ of God, Consolation of Israel, Capstone, Counselor, Creator, Rising Sun, Deliverer, Desire of All Nations, Gate, Chosen of God, Faithful Witness, First and Last, Firstborn, Forerunner, Glory of the Lord, God, Good Shepherd, Great High Priest, Head of the Church, Heir of All Things, Holy Child, Holy One of God, Holy One of Israel, Image of God, Immanuel, Jesus, Jesus of Nazareth, Judge of Israel, Righteous One, King, King of the Jews, King of kings, King of the Ages, Lawgiver, Lamb, Lamb of God, Life, Light of the World, Lion of the Tribe of Judah, Lord of All, Lord of lords, Lord Our Righteousness, Man of Sorrows, Mediator, Messenger of the Covenant, Messiah, Mighty God, Mighty One. And that's not even the end of all the nicknames of Jesus found in the Bible!

Jesus our Saviour is all of these things. Even more amazing, He gave them all up for us when He died on a cross for our sins. Aren't you glad that someone with that kind of influence—and all those nicknames—is your friend? **Jim**

Man Under Board!

When you pray, I will listen. Jeremiah 29:12, TLB.

Ya-hooooo!" cried Andrew joyfully as the nose of his sailboard sliced into the wind and through the white-capped waves of Beardsley Lake. Feet pushing hard in the foot stirrups, Andrew pulled against the boom (the mast holding the sail) and tilted his head way backward. Just then the wind began to die, and he felt the icy water drench his scalp—and then the rest of his body.

Normally he would have swum out from under the board, but his feet, still jammed in the stirrups, were stuck *above* water. The rest of his body sank as the sail collapsed on top of him. Andrew was trapped underwater, inches from air. Then his oxygen ran out; his lungs grew hot. He lunged at the sail with his nose, grabbing a gulp of air before being pulled down again.

I'm going to die! he thought. *God, help me, or I'll die!*

Instantly Andrew lost his sense of panic and seemed to be able to think logically.

Your energy's gone—loosen your feet, he said to himself. He managed to draw one last breath and curl his legs up, making him sink even lower—almost upside down. He grabbed hold of the board and tilted it toward him, pulling with all his remaining strength.

One foot slipped out of a stirrup . . . and then the other one broke free. The teenager's head broke the water's surface, and he could breathe at last. Soon he was up on his board, galloping across the waves once again.

Andrew's sailboard experience happens to us every day, spiritually speaking. We're windsurfing along, everything going just fine in our lives. Then the wind dies down. We stop being faithful in our Bible reading, or we give in to an unexpected temptation. Suddenly we're sinking down into the icy chill of discouragement or sinful thoughts or some other sin that controls us. Satan's goal is to make us drown in that sinful condition.

Only when we ask Jesus to help us get "unstuck" and "on board" again can we be saved from drowning. Jesus always hears our cry to get out of the lake of sin, and He always shows us how.   **Carolyn**

E-7

All Is Fish That Comes to His Net

Perhaps dolphins are the most loved of all the sea creatures, because they are one of the few ocean creatures that has actually gone out of its way to interact with humans. There are many stories about dolphins guiding ships through dangerous waters, tossing lost beach balls toward wave-jumping tourists, and keeping drowning people afloat till help arrives. Perhaps because of this there's been a drive to boycott tuna companies that use nets that catch both dolphins and tuna.

Catching more than one species of fish is not uncommon to those who fish. Often more than fish show up in a fishing net. There may be seaweed or other debris, inedible fish, and eels in a net. These undesirables must be separated from the edible fish and tossed overboard. It's a nuisance to have anything except fish in one's net.

Someone whose net brings up only the desired fish is very lucky. And that is where the statement for today comes in. "All is fish that comes to his net" means someone has the unique ability to get just what is wanted, when it is wanted.

There's one necessary requirement for getting along with others, however. The Bible says it very clearly in **Matthew 23:12: For whoever exalts himself will be humbled, and whoever humbles himself will be exalted (NIV).** Humble people don't think they're better than others—they're interested in others. One of the secrets to a happy life is that as you live your life humbly, willing to help others, God will exalt you, and your net will be overflowing with love. **Nancy**

The Aspirin That Cured More Than a Headache

Don't let anyone look down on you because you are young, but set an example for the believers. I Timothy 4:12, NIV.

Bobby loved to read, so when he picked up a book on Albert Schweitzer at the library, he couldn't wait to get home and read it from cover to cover. He had no idea who Albert Schweitzer was when he started the book, but by the time he was finished, Bobby had a mission.

Albert Schweitzer was a missionary doctor in Africa during World War II. He had sacrificed much to help the native people there. When Bobby read about Dr. Schweitzer he was moved with compassion and wanted to go directly to Africa and help this courageous doctor. But how could he do that? He was only 13, and he couldn't go to Africa. So Bobby did the only thing he could do—he went to the medicine cabinet and got a bottle of aspirin.

Bobby's dad was in the Air Force in Southern Europe. He figured if he sent the aspirin to his dad's boss, the boss could do something about it. So Bobby sent that bottle of aspirin to Lt. Gen. Richard C. Lindsay, commander of Allied Air Forces in Southern Europe. In his letter Bobby asked Lt. Gen. Lindsay if "any of your airplanes" could drop the aspirin over the part of Africa where Dr. Schweitzer worked.

Somehow Bobby's letter made it to radio stations and newspapers in Italy. Soon the commander had more than $400,000 worth of medical supplies to fly to Dr. Schweitzer for his work in the jungles of Africa.

Bobby had no idea how powerful one little boy could be when he decided to do something instead of just sitting around waiting for things to happen.

How about you? Would you like to make things happen for God? Ask Him to show you a project that He'd like you to work on. Maybe it's feeding homeless people or helping your neighbor next door. Whatever it is, God will bless your work as you do great things for Him. **Jim**

Jul 11

English as She Is Spoke

Therefore is the name of it called Babel; because the Lord did there confound the language of all the earth. Genesis 11:9.

One of the funniest books I ever read wasn't even meant to be funny. It was written during the past century by a Portuguese man named Pedro Carolino. In it he translated a lot of Portuguese expressions into English. The only problem was that he didn't know English! Pedro thought that if Portuguese travelers to England used his book, they would be able to "speak" English in any situation. So he entitled his book *English as She Is Spoke*.

For example, Pedro suggested that if you wanted to compliment someone's handsome nose you could say, "Ah, he has a good beak." Among the "helpful" phrases Carolino recommended for discussing the weather were "It rains" and "It not rains."

Words of encouragement to an English fisherman that the Portuguese-speaking tourist might say include, "That pond it seems me many multiplied of fishes" and "Here, there is a wand and some hooks—dip again it in the water."

Sin has caused a big language problem on this earth. After the Flood, humans chose to not trust in God's promise that He wouldn't send another flood. Instead, they chose to trust in themselves and build a high tower for protection. Their plan was to stay together instead of spreading out over the earth as God had asked them to do. Because of their pride, lack of faith in God, and disobedience, God confused the languages of the people working on the tower. Because of the resulting communication problems, this place became known as the Tower of Babel.

The people of various language groups had to spread out over the earth and accomplish God's will better that way. But as Pedro Carolino's funny expression book proves, different language groups still cause misunderstandings among people.

Someday soon, though, after Jesus returns, we will all speak the same heavenly language. Never again will there be confusion or disharmony among peoples of the earth made new. I can hardly wait! **Carolyn**

The Tables Are Turned

H ave you ever played Boggle? That's the game in which you have to make words out of randomly-placed letters in a grid, using only the letters that touch each other. Often you get stuck and can't see any more possibilities until the grid is turned and you see it from a different direction. Then all sorts of new words you couldn't see before seem to jump out at you.

The phrase "Turn the tables on someone" in a positive sense means to see something from someone else's point of view. In a negative sense it means that you put someone who thought they were powerful in a position of powerlessness so they can see what that feels like for a change.

Someday God is going to turn the tables on bullies. You can read about it in **Matthew 18:6: But if any of you causes one of these little ones who trusts in me to lose his faith, it would be better for you to have a rock tied to your neck and be thrown into the sea (TLB).** Today's verse says that if anyone causes a little child to lose their faith in God, it is better if that person were drowned. You might know someone who acts like a Christian at church but belittles you or hurts you at home or in private. You might think this person is a Christian—certainly he or she acts like a Christian by going to church—but a true Christian doesn't hurt little children.

Please don't mistrust Jesus because of the example of these people. Jesus is on your side. He's angry at what these bullies are doing because He loves you. Tell your pastor or a trusted adult what the bullies are doing, and turn the tables on them. Let *them* be afraid for a change. Telling is the right thing to do, no matter what the bully may say. True Christians keep little children safe; they don't hurt them.

Jesus is on your side against pretend Christians who hurt children.

Nancy

Persepolis

They could find no corruption in him. Daniel 6:4, NIV.

It had 40-foot walls and a beautiful staircase made of 111 stone steps that led to a terrace. The remains of several enormous buildings, made of huge slabs of highly polished gray stone, still exist. Thirteen columns that helped to support the great hall still stand. It was indeed an impressive complex.

The man who had it all built was an extremely powerful man. He had hundreds, maybe thousands, of men and women who served him night and day. He had governors, prefects, satraps, and advisers who ran his kingdom for him and reported directly to him. His name was Darius. Do you recognize that name? Remember the story of Daniel in the lions' den? Yes, Darius was the king who was tricked into putting his favorite governor, Daniel, into a den of hungry lions.

How is it that a man from a foreign country could impress the king of the most powerful empire on earth? What was it that Daniel had done to cause King Darius to think so highly of him? The Bible says that Daniel was "trustworthy and neither corrupt nor negligent" (Daniel 6:4, NIV). The men who were after him could find nothing to accuse him of.

I'm sure the strong character Daniel had was formed when he was very young. Daniel learned important lessons about life and about God, just as you are doing right now. But it was more than just learning them. Daniel also made good choices.

You might be in a place of greatness someday, just as Daniel was. But even if your job is rather ordinary, your character doesn't have to be. Daniel had a character that made him stand out from the rest, and he was rewarded for it. He also made some people angry, but he stayed true to God through it all.

Daniel did his best to serve Darius, but it wasn't the king of Persia he was trying to impress. He simply wanted to be faithful to the King of the universe.

Jim

Rattlesnake Canyon

The eternal God is thy refuge, and underneath are the everlasting arms. Deuteronomy 33:27.

The granite boulder looked like a giant pie with one piece missing. And I, on a slippery slope, was facing the inside of the "pie." I, with my uncle and two cousins, Gina and Jared, was on a Sabbath afternoon hike up Rattlesnake Canyon in Joshua Tree National Monument. But my cousins' 13-year-old legs carried them faster than my 11-year-old ones could go. They were choosing the route, I was trying to keep up, and Uncle Wally was bringing up the rear. Losing sight of Gina, I took a route I *thought* she and Jared had taken. But suddenly I was in this "pie" with my tennies slipping on the slick surface and the canyon suddenly far below me.

"Uncle Wallee-e-e!" I shrieked.

"Here I am," he said as his head suddenly appeared over the ledge.

He pulled himself onto my slippery slope, and I realized he was the only thing between me and the bottom of Rattlesnake Canyon.

"Uncle Wally," I said in a trembling voice, "I'm so scared!"

"You have to trust me," he said kindly but firmly. "Jared!" he called.

"Yo!" answered Jared, not far above us.

"Get down on your stomach and be ready to pull up your cousin."

"OK, Dad."

"We must change places," said my uncle, "so I have enough leverage to boost you over the ledge."

I closed my eyes and shook my head.

"I won't let you fall—I'll have my arm around you the whole time." I knew I had to trust him.

Trembling, I followed his directions. Wedging in my right foot . . . Letting go with my left hand . . . Leaning out over the canyon. . . . All the while, my uncle's strong arm—my only hope—remained firmly planted about my waist.

Soon we'd traded places and I was being pushed and hoisted to a higher, flatter, safer granite slope.

Sometimes, when I feel my feet slipping, I think about Rattlesnake Canyon and remember that Jesus, like my uncle, has His strong arm around me. And somehow, it's just a little easier to make the right choice.

Carolyn

Jul 15

In the Nick of Time

Have you ever wondered why bad things happen to good people? Even Jesus wondered "Why?" Read **Matthew 27:46: About three o'clock, Jesus shouted, "Eli, Eli, lama sabachthani," which means, "My God, my God, why have you forsaken me?" (TLB).** As Jesus was dying He asked God "Why Me?" but there was no answer. There may not be an answer until our life on earth is over, but that is no reason not to trust in God.

The phrase "in the nick of time" comes from the Middle Ages. If someone owed you something, a time was set up for him to make a payment to you. The meeting place might have been at the city gates or in the town square. Wherever it was, you would arrive ahead of time with a stick, a knife, and a good pocket watch.

The instant the time for the meeting came, you would look around for the person who was to make a payment. If that person wasn't there, you'd make a notch in the stick, indicating that they had not come in time, and you would then have the right to claim some of their property as your own.

Believe it or not, there were people back then who were always late, just as there are today. Only they weren't exactly late; they arrived "in the nick of time." Before you could finish cutting a nick in the stick, they would show up and pay you. So doing something in the nick of time means doing it at the last possible second, before the permanent mark is made.

Just before Jesus comes it's going to be both scary and exciting here on earth. But God will be with us. And Jesus will appear just in the nick of time, before Satan's people win. Whose side will you be on? You have a choice that you're making right now. And I've got a good idea that it's going to be with God.

Nancy

Directory Assistance

There is only one Lawgiver and Judge, the one who is able to save and destroy. James 4:12, NIV.

G o get your yellow pages. Go ahead; I'll wait. Do you have them? OK, look under the word "attorneys." Do you know what an attorney is? That's right, an attorney is a lawyer. Lawyers are people whose job it is to work with those who are involved in legal matters. The people might be in trouble for doing something wrong, or they may be owed money by someone and are trying to get what belongs to them.

You'll notice that there are different kinds of attorneys. Some specialize in helping people who have been in accidents; some help people with their property; some help those who are in financial trouble.

Yes, attorneys are people who help other people. But I don't think any of those lawyers you found in the yellow pages would be willing to take their clients' punishment. If you had to go to jail for stealing a car, do you think any of those lawyers would go to jail for you? If a murderer had to go to the electric chair to pay for their crime, do you think their lawyer would go for them, and let the murderer go free? I'm pretty sure that none of the attorneys in the yellow pages would do that.

But wait! I know Someone who did just that. Jesus is our lawyer and judge, and He's already served our sentence for us. He took the punishment that we should have taken when He died on the cross so our sins could be forgiven. If we'll accept the free gift of salvation, He will write our names in the book of life and free us from the penalty of sin.

You would probably never ask an attorney in your town to serve a sentence that you deserved. But Jesus, our judge and our attorney, volunteered to take our place before we ever asked. **Jim**

Jul 17

"It Is Good for You to Rot"

Pride . . . do I hate. Proverbs 8:13.

Some attempts at translating things from one language into another one can be pretty funny if the translators don't know what they're doing. I once heard of a British missionary who was trying to translate an English hymn into a Bantu (African) language. One line of the English hymn went like this: "Sin dies, simply to rot." But the missionary's translation of the line became "It is good for you to rot."

More recently an American missionary in Africa attempted to translate the line "I gave my heart to Jesus. How about you?" Unfortunately, her translation gave it this meaning: "I gave my heart to Jesus. What's the matter with you?"

As a missionary in Africa with limited knowledge of Kinyarwanda, the very complicated local language, I knew better than to attempt translating. Nevertheless, my few language lessons—and the praise I received when attempting to speak that language—fostered something inside me. That something was pride.

Although a wise old pastor translated most of a song for our school choir to sing, I decided to translate the last line by myself. My little secret. Two weeks later, the choir performed that song before a 600-member outdoor camp meeting congregation, and I felt so proud, hearing a big choir sing *my* translated line.

After the service a pastor respectfully approached. "Nice music," he said, "but I'm puzzled by that song's last line. What is it in English?"

"In English," I answered, "it's 'I believe, so why should I worry or fret?'"

Gently the kind old man explained that what I had *actually* translated—and had the college choir sing at the top of their voices—was "I believe, so why should I throw up all the time?"

Oops! This whole thing happened because of my pride. Pride takes our love and focus off God and puts it on ourselves. As I found out at that African camp meeting, pride will eventually embarrass or hurt us (see Proverbs 16:18).

But worst of all, pride—in Christians—will embarrass and hurt the cause of God.

202

Carolyn

Get Someone off the Hook

If fish have emotions, there is a moment in every fish's life when it may wonder for a second if it's lucky or unlucky. It's the moment it's taken off the hook. Writhing in the hand of the person who caught it, the fish will be sent in one of two directions: back into the lake, or into the skillet for supper.

When we say someone is let "off the hook," it means the pressure is off, and things are going to be OK. **Matthew 10:19** promises the same thing. **When you are arrested, don't worry about what to say at your trial, for you will be given the right words at the right time (TLB).** If you are ever called into court to testify for your faith, God promises He will impress you with the right words to get you "off the hook," and everything will turn out right.

Of course, this doesn't happen magically. You have a part to play in how easy it is for you to stand up for God in court. God uses the texts and promises you have already learned and helps you recall them. So when you study for Bible class, don't just memorize your lessons—make sense of them! Put yourself in a Bible person's shoes, dust off your imagination, and think about how it must have felt.

Jonah, for instance. We think of him as a pathetic coward, but he didn't want to go to Nineveh because the people there skinned their enemies alive. No wonder Jonah didn't want to make them mad! But what was it that gave Jonah the courage to preach to the people once he got there? You decide.

Now think about your own life. Have there been times when you thought it was wiser to keep silent, but somehow things worked out so that you spoke up for Christianity? How did it feel? The more positive you feel about the value of Christian ethics in your life, the easier it will be to defend them. You can be proud that Christians are kind, honest, hardworking, and patient. Each of those traits points back to God.

When you have personalized the Bible, its verses are much easier to recall.

Nancy

Fire

Do not put out the Spirit's fire. I Thessalonians 5:19, NIV.

Campfires are the best. But a good campfire isn't as easy to build as it seems. You've got to have the right conditions and ingredients. Never do this without adult supervision, but here's what a camper needs to build a roaring fire:

The fire starts with kindling. I like to shave small pieces of dry wood from a dead branch. Next, build a tepee of medium sized sticks over the kindling. Finally, build a larger tepee over the smaller tepee. This helps the fire to build slowly and steadily. A good supply of air keeps the fire healthy. A gentle breeze is good, but when the air is absolutely calm, I blow steadily at the glowing coals to help increase the flame.

Keeping your fire alive for Jesus is even more important than a good campfire. It warms the soul and keeps you encouraged. It also brings others to Jesus, the Light of the world.

To keep your zeal for Jesus, you need the right ingredients, just like a campfire does. You need to spend time each day with Him. Talk to Him often and read the letters He's sent to you in His Word. But don't leave it there. Sharing what you've discovered about Jesus is like a fresh breeze blowing on a campfire. It fans the flames and keeps you afire for Him. Others need to see the excitement in your eyes when you share what you know about Him. After all, if you aren't excited about the Saviour, why should anyone else be?

Building a good campfire takes time and careful work. Building a fire for Jesus does too. Don't let the things of this world take you away from building a fire that others will be attracted to. Allow the Holy Spirit to keep your flame alive as you share God's love with others. As you do, you'll find that others will begin to gather around as the light of Jesus shines through you.

Jim

Fire in the Fuel Supply!

"Then he will say to those on his left, 'Depart from me, you who are cursed, into the eternal fire prepared for the devil and his angels.'" Matthew 25:41, NIV.

*K*afoom! The explosion ripped through the cold African night and shook our house. In horror we watched the roof lift off the campus fuel storage shed across the little dirt road. In the swirling red-orange columns of flame shooting toward the eucalyptus trees overhead, we saw tiles and pieces of rafter go flying.

Hundreds of miles from the nearest fire department, we hovered against the far wall of our living room, afraid that our own front windows might blow out during the continuing explosions. The heat penetrated our brick walls and sent us scurrying to the huge pot of drinking water in the kitchen.

It seems that someone on the staff, wanting to evaluate the school's fuel supply, had held a kerosene lantern above a gasoline barrel whose small lid he'd just twisted off. While he strained to see the level of fuel in the large container, his lantern's flame suddenly ignited the escaping fumes. Fortunately, the man escaped that first explosion with only second-degree burns to his face and neck.

Until the early-morning hours we heard containers of fuel exploding, demolishing the wooden shed, crisping nearby trees, and burning until there was nothing left for the flames to consume. But the pile of twisted metal and ash on the concrete slab stayed red-hot for days.

A fuel fire is coming soon to this old earth. Before that time, though, we'll be so sick of sin's atmosphere that we'll want only one thing: to be "outta here" and home safe with God. And God will want that too. In heaven He'll give us plenty of time to look through all His record books and see for ourselves how loving and fair He is. When that's done, He'll take His own kind of "kerosene lantern" and allow its flame to ignite the stinking fumes of this world's sin. And the resulting fire will burn up all the cruelty, pain, injustice, and filth . . . until there's nothing left to consume.

Then, in the earth made new, we'll be happy, safe, and pain-free— for always and always. **Carolyn**

Jul 21

Flannelmouth

Daddy, does God know everything?" a little boy asked his father. "Yes, Bobby, He certainly does," his father replied. "He knows everything that everyone is doing right now, all around the world. But why do you ask?"

"Well, I just wondered, because at church the preacher prays so long about so many things it's as though God doesn't know what's going on down here or something."

When God sees His children making decisions that hurt themselves or others, maybe He does wish He didn't know everything that's going on. I'm sure there were many times Adam and Eve wished they didn't know so much, either. But Satan had tricked them (as he always does) into thinking that what they didn't have or hadn't experienced was something they should risk everything for. Read in **Genesis 3:4, 5** what the serpent told Eve she was missing out on. **"You will not surely die," the serpent said to the woman. "For God knows that when you eat of it your eyes will be opened, and you will be like God, knowing good and evil" (NIV).** Satan suggested that God was trying to keep something from them. Satan was a flannelmouth, a smooth talker, in the same way that flannel is soft and smooth. And Satan talked softly and convincingly, almost hypnotically. He still talks to us that way today.

There are many things he may lead you into thinking you must experience right away. Your friends may say you're missing out on something if you don't experience sex, drugs, or alcohol. And you may give in, as Adam and Eve did, and go for it. But you will find, as Adam and Eve did, that knowing too much about sinful things brings you only pain and misery and a guilty. conscience.

God will still love you if you have experienced these things, but you may not love yourself until you stop doing them. The best decision is to stand firm against the flannelmouths. Be good to yourself. Don't let anyone talk you into doing anything you couldn't tell your parents about later.

Make the choice to recognize flannelmouths and disbelieve their lies.

Nancy

The One and Only

You alone are God over all the kingdoms of the earth. Isaiah 37:16, NIV.

Long ago, if you were the king in some ancient countries you were also considered a god, or at least special friends with the gods. In Egypt the pharaohs were thought to be gods. So when Moses and Aaron challenged the pharaoh, it was a big deal. You can see why the pharaoh may not have wanted to let the Israelites go. Why should a god back down and grant the wishes of mere human beings?

If you were a Hittite king, you became a god when you died. In many other places, such as Crete and some of the tribes in Asia and Africa, if you were king you were identified as a divine animal. Alexander the Great had himself made a god about a year before he died. (I wonder why he waited so long?) Later the Roman emperors, who were in charge at the time of Jesus, were also worshiped as gods.

Really, it's pretty silly, isn't it? Men thinking they were gods, and the people of their kingdoms giving them all their money and honor. I wonder why the people didn't figure it out when their kings made mistakes or when they got sick and died.

Of course, there's really only one true God. He not only *rules* the universe; He *made* the universe. There will always be people who believe that someone else is God, or that God doesn't really exist, or that God doesn't really care. But if they knew Him, they'd know how much He loves them.

Ancient kings who thought they were gods were only fooling themselves and their people. They had no power over death or the laws of nature. But we worship a God who not only conquered death, but will give us eternal life. Let Him reign in your heart today, and find out how great life can be when you know the One and Only. **Jim**

Jul 23

3-D!

Now unto him that is able to do exceeding abundantly above all we ask or think, according to the power that worketh in us. Ephesians 3:20.

"See it yet?" a total stranger asked me the first time I stood staring at a yellowish-orange three-dimensional illusion in the center of a mall display.

"See what?" I asked.

"Why, the bomber!" he answered matter-of-factly. "And there's a school of dolphins in that blue hologram there, and tropical flowers in the red one."

I stared again at the pieces of computer-generated art. Honestly, all I could see were framed hodge-podges of tiny color spots. The thought occurred to me that the stranger might be hallucinating—and dangerous. So I quickly left the display and resumed my shopping.

In the months that followed, people I knew—and respected!—started telling me they saw 3-D pictures in holograms. So I kept looking, and do you know what? One day about two years later, when my son and I were staring at a green 3-D illusion in an art shop, my eyes relaxed, or something. Suddenly, almost bursting through the borders of the shiny black frame, was a huge dinosaur! Whoa! Totally 3-D! It seemed as though I had entered the picture. Then I spotted a grazing *Brontosaurus* just beyond this fearsome beast. And that's when I first saw the long-beaked, huge-winged *pterodactyl* flying overhead. Scary!

Then someone gave me my very own 3-D hologram. So now when my eyes get tired of looking at the computer screen at the office, I glance up at the thousands of blue and lavender spots in *my* picture. In a matter of seconds I'm standing at the foot of Jesus' cross, which is flanked by the Bethlehem manger in the lower left-hand corner and an empty tomb in the right.

And you know what? Just as a picture of Jesus emerges in the hodge-podge of all those color spots when I focus my eyes just right, so He emerges in our lives. When we give our lives over to Him, His power works with all the color "spots" that make up our lives.

If we trust Him, we will begin to see His protection, His plans, His power at work for us. God's 3-D "picture" will bring it all together.

Carolyn

Let the Cat out of the Bag

Many years ago in England there was the practice of selling suckling pigs at county fairs. While it was still alive, a poor little pig would be selected by the buyer, and then, out of sight of the buyer, the pig was butchered and placed in a gunny sack for the trip home. However, there were quite a few dishonest merchants who would not actually sack up the little pig. Instead they substituted a dead cat, sealed up the bag, and passed it off as the little pig the customer had chosen. Only when the customer got home and "let the cat out of the bag," did they know they had been tricked. The secret was out.

Have you ever noticed how some people seem to be very nice until a certain situation comes up? Then they let the cat out of the bag and lead you into trouble. A young woman in our town was out with some friends who suddenly decided to spray some graffiti on a neighborhood fence. She didn't do any spraying; she just sat in the car. But by the time the police came, everyone else was in the car too, and the police had no way of knowing whether or not she was one of the vandals.

The best way to be sure there are no "cats in the bag" is to know your friends' characters. Are they always honest? Must you always be doing something when you're together, or can you just sit and talk and do nothing together except watch the waves or something else utterly simple?

If you choose your friends only because they're physically attractive or popular, you may be sorry. There could be a shocking surprise in the bag, inside the heart, where things really matter.

Proverbs 27:19 has some good advice about people. **As water reflects a face, so a man's heart reflects the man (NIV).** Be careful who your friends are. If your parents are uneasy about them, it could be for a very good reason. **Nancy**

Jul 25

Parable of the Wrong Road

"There is no other name under heaven given to men by which we must be saved." Acts 4:12, NIV.

The Jacobs family was on vacation, and they were lost. They had wanted to see the sights, but all they could see were trees, dirt roads, and a very confusing map. As they studied the map carefully, it appeared there was more than one way to reach their destination.

One road would make the trip very short, but the map said "Four-wheel-drive Vehicles Only." They could try it, but they might end up in the wilderness with a broken car. No, they wouldn't try that one.

The map did show another road. It looked like a good one, but there were sections that said "Incomplete." What did that mean? Were sections of the road missing?

There was yet another road. It looked longer than the first two, but it was all there. The map even said "The Only Way." What did that mean? Why were there other roads if this one was supposed to be the only way?

"Well," Dad said, "I've made a decision. We're going to take the incomplete road. I'm sure we can make it past these blank sections. Besides, it looks a lot shorter."

So off they went. It wasn't too rough, and there were plenty of rest areas. But when they came to their first incomplete section of road, they hesitated. The road looked swampy, and they couldn't tell where it led. Even though a sign said "Enter at Your Own Risk," Dad said, "We're going." Soon the car began to sink slowly into the marshy path, and the family knew they had made a terrible mistake.

Some people say there are many ways to get to heaven and to God. But what do you think the Bible means when it says "There is no other name under heaven given to men by which we must be saved"? I think it means just what it says. Follow Jesus. He's the only way, and He will lead you down the right road toward your eternal destination.   **Jim**

"Don't!" Or Was That "Do!"?

Exodus 20.

Don't! Don't! Don't! That's all my little book is about. All 104 pages of this book, published in 1889, tell me "don't." In fact, the book's title is *Don't*. "Don't wear fancy-colored shirts" (p. 28). "Don't be a 'swell' or a 'dude'" (p. 29). "Don't carry your hands in your pockets" (p. 31). "Don't whistle in the street" (p. 33). "Don't have the habit of letting your lip drop and your mouth remain open" (p. 35).

I get the feeling the author of this book didn't like others to have fun. And that's what a lot of people think about God. That's because He said "Don't" or "Thou shalt not" so much when He gave the Ten Commandments. Yet the whole Bible shows us He's a God of love. Here's why I think He sprinkled so many don'ts in the commandments.

Sometimes parents say "Don't," as in "*Don't* step off the curb—there's a big truck headed right for you!" Other times they say "Do," as in "Although there's no traffic now, *do* stay on the curb so you won't get hurt." They say "Don't" in an emergency situation. They say "Do" to help us develop a safety habit. Both "orders," however, are prompted by love.

When God, our heavenly parent, gave the Ten Commandments to the children of Israel, they were about to step off the curb and get hit by a truck, so to speak. For many years idolatry, murder, impurity, and dishonesty had made them unsafe for being around each other. So God, in His great love, had to get their attention with some very strong don'ts.

If Israel hadn't been so sinful, maybe God could have worded the Ten Commandments with more *do's*.

Commandment 1. To find true happiness, *do* let Me be your only God.
Commandment 3. To honor Me, *do* always speak My name in respect.
Commandment 6. To have safe neighborhoods, *do* preserve the lives of all around you.
Commandment 7. In order to assure happy, unbroken families, *do* be sexually pure and faithful to your spouse.
Commandment 10. *Do* be happy with what you already own.

The great principles of God's love—and our happiness—are behind the Ten Commandments—even if our heavenly parent originally had to get our attention with *don't*.   **Carolyn**

J_ul 27

Come Out in the Wash

While we were waiting in line at Disney World my brother remarked, "I think this is what heaven will be like—marching bands and parades and all kinds of thrilling things to see, but we won't have to stand in line!"

We laughed. We usually think of heaven as a rather quiet place, where beautiful smiling people in long white robes glide past, strumming their harps. There may be some of that, but I think there will also be more active things going on too.

One time I heard Morris Venden talking about heaven. He said that in heaven our senses will be more sensitive than they are now. The flowers will smell sweeter. Our sight will be a thousand times better. And if we think rabbits and kittens feel soft down here, wait till you see how wonderful they will feel in heaven!

Have you ever looked at your reflection in a shiny spoon or on the side of the toaster? That's how the mirrors were in the apostle Paul's day. Read how he described it in **1 Corinthians 13:12,** when he talked about heaven: **Now we see but a poor reflection as in a mirror; then we shall see face to face. Now I know in part; then I shall know fully, even as I am fully known (NIV).**

You know how faded a shirt can seem when it's dirty? But when it's washed and the dirt comes out, the shirt looks very different. To "come out in the wash" means that something we're not sure of right now will be OK. When we get to heaven and all the ugliness of sin is removed, we'll be beautiful, kind—heavenly!

Heaven will be a fun place. Everything wonderful in this life is only a substitute for the joys of heaven. Friendships will be deeper and will last forever. In heaven those you love will never leave you or betray you— guaranteed! Everything's going to come out in the wash.   **Nancy**

What's Your Opinion?

"How long will you waver between two opinions? If the Lord is God, follow him." I Kings 18:21, NIV.

Well, my dad says there is no right and wrong. It's all just a matter of opinion." Calvin was sure his dad was right.

"My dad says there is a right and wrong," Ted said just as firmly.

"My dad is right, and I know it!" Calvin shouted.

"I thought your dad said there were no rights and wrongs. If there are no rights and wrongs, how do you know he's right?" Ted knew he had stumped Calvin, because Calvin just stood there with his mouth hanging open.

Are there rights and wrongs? Daniel thought so when he was thrown into a den of lions. Moses believed it when he challenged Pharaoh to let the Israelites go free. I'm sure Abraham thought there was a right and wrong when he was willing to offer his only son, Isaac, as a sacrifice. The apostle Paul knew what was right when he was put into prison for preaching Christ. And I'm absolutely sure Jesus was convinced there was right and wrong when He died on the cross for you and me.

If there were no rights and wrongs, why would you pay attention to stop signs? Why not just take what belongs to your neighbor? It's obvious that if everyone started ignoring rights and wrongs, there would be a big mess.

Yes, there are definitely rights and wrongs, but there are also matters of opinion. You may think that red is a better color for carpet, and I may believe that blue is the best. Those are opinions. Some think that Jesus is the Son of God, and others think He was just a good man. There is a right and wrong belief when it comes to Jesus.

So how do you know the difference? Well, you can certainly ask the advice of trusted godly men and women. But only the Bible can really help us sort out the difference between opinions and what is right and wrong. Seek God today in His Word. His opinion is the one that really counts.

Jim

Jul 29

Shredded by Sin

Save me from all my transgressions. Psalm 39:8, NIV.

"Oh, no!" exclaimed Mother, looking at the shreds of fabric hanging at the living room windows. Only 90 minutes earlier the fabric had been beautiful newly made African-print curtains. The whole family had been proud of them—even Daji, the dog.

"Has our house been vandalized? Nick? Marte? All you all right?"

Mother, who had just returned from the students' Saturday night program, sank down in the nearest chair. Nick and Marte, his student baby-sitter, sat soberly on the couch.

"Oh, Mom, it's all my fault!" blurted Nick, bursting into tears.

"No, it's mine!" insisted Marte, wiping her eyes.

Little Daji wagged his tail and tried to lick her hand.

Staring at the ruined curtains, Mother seemed to be in shock. Since she and Dad had had to supervise a film program for the students, they'd asked Marte to stay with Nick, who was sick with a bad cold. She shook her head in disbelief. "What happened?"

Nick recounted how badly he'd wanted to see the films. He said he kept thinking about how he was missing out. He'd asked Marte to sneak up to the school with him so they could watch the movies outside the auditorium through the back windows.

"She said no at first," admitted Nick through his sobs, "but then she agreed to. I wasn't going to tell you, of course. Just lie about it, if you asked me. But you know how Daji hates to be left alone and tries to get out. Well, that's what happened. He tore up the curtains trying to get out of the house to follow us. I'm so-o-o-o sorry!"

The next morning Nick, Dad, and Mom had a family council and talked about the consequences for everyone—and all because of Nick's poor choice. Dad had to punish; Mother had to repair curtains; Marte had to somehow prove she was trustworthy. (Little Daji got off scot-free). Nick was amazed how his choice had affected everyone around him—even his dog and the environment. He realized the importance of asking Jesus to help him stop sin at the thought level—when it's still a temptation. Nick found out that if he didn't shred temptation, it would certainly shred him!

Carolyn

Do a 180-Degree Turn

E ver had this happen to you? Your friend tells you she likes your new dress and thinks it looks good on you. You feel good and go through the school day with a smile on your face. Then after school, as you're waiting for the school bus, another friend comes up to you and wrinkles up her nose and asks, "Where'd you get that?"

You look over at your first friend (who had said the dress was flattering) and raise your eyebrows, hoping she'll say she likes it. But she laughs. "I'm glad you said that; I didn't want to ask!" Then they laugh together at you.

How long would it be before you would ever trust your first friend's compliments again? When people contradict themselves, we say they make a "180-degree turn." In other words, they've turned right around and headed the opposite direction.

How about God? Can you trust Him? Read **Malachi 3:6: I the Lord do not change (NIV).** But what about the time He said He would destroy Nineveh, and then He didn't? Did God change, or did He change His mind? His loving character didn't change. In fact, He showed Himself to be more loving by giving the Ninevites a chance to live when they changed their ways. There are other things about God that will never change. The Sabbath will always be the seventh day of Creation, and it will always be hallowed. God won't pick another day and hallow it next year. The laws of gravity will always be in force. There will always be some sort of penalty for sin. God will always love you. He will always want you with Him in heaven. That will never change. And He will come again. There will be no 180-degree turns on those things. You can count on that! **Nancy**

Jul 31

Penguin Parents

He cares for those who trust in him. Nahum 1:7, NIV.

Have you ever heard of an emperor penguin? These are amazing birds. First of all, they're about four feet tall. That's a big bird! They're not that heavy, because two thirds of what you see is feathers—only one third is bird.

The most amazing thing about emperor penguins is how they hatch their young. It's about 80 degrees below zero during a cold arctic night, and penguin eggs, just like every other bird's eggs, have to stay warm in order to hatch. So how do they do it? Well, since the egg is laid in the middle of winter, it would freeze right away if it were to hit the ground. So dad helps out here. He rolls the egg onto his feet, covering it with the lower part of his warm tummy.

Then mom walks away, leaving dad holding the egg. She hasn't eaten in a while, so she decides to go fishing. You'd think she wouldn't want to spend too much time away from her new egg, but you're wrong. Actually, she's gone for about two months. That's right, 60 days. Poor dad. He huddles together with other dads keeping their eggs warm for 60 days! He doesn't even eat all this time. After her two-month hunting trip mom comes back, just in time for her new little chick to hatch. Then she takes over, and dad saunters off to find some fish for himself.

What an incredible thing the emperor penguin dad does for his little baby! But your heavenly Father cares for you even more than that. Not only does He provide you with everything you need to live, He sent His only Son to die for you. Without Him we would die, just like the tiny baby penguin would die without its parents' care.

Emperor penguins got their name because they look sort of regal. Our heavenly Father is the actual Emperor of the universe, and He'll hold and protect you, too! **Jim**

Whiteout!

The angel of the Lord encamps around those who fear Him, and rescues them. Psalm 34:7, NASB.

Thick flakes of heavy snow swirled like New Year's Eve confetti through the beams of Miss Branson's car headlights. Suddenly everything went white.

School had dismissed a little early that Friday afternoon because of the blizzard warning for the Sierra Nevadas. "That will give me plenty of time to get home safely," Miss Branson assured her junior high students as they helped her chain up her tires. "My dog and cat will need food and a warm house during this storm. Otherwise I wouldn't risk the drive."

Because of snow and heavy traffic, it had taken Miss Branson nearly two hours to make the normally 20-minute drive on the winding mountain road. Looking out at the dangerous whiteness, she said, "God, I know You're with me."

Finally her headlights lit up the railing of the last bridge before her turnoff. *Thank You, Lord!* she prayed with a sigh of relief. Then, just as she crossed to the other side of the bridge, her car suddenly went into a slow-motion 360-degree spin toward the shoulder of the road—beyond which an 80-foot drop-off yawned into a thickly forested canyon.

With a *foof!* the car came to rest in a deep snowbank, the windshield wipers still struggling to move the ever-increasing deposit of snowflakes.

Oh, dear God, breathed Miss Branson, *here we are with the rear wheels possibly hanging over the canyon. Should I try to get out?*

"Ma'am, are you all right?" Someone was pounding on her hood.

Where had he come from? Moving as little as possible, she rolled down the window. "Yes, I'm fine, but—"

"Don't move!" ordered the man in a hooded parka. "I'm gonna pull you out!"

Later that night, as she sat in front of her wood-burning stove with Sebastian and Nomad, she told her pets, "I don't know if an angel kept me from going on over the bank, or if an angel pulled me out of the snowbank—or both. All I know is that I didn't drive home alone."

Carolyn

Aug 2

Egg on Your Face

On a quiet, moonlit night the old fox made his way soundlessly across the pasture toward the little building the humans owned. He knew he had to be careful; they'd been after him before. But he always got away safely. He had been watching the place for some time and knew just when the humans locked themselves away for the night.

Crouching, then darting quickly across the backyard, the fox approached the chicken coop and tried to push the door open with its nose. No luck. So it began to dig under the wall. At last the hole was big enough, and the fox wriggled through. The chickens crowded high on their perches, leaving their nests unattended. With lightning speed, the fox devoured all six eggs in the first nest, licking its lips with satisfaction. It was just starting on the next batch of eggs when the door to the chicken coop flew open, and there was the big human looking down at it from behind that long, black stick that spit fire and noise.

"There you are!" the human bellowed. "With egg all over your face!"

Quick as a flash, the fox vanished back down through the hole. Across the pasture it flew to safety.

To have egg on your face means to make a mistake that everyone knows about. It's humiliating. In the last days there will be those who choose to live their lives with no thought about God. When things get serious—especially when Jesus is seen in the heavens for the first time—they'll have egg on their faces. Everyone will know they made a serious mistake in disbelieving. They'll be so frightened they will plead for the rocks to fall on them and put them out of their misery. In an instant they'll realize what they have lost.

The Bible urges us to get to know and believe in Jesus right now: **Seek ye the Lord while he may be found, call ye upon him while he is near (Isaiah 55:6).** While you're young and can see the beauty and mystery of things in this world, Jesus seems very near. Build a trust relationship with Him that starts now so you can be joyful when He comes. With a clean face, clean hands, and a thrilling anticipation you can look forward to the delights waiting for you in heaven.

The next time you eat eggs, remember the fox—and make a choice to be among those who will welcome Jesus. **Nancy**

Pass It On

You, O Lord, reign forever; your throne endures from generation to generation. Lamentations 5:19, NIV.

B ible quiz time: Who were the first three kings of Israel? If you guessed Saul, David, and Solomon, you were right! They each reigned 40 years. And then the nation of Israel split into two kingdoms with many kings. The nation of Israel had 19 kings, and the nation of Judah had 20 kings. It was sad that God's own people couldn't manage to stay as one kingdom.

All those kings did have some things in common, however. They all died, and their throne was given to someone else. Each new king who took over changed things. Sometimes for the better, sometimes for the worse. Sometimes a new king would throw out—or even kill—the old king's family, friends, and workers. Nothing seemed to stay the same. When King Saul saw that David was gaining more popularity among the people than he was, he tried to kill David several times. David found himself running for his life.

We as God's people have it much better today. If God is our king, we can be sure of this: His kingdom will never change. His rules and His love will always remain the same. We don't ever have to worry about God wanting to get rid of us. He will always be waiting for us to come to Him each day.

In Israel, when the king died, people knew that things would never be the same. It was a scary time. God was sad when the people of Israel wanted an earthly king. He knew they would begin to depend on their worldly king more than they did on Him. He also knew that many of the kings the people chose to rule them would not be kind or godly men.

God wants to rule in our hearts. I think He's the best choice to be the king of my life, because He'll always be here and always be the same.

Jim

Aug 4

My Way—Or His?

The way of the Lord is strength to the upright: but destruction shall be to the workers of iniquity. Proverbs 10:29.

People are so eager to do things their own way. There was once even a hit song about it. But doing it "my way" isn't always the safest way to go.

Floyd Collins was an experienced caver who liked to do things his way. His way often included (1) caving alone and (2) not telling anyone where he'd be caving. He even boasted to some acquaintances that he was always safe underground because his own internal compass helped him find his way out again. But on January 30, 1925, Floyd did things his way once too often.

Crawling up a passage on his belly, Floyd got within 115 feet of the cave's entrance when the lantern he was pushing ahead of him flickered and went out. In the darkness Floyd's foot kicked and dislodged a ceiling rock hanging behind him. It fell, pinning his left leg. Then loose gravel poured down and pinned his right leg as well.

Because he had no one to send for help and hadn't told people exactly where he was going, rescuers didn't locate Floyd for 24 hours. And even after they found him, they couldn't get him out.

After digging from different directions, volunteers finally tunneled down to 55 feet below ground level, just above where Floyd was trapped. Then a volunteer weaseled his body through the last few feet of tunnel into Floyd's underground prison. He signaled the other diggers to pull him back by the feet. Then he said one word to them: "Dead." The coroner's report stated that Floyd Collins, the caver who did things his way, had probably died of starvation two or three days earlier.*

In discussing our choice to do things our way or God's way, King Solomon wrote, "He who heeds discipline shows the way to life, but whoever ignores correction leads others astray" (Proverbs 10:17, NIV). Making commonsense decisions based on advice given us in the Bible is how to do things God's way.   **Carolyn**

---

*Donald Dale Jackson, *Underground Worlds* (Alexandria, Va.: Time-Life Books, 1982), pp. 97-103.

The Bottom Line

S hannon was feeling good about her grades by the time the midterms in her last semester crept up. Solid A's and B's in every class. She was sure of it. She sailed through the midterms easily and settled in for the short run to the end of the semester, when the grades would be finalized and permanently placed in her educational file—for the rest of her life. Did you catch that? Her grades would remain in her educational file *for the rest of her life.*

Shannon didn't realize how important her grades were to the rest of her life. She became overconfident and started skipping classes. Papers weren't completed on time. Some of them weren't completed at all. By the time her finals were over, the bottom line in the teacher's grade book didn't show any A's or B's; they were C's and D's.

Shannon didn't get into nursing school as she had hoped to, because her GPA wasn't good enough. When she finally started college with a general education major, she discovered, to her dismay, that much of the stuff she was learning was similar to what they had taught in high school, only the teachers went faster, with more detail, and graded harder. She wished she had done better in high school so it would be easier now. Regrets, regrets, and no way to change the past.

When we talk about something being "the bottom line," we mean it's the final outcome. It's an accounting term that means you can put numbers in a column as long as you want. Individually, it doesn't mean much if you add a number or subtract a number from the column as you go along. What really counts is the bottom line—the number you have when all is said and done.

God has given us a promise found in **Romans 8:28: All things work together for good to them that love God.** If things aren't going very easy for you right now, try to find out what you can learn from the process. Maybe someday you'll be a very effective counselor because you'll have come through so much. You'll have learned that feelings come and go; disappointment has a life span. Hold on! God can use everything life throws at you to make something beautiful of your life—on His timetable. You've just got to trust Him to balance out the bottom line.

Remember that two odd numbers added together always turn out even. Everything will work out OK for those who love God. That's the built-in bottom line from God, the Father of mathematics. **Nancy**

Aug 6

Buried Treasure

The kingdom of heaven is like a merchant looking for fine pearls. When he found one . . . he went away and sold everything he had and bought it. Matthew 13:45, 46, NIV.

What's buried, starts out as a piece of dirt, is hidden in a shell, and is worth a whole lot of money? Give up? A pearl, of course. It's buried in water. It starts out as some piece of foreign matter inside the shell of an oyster. And it ends up as a precious gem. Somehow an impurity finds its way into an oyster (probably when the oyster is eating). In order to protect itself, the oyster puts a hard coating around the foreign matter. It adds more and more of this hard shiny substance. Finally, the object becomes round and shiny. Pearl divers go underwater to harvest these valuable pearls.

The pearl of Allah may be the most beautiful pearl in the world. Not because it's perfectly round or particularly beautiful, but because it's just plain big. It weighs more than 14 pounds! Pick up two gallons of milk at the same time, and you'll know approximately how heavy the pearl of Allah is. It's valuable, too—worth about $4 million.

Although the pearl of Allah is worth a lot of money, it's not the most valuable pearl in the world. The most valuable pearl is the pearl of great price. And it's not found in any museum. It's not even found in an oyster. It's Jesus. And He's knocking at your heart's door. Read the story in Matthew 13:45, 46. That man sold everything just to get the pearl he had found. Nothing was more important to him. That's the way it should be with Jesus and us. Nothing should be more important to us than Him.

Today Jesus wants to be our Pearl of great price. Won't you let Him into your heart and allow Him to make you into His precious gem?

Jim

"Deplane, Deplane!"

Let each one do just as he has purposed in his heart; not grudgingly or under compulsion; for God loves a cheerful giver. 2 Corinthians 9:7, NASB.

Deplane if you would like to," boomed a good-natured voice through the overhead speakers in the 737. "This most recent blizzard will have us on the ground for at least another three hours!"

A frightened voice beside me pleaded, "What? Help, please!"

Only a few minutes earlier my seatmate, an elderly tourist from Sweden, had been escorted aboard by one of her daughters. "She can't speak English," the younger woman told me, "but my sister will meet her in Los Angeles."

"I'll look out for her," I volunteered, "and stay with her until she finds your sister."

Now with my own made-up sign language, I tried to explain to the woman what was happening. Through return sign language she indicated she did *not* want to leave the plane.

So I stayed with her.

Eight long hours later we touched down at the international airport in Los Angeles. As the Swedish grandmother and I walked into the terminal, a woman cried "Mama!" and pushed her way through the waiting crowd toward us.

Wow! I thought, looking at a white package tied with gold ribbons in her hands. *This family likes to give presents to each other!*

But instead of giving the gorgeous gift to her mother when she hugged her, the daughter held out the beautiful gift to me and said, "This is for you! Just a little thank-you from our family. My sister phoned from Baltimore to say that Mother was in good hands—yours."

I almost felt guilty taking the gift when all I'd done was smile a lot and give up a little of my reading time.

God wants us to give of ourselves to others cheerfully—but not because we want some kind of reward. Although He wants us to be givers simply out of love for Him, God does have plans to reward us someday for our selfless giving. He can't help doing that, because that's how *He* is—the most "cheerful giver" of all!

Carolyn

Aug 8

Upstaged

It was a silent feud between two of the cast members in the school play. One of them had a bigger part than the other one, and this had stirred up a smoldering jealousy. Sue had the bigger part—her first big part, in fact. And Jill, who had had the biggest part in every play for the past two years, was miffed that Sue was stealing the show.

No one knew anything was amiss until the dress rehearsals started and the director began marking the places where everyone was to stand on stage. Now, if you haven't been involved in acting, you might need to know that stage directions are given from the actors' point of view. Therefore, "stage left" is to the actors' left (the audience's right) as they face the audience. "Downstage" is the very front of the stage, closest to the audience. The actors have to walk down to it. "Upstage" is at the back of the stage.

Though Jill was told to stand downstage of Sue, near the audience, she inevitably made her way upstage. The reason? By standing at the back of the platform, Jill forced Sue to turn her back to the audience to talk to her, effectively taking the audience's attention away from Sue. All the audience could see was the back of her head.

You may have a classmate who tries to "upstage" you by bragging or playing up to the teacher. These kinds of people seem to draw attention away from you to themselves. It's as though everyone has their back to you to look at the braggart. Try not to let it get to you. God has given you talents of your own that you may not have discovered yet. Maybe your talents are quiet ones, such as organization, kindness, or being someone others confide in because you listen so well. Find out what you do well, and then do it— silently. It's OK to be proud of the talents God has wrapped up inside of you.

Read **Psalm 139:14: Thank you for making me so wonderfully complex! It is amazing to think about. Your workmanship is marvelous— and how well I know it (TLB).** *Good* pride recognizes that you are a special and unique person. Good pride helps you be all you can be, without bragging about it. And that is what God wants for you. No one can upstage you in God's eyes.

You have a part to play in your circle of friends that nobody else can fill. Find out what it is and play it well.   **Nancy**

224

The Big Lie

They acted with complete honesty. 2 Kings 12:15, NIV.

You've probably heard the old saying "Honesty is the best policy." Once you start telling lies, you have to remember which lie you told so that you don't contradict yourself. It seems that when a person starts telling lies, they just get in deeper and deeper.

There was a pharaoh who once told a lie, and people believed it for thousands of years. Pharaoh Ramses II didn't like the fact that his army had been defeated in the Battle of Kadesh about 1285 B.C. The pharaoh didn't like to lose battles, so instead of admitting that his army had been whipped, he built a memorial to let everyone know that he had "won" the battle. I suppose many people knew the Egyptians had actually lost, but after a while all those who knew that died, and the monument lasted. For thousands of years after that people believed the pharaoh's army had won the Battle of Kadesh.

Recently archaeologists discovered that Pharaoh Ramses II had lied and that historians had believed his fib all these years. I wonder what else the pharaoh lied about? I'm not sure I could believe anything the king said. You see, when you tell a lie, people lose confidence in the things you say. Your reputation becomes soiled. People have a hard time believing you.

I suppose the pharaoh thought he was doing a good thing. Maybe he thought it would make his country look great. In reality, it made his country look bad.

Make it your policy always to tell the truth. It may not be easy at times, but people will believe you when you say things if they know you have a reputation of always being honest. God has always been honest with us. We know we can trust what His Word says because He's never lied. Ask Him to give you the courage to be totally trustworthy, and build your own monument to honesty. **Jim**

Aug 10

Silver Spoons

Blessed is the man who finds wisdom, the man who gains understanding, for she [wisdom] is more profitable than silver. Proverbs 3:14, NIV.

We've been ripped off!" I exclaimed to my husband. "But why did those trusted students steal three of our silver-plated spoons?"

Deeply hurt, I thought over the day's earlier events. After church I had asked three students from the African school where we taught to come home with us for Sabbath lunch. We'd had such a wonderful time visiting and swapping stories. As we cleared the table in preparation for dessert—homemade ice cream—I had instructed them to keep their spoons.

Flash! The lightbulb inside my head suddenly exploded! I had told them, "Keep your spoons"!

Well, they certainly had! And I had just lost three spoons from my wedding present silverware because I hadn't communicated wisely enough. My unwise *partial* communication had left me with a *partial* set of silverware. My earthly riches had been diminished by three precious spoons.

Yet even the silver in a *whole* set of silverware is worth nothing compared to what God says real riches are. And the good news about real riches is that they're available to anyone who asks for them.

What is this treasure that's worth much more than silver and "yields better returns than gold"? Proverbs 3:14 tells us it is wisdom—the wisdom that comes from God. How do we get it? Verse 7 tells us how: "Do not be wise in your own eyes; fear the Lord and shun evil" (NIV).

What a God we have! He will make us truly rich just for our asking!

Carolyn

226

Get Off on the Right Foot

A very wise professor told one of his friends, "I try to get along well with my A and B students, because they may someday come back as fellow professors." Then he added, "I try to get along well with my C students, too. They may someday donate enough money to build a whole new wing on the university."

This man knew the importance of "getting off on the right foot" in a relationship.

Some say the Romans started the superstition of getting off on the right foot. They believed that unless a person entered or left a room with the right foot, something bad would happen to them. When you're grouchy in the morning, someone may say you "got up on the wrong side of the bed." That implies that you got up on the left side—the wrong side—and that's why your day is going badly.

We want to get off on the right foot. We like to make a good first impression and not have any misunderstandings to get in the way of our new friendship. Every friendship may be important, whether or not you realize it at the time.

There were those who thought Jesus didn't get off on the right foot as far as His life on earth was concerned. He was often in trouble with the leaders of His time (sometimes that happens when your integrity is at stake). **Hebrews 12:2** talks about Jesus' example. **Keep your eyes on Jesus, our leader and instructor. He was willing to die a shameful death on the cross because of the joy he knew would be his afterwards; and now he sits in the place of honor by the throne of God (TLB).** Sometimes when you get off on the right foot with Jesus, it seems you're on the left foot with the world. You may be misunderstood by nonbelievers, but that's only temporary. Like Jesus, you'll finally receive what you deserve: a place of honor by the throne of God.

Share a kindness with everyone who crosses your path today, not because you may need their friendship someday, but just because it makes you feel better, and just because you follow Jesus. **Nancy**

Ping-Pong

Be faithful, even to the point of death, and I will give you the crown of life. Revelation 2:10, NIV.

We had a Ping-Pong table in my fifth-grade classroom. I remember playing with my friends and counting how many volleys we could make in a row without missing. I don't remember what our record was, but it wasn't that many times. If you have a Ping-Pong table, try this:

Gary D. Fisher, of Olympia, Washington, has the world's record for consecutive volleys with a Ping-Pong ball. Using two paddles, one in each hand (actually, that sounds like a disadvantage, doesn't it?), Gary completed 5,000 consecutive volleys in 44 minutes and 28 seconds. Can you imagine hitting the Ping-Pong ball *5,000 times?* Or how about playing almost 45 minutes without stopping? Imagine the concentration that kind of playing would take. You would have to be really committed to Ping-Pong to stay with it that long, wouldn't you? I'm sure Mr. Fisher practiced hundreds of hours to be that good.

Jesus said He would reward those who endured until the end with a crown of life. But, you might ask, if Jesus saves us by His grace, why should there be so much work involved? It's true that only the kindness and grace of God saves us. No amount of work will measure up to His standards. I'm so glad salvation is a free gift. But Jesus does want us to give our whole lives to Him. Each day He wants us to make sometimes difficult decisions to follow Him and stay with Him until the end.

Some of you may be ready to give up now. Don't do it, because the same God who saves us by grace is ready to give us the strength to stick with Him. He never asks us to do anything that He's not willing to give us the power to do.   **Jim**

Aug 13

Don't Bend Over!

The fear of the Lord is the beginning of wisdom. Psalm 111:10.

R*ip!*
"Oh, no!" I cried, quickly standing up.
"What's wrong?" asked Janet, another first-time camper, still bending over to touch her toes during early-morning exercises.
"I ripped out the seat of my pants when I bent over."
"So go put on another pair," she counseled wisely.

Mom had sewn me all new camp clothes, including my pants—but she hadn't reinforced the seams. Well, I was definitely having a clothing emergency. Mom had packed all my clothes in bags marked "Tuesday," "Wednesday," "Thursday," etc., but today was only Monday. Nothing to do but pull on the stiff new "emergency jeans." As they rubbed my legs raw that day, I thought about the relief I'd have when I opened the "Tuesday" bag the next day.

On Tuesday morning, as we shivered outside in the frigid mountain air, the girls' director yelled, "Everybody, touch your toes—no exceptions!" just as Janet gave me some very mature advice. "If you don't want to ruin your pants," she said matter-of-factly, "then just don't bend over!" What wonderful wisdom! But it came too late, for I had just bent down. Both Janet and I heard the dreaded *rip!* The emergency jeans were now even scratchier with the accumulation of a day's worth of rain-stiffened dust and perspiration from hiking and horsebackriding.

Like Janet, God gives us commonsense advice. It's called wisdom. It's possible to have a lot of *knowledge*—even Bible knowledge—but not much *wisdom*. For example, I heard of a man who wouldn't wear a necktie because there's no record in the Bible that Jesus wore neckties. (Of course Christ didn't—neckties didn't even *exist* back then!)

True wisdom begins with "the fear of the Lord"—loving and respecting God. We love and respect God by the kinds of choices we make. At camp that first summer, if I'd used commonsense wisdom, I would have avoided ripping out all those pairs of pants. If we use the commonsense wisdom that comes from loving and respecting God, we'll avoid a lot of damage in life as well.
Carolyn

Aug 14

Warts and All

In the time before photographs, only the rich could afford to hire a portrait artist to paint their picture. And I would guess at least some of them demanded that the artist show them only at their best by leaving out all flaws—warts, crooked noses, and wrinkled skin. However, if a portrait was painted truly lifelike, it was worth commenting on. It was a portrait with "warts and all"!

Sometimes we prefer to think of ourselves without any annoying character "warts." We want others to see us as a portrait artist of long ago might have painted us, concealing our meanness or weaknesses.

The strange thing is that the more we try to cover up our meanness, the more we may actually become kind. The Bible explains how this happens in **Proverbs 11:17: Your own soul is nourished when you are kind; it is destroyed when you are cruel (TLB).** Even criminals who are forced to do community service feel nourished—just a little. And when they go back to being cruel, their darker natures become stronger. Eventually, if the soul is not fed often enough by doing kind deeds for others, it may be destroyed.

How is the picture of your life looking? Has it been nourished lately by doing something for someone else? You are in charge of that picture. Make it beautiful!   **Nancy**

Thirty Years on a Pole

Now get up and stand on your feet. I have appeared to you to appoint you as a servant and as a witness. Acts 26:16, NIV.

Have you ever heard of a pole sitter? It's actually a pretty simple thing to do. The pole sitter finds a pole, nails a wooden platform to the top, sits on it, and doesn't come down for a long time. How long, you ask? Well, days—or even months. Would that be boring, or what? If you think that sitting on a pole for a few *months* is a long time, what about 30 *years?*

Simeon Stylites, a Syrian monk, lived on a column 60 feet high for more than 30 years. He was brought down from the pole only when he died. Monks are people who try to be very close to God. So what did he do all that time? Well, he prayed a lot, and did sit-ups.

Do you think God loved Simeon more because he sat on the top of a pole for 30 years? I don't think so. God would have loved Simeon just as much had he been on the ground. And think of all Simeon could have done for God on the ground. He could have taught many more people about how much God loved them if he hadn't been so far up in the air. He could have been an example in daily life of the kind of person that God can make us. If only Simeon had had his feet on the ground, he could have helped so many people, and God would have loved him just as much. God could have heard his prayers just as well.

God puts each of us where we'll do the most good. It won't always be easy, but if you'll talk with Him each day and study His Word, He'll work through you to help others know of His love. You can do so much for Him if you'll just keep your feet on the ground and your face to the Son.

Jim

Aug 16

Break-in!

For he shall give his angels charge over thee, to keep thee in all thy ways. Psalm 91:11.

W
e've been robbed!" Mother's frantic cry rang down the hallway from the living room.

Terrified, Andrew jumped out of bed and rushed down the hallway right behind Dad. At the end of the hallway Mother pointed to a big gaping space in the cabinet.

"The stereo's gone!" Andrew exclaimed.

"And a lot more," murmured Mother in shock.

Andrew had overheard his parents talking earlier that week about a gang of thieves committing violent thefts in the hills near the mission school where his family lived. The thieves did not hesitate to use their machetes on anyone catching them in the act.

"Someone's been all through my desk!" called Father from the study.

"Mom, did you leave this suitcase by the front door?" Andrew asked suddenly.

"No," answered Mother. "Last night it was right by the side of our bed—we hadn't finished packing for our trip. Oh! That means the thieves were—"

Father came back down the hall holding two skeleton keys. "They didn't find the keys to the doors."

"Whoever came in sure had to be skinny!" Andrew observed. "They had to climb through the gridwork on our windows."

"Andrew," said Father, blinking back tears, "your guardian angel must have been working overtime. Come, look at this." Father led the way to Andrew's bedroom. Mother gasped as she saw the broken screen on Andrew's window and the dusty footprints leading across the floor toward the hall.

"One or more thieves came right across the foot of your bed!"

"Oh!" Andrew was speechless for moment. "I heard my screen fall last night and thought it was just one of you guys shutting the window. I almost said hi; then I just fell asleep again."

Although Andrew is a grown man now, he continues to thank God for one very special guardian angel who continues to make life safer for him.

Carolyn

Have the Ball at One's Feet

When I was a little girl and first read the phrase "Have the ball at one's feet," I imagined a statue with its feet on a ball—a precarious position for trying to keep one's balance! Actually, today's statement refers to the game of soccer. A player who has the ball at his feet has an advantage over all the other players. He is not in a precarious position at all. Rather, he's in control of the game at that moment; he calls the shots.

Christians also have the advantage of having the "ball" at their feet in the game of life. They can pass on the good things in their life to the "rich" people, who already have their own good things, or they can pass their blessings on to the "poor" people, who really need something good to happen in their lives. For Christians, there really shouldn't be any question as to how we treat the poor. Read **James 2:1. Dear brothers, how can you claim that you belong to the Lord Jesus Christ, the Lord of glory, if you show favoritism to rich people and look down on poor people? (TLB).**

So who's rich and who's poor? I suppose if we compared ourselves to Donald Trump we might think we're poor, but actually, most of us are not poor. I think of the poor as those who do not have enough food or clothing or even a place to sleep. If your life has been going well, in spite of having less than Donald Trump, it might be good to remember why those with less than you do need something "good" from you. There's a reason they need the warmth of human kindness.

Psychologists say we have particular needs that must be filled in a certain order. Our most basic need is the need to survive—the need for food, water, and shelter. If someone doesn't have the security of these things, they cannot move on to the other needs that "rich" people may have. If you have food, clothing, and shelter, you can look for fulfillment of your other needs, such as recreation and fun and the pursuit of happiness. If you can help a needy person satisfy their basic survival needs, you free them to go a step higher and meet the pleasure needs that make life enjoyable.

So you have the ball at your feet. What will you do? Just by smiling at a person in the hallway at school you can pass on some warmth and make that person feel safer. It's not hard to do, and it makes you feel really good!

Nancy

233

Aug 18

Any More Questions?

Do not believe every spirit, but test the spirits to see whether they are from God. I John 4:1.

It was dinnertime, and I was hungry. My wife had made vegetables, a vegetarian loaf, and stuffing—one of my favorites. That warm summer night in Florida the table was set, and we were ready to eat. I liked Florida except for two things: the humidity and the cockroaches. Actually, what we called cockroaches were palmetto bugs, some as large as two inches long, and they were everywhere. They scurried under doors, in through windows, and anywhere else they could get in.

After we said the blessing, we began to eat. I was enjoying my meal immensely when my wife asked, "What are these?"

I looked up from my forkful of food to see my wife holding up a little dark speck from her stuffing. "It's probably some kind of spice," I said as I continued to put more food into my mouth. I didn't notice that while I was shoveling more food down, my wife was still playing with that little dark speck.

"I don't think these are spices," she said.

"Why not?" I said in between mouthfuls.

"Because they have wings."

Now I stopped eating. My wife had a little brown object with little tiny wings that, under close observation, was obviously a baby cockroach. There was no telling how many I had eaten. I was suddenly finished with my supper.

Did you know that God wants us to ask questions? David asked God all kinds of questions when he didn't understand what was happening in his life. If we believe everything we hear, we might just swallow something that is false. Of course when we ask questions of our parents, teachers, and other adults we need to be respectful, but asking questions is a good thing, because we learn when we ask.

I guess I should have asked a few more questions about what was on my plate for supper. Ask lots of questions about God and about life. That way you won't swallow just anything. **Jim**

234

Guano Lesson

God has deliberately chosen to use ideas the world considers foolish and of little worth in order to shame those people considered by the world as wise and great. I Corinthians 1:27, TLB.

P eee-yew!" exclaimed Kara. "This guano smells so bad in this part of the cave!"

"The what-o?" Tim asked.

"The guano. You know—bat droppings."

Later, while the Pathfinders were eating their lunches outside the cave's entrance, the subject of guano came up again.

"Did you know that guano has some practical uses—for instance, protecting our country against enemy invaders?" asked Mr. Kooper.

"No way!" exclaimed Derrick.

"Yes, indeed," insisted Mr. Kooper. "A necessary ingredient for gunpowder is saltpeter, which can be found in guano-enriched cave soil. During the War of 1812 against Great Britain, more than 70 men mined the nitrate-rich soil of a Kentucky cave. They shoveled it onto carts that oxen pulled to the cave's entrance. By the end of the war—which we won—the cave had produced around 400,000 pounds."

"What's another use for guano?" Kara wanted to know.

"Well, waste matter of bats and sea birds, when mixed with four to five times as much soil, makes great fertilizer."

"It's hard to believe that anything so stinky and disgusting as guano has helped protect our country and helps new plants to grow. That just doesn't make sense."

"No, it doesn't," agreed Mr. Kooper. "But it's a wonderful illustration of how God operates sometimes. In the Bible He tells us that sometimes He uses what seems totally worthless to us to perform mighty miracles. You can read His exact words in 1 Corinthians 1:27-29."

"Yeah," said Derrick thoughtfully. "He used Moses' rod to part the Red Sea, and a kid's little lunch to feed more than 5,000 people. But why?"

"So that no one can brag that he or she did anything great without God's help," answered Mr. Kooper.

"Know what?" laughed Tanner. "The next time I'm feeling worthless, I'm going to think about the guano lesson and remember that there's hope for me after all!" **Carolyn**

Penny-wise and Pound-foolish

The strange thing about Marc was that the hearing problem he had during the week miraculously cured itself on Sundays. Monday through Sabbath the alarm would buzz, and Marc would sleep on and on and on until he had only 15 minutes to get up, comb his hair, and grab a bite of toast before rushing off to school or church.

But on a Sunday, when snowboarding was on the docket, he was up with the first beep. Into the shower and down to the kitchen he raced for a hearty breakfast of hash browns and fried eggs. Then he threw together a lunch and was heading down the road before the sun was up.

What made the difference? His motivation.

Sometimes Christians experience a lack of motivation to know Jesus better and to share Him with others. You could call this being "penny-wise and pound-foolish," a phrase that comes from England. (Americans might say it's "penny-wise and *dollar*-foolish.") This phrase describes someone who is very prudent and careful with the small, unimportant things (the pennies), but careless with the most valuable things (the dollars).

When Jesus was here, He kept encouraging His disciples to raise their sights from earthly life—the pennies—and keep their goals in line with heaven—the dollars.

Are you making good choices about the pennies in your life (what you wear, what you do for entertainment, what you eat)? And how about the dollars—the more important things (living with a clear conscience, trusting Jesus more, being responsible, encouraging others)? The Bible tells us something about those decisions. You'll find it in **Ecclesiastes 11:9. Young man, it's wonderful to be young! Enjoy every minute of it! Do all you want to; take in everything, but realize that you must account to God for everything you do (TLB).** **Nancy**

What a Racket!

Be still, and know that I am God. Psalm 46:10, NIV.

Has your mom or dad ever said, "Turn down that noise! I just want some peace and quiet"? There are times when we need to sit and think without anyone talking, or even the radio playing. But if it's real peace and quiet you want, let me tell you about a place in Africa where you'll want to spend your vacation.

The Mabaan tribe in the Sudan of Africa have a religious belief that prohibits noise. The only noises you'll ever hear are animal sounds and rain. It's so quiet in their villages that if you turned on your microwave (they don't have any), you'd be disturbing the peace.

Do you think all that quietness would drive you crazy—nobody to talk with and no one to listen to? Think of the things you'd hear. Birds you'd never noticed before; mice nibbling at things in your room. Maybe you'd even hear God. That's right, God!

When God asked us to "be still," what do you think He meant? Do you think He meant to get rid of all our radios and televisions and video games and friends? God doesn't mean we have to be like the Mabaans. What He wants us to do is spend some quiet time with Him each day. Just us and Him. Even Jesus, God's own Son, would leave His disciples and take off into the hills to be alone with His Father. If Jesus needed to do that, I know we do.

Let's try an experiment right now. Someone watch the clock. For exactly one minute, no one say anything. Not a word; not a sound. Ready? Go! . . . Well, how was that? Was it difficult, easy, nerve-racking? You might have to train yourself, but after a while, in the stillness, you'll begin to hear God speak to you. Once you do, you'll never want to miss your special time with God again.   **Jim**

Aug 22

Compassion With Wings

So God created . . . every winged bird. . . . And God saw that it was good. Genesis 1:21, NIV.

Although birds seem to operate mostly on instinct, biologists have noticed unusual behaviors from time to time that suggest birds are capable of compassion.

A scientist on a bird-banding study watched two savanna sparrows build a nest.* But soon after the eggs were hatched, a snake killed the mother. Immediately the father attracted a second female to help him feed the hungry young. When the father was killed, the "stepmother" bird attracted a "stepfather" to the nest, and these two foster parents faithfully and untiringly raised the baby birds to adulthood.

This same scientist was once on a multistate camping trip with his wife. They had their pet baby owl along that they tied to a perch near their sleeping area each night. Soon a mystery began to develop. They'd hear the owl make "hungry cries" in the night, but in the morning when they took it a mouse to eat, its crop was already full. Then one night they saw two large owls fly out of the darkness, stuff mice into the youngster's mouth, and fly off. The two owls were responding to the hunger cries of the baby stranger.

This couple's son, Craig, once became very sick with a high fever. Their pet crow sat on a limb outside the boy's bedroom window and cawed an "alarm." Craig's mother watched in amazement as wild crows from miles around answered, flying in to join the pet crow. Then, not seeing the large rodent or bird of prey they thought they'd be pestering, they soon flew away. But the pet crow continued his cawing alarms.

Three days later Craig was well enough to take a walk outside. The pet crow hopped along after the boy, sat down when he sat, then rested his beak upon his knee and swayed in happiness at being with his young friend again.

If our Creator is a God of compassion and love, don't you think He instilled this quality in all the creatures He created? How wonderful it will be in heaven when everything in nature—including us—lives just to make God and each other happy!

Carolyn

*Anecdotes found in Reader's Digest Association, *Marvels and Mysteries of Our Animal World* (Pleasantville, N.Y.: Coronet Books, 1964), pp. 284, 285.

Aug 23

On Tenterhooks

There is probably a moment in the life of every tent when it must feel pulled in all directions. You know, when the wind is blowing from all directions and the stakes, or "tenterhooks," pounded firmly into the dirt, pull it tightly over the frame.

If someone says they're "on tenterhooks" as they wait to learn the outcome of something, it means they're feeling tense and tight, anxious and very stressed.

Anxiety is a normal part of being alive. It can energize you into studying for a test or learning your lines in the play. It all depends on what is called "self-talk"—the things you tell yourself inside your head. If you keep your self-talk positive, you experience less anxiety. Even if you expect to hear some bad news, you can tell yourself, "Whatever happens, I will get through it." Plan an alternate course of action, if possible—your Plan B. If you get the news you want, you will be happy. And if you don't get the news you want, Plan B is ready to go, and you can pick it up and run with it.

Many people are on tenterhooks about their salvation. They worry that they're not good enough or kind enough or knowledgeable enough about the Bible to get to heaven. They don't think God can love them if they're smoking or drinking or breaking the commandments. The truth is, Jesus loves you in spite of your sins. But He doesn't let it rest there. *Because* He loves you, He wants you to stop sinning. "Making good decisions" means the same as "avoiding sin." Jesus doesn't want you to be tense about your salvation. So get off those tenterhooks. You don't have to change yourself before you come to Him—He'll change you! **Romans 3:22 tells us how. This righteousness from God comes through faith in Jesus Christ to all who believe (NIV).** He changes your desires if you ask Him to, because He loves you!   **Nancy**

Auto Worship

Great is the Lord and most worthy of praise. I Chronicles 16:25, NIV.

"Hey, guys, guess where we're going tonight."

"Probably to feed Aunt Bertha's parakeet while she's gone on vacation," said Jason glumly.

"No," Dad said with a sparkle in his eyes. "We're going to buy a new car."

"Yea, yea!" yelled Morgan and Tiffany.

"Are you serious?" Jason said, perking up. "Can I drive it, Dad?"

"Now, Jason, you've had your license for only one month, and this is a brand-new car. I'll have to think on that for a while."

As everyone piled into the station wagon, Jason dreamed of driving a brand-new car. The power of that big engine cruising down the road would be exciting. And what would his friends say? He could hear it now: "You're driving a new car? My dad won't even let me drive our old junker."

As Dad pulled the old wagon into the new-car lot, the glint of the lights shining off the hoods of the brand-new cars was exhilarating. Jason immediately began looking at the new vehicles, touching them, opening doors and pressing buttons.

Two hours later the family drove out of the lot with their brand-new car, inhaling that new-car smell. "OK," Dad said, "I'm going to lay down some ground rules for our new car. We want it to last, so we need to take care of it. First, there is to be no food in this car. No food, no exceptions. Second, do not play around it when it's parked in the yard. I want no scratches on this new paint. And third, if anyone messes anything up on this car, they'll be grounded for two months. Everyone got it?"

"Boy," Tiffany whispered, "Dad takes all the fun out of having a new car."

Sometimes people worship their possessions more than they worship God. Oh, there's nothing wrong with taking good care of your things, but be careful that they don't become more important than the people around you, and especially God. He's the one who deserves our worship.   **Jim**

Oooooh, Gross!

Dead flies will cause even a bottle of perfume to stink! Yes, a small mistake can outweigh much wisdom and honor. Ecclesiastes 10:1, TLB.

Hey, Ms. Jennings," Angelina asked her teacher across the lunch table, "did you ever see anything that really grossed you out?"

"Yes, girls, but we are *eating*."

"That's OK. Tell us!" they begged.

"Well, last Sabbath morning it was really cold. So, I decided to wear a wool dress to church that I hadn't worn yet this winter. I also fished around on the top shelf of my closet for a small purse I hardly ever use—but it goes with that dress. When I opened the purse to put in my offering, I saw a sealed plastic bag. It was filled with—with brown slime."

"From what?" asked Angelina.

"From these," answered their teacher, holding up two orange carrot sticks.

"Carrots?"

"Yes, evidently I'd thrown a couple into my purse for a snack on September 13 of last year. I know the exact date because the only other thing in my purse was a dated bank deposit slip."

"And you found the carrots just last Sabbath?" said Angelina.

"That's right—on January 11 of *this* year."

"Oooooh, gross!" screamed the girls.

"So did you open up the plastic bag and take a whiff?" Starr wanted to know.

"Yes," answered Ms. Jennings, involuntarily making such a face that her listeners once again dissolved in laughter. "And know what else I did?" Ms. Jennings' face grew thoughtful.

"What?" asked Angelina.

"As I threw away the bag of brown slime, I thought of how even a small mistake—like leaving carrots in a purse—can cause a really big stink, just as the Bible says."

"The Bible talks about carrots in your purse?" Starr stared at her teacher.

"Not exactly," answered Ms. Jennings. "But Ecclesiastes 10:1 talks about small things that can stink up our lives. Little mistakes—and dead flies."

"Oooh, gross!" exclaimed Angelina again. "I guess that means, then, that God likes fresh-smelling air."   **Carolyn**   241

You're off Your Rocker

When trolley cars, or streetcars, were first installed in American streets, they left much to be desired. The most common problem the motormen encountered was keeping the contact wheel of the trolley car attached to the overhead wire. Without this contact the trolley couldn't run because there was no electricity to run on. Many a motorman spent a portion of each day squatting on the top of the trolley car, struggling to regain the connection. And much to the chagrin of the motormen, a common expression was born: "He's off his trolley." It meant "Something's wrong with him; he isn't working right."

The expression "He's off his rocker" was born about the same time. And although it referred to a rocking chair without its rockers, it meant much the same thing—someone wasn't going anywhere because something was missing or wasn't working right; things weren't normal.

The Bible tells us that Jesus loves people who are "off their rocker" in the sense that they know something is missing in their lives. **Mark 10:49** tells us that Jesus called for the blind man Bartimaeus by name so He could heal him. **Then they called the blind man, saying to him, "Be of good cheer. Rise, He is calling you" (NKJV).** Bartimaeus thought he was a nobody, but Jesus knew his name, and Jesus was calling him to Himself so He could heal Bartimaeus.

From time to time everyone thinks they're insignificant for one reason or another. But you know what? Nobody is a nobody to Jesus. Jesus is the best motorman there is. He can help put you back on your rocker, back on your trolley. Live your life so that you have nothing to be ashamed of. You'll really like yourself. And you'll have incredible power to help others once you're "on track."

Nancy

The River of Life and Death

Then the angel showed me the river of the water of life, as clear as crystal, flowing from the throne of God and of the Lamb. Revelation 22:1, NIV.

There is a river whose water the Hindu people of India believe cleanses the soul. I call it the "river of life and death." People bathe in the river Ganges because they believe that its waters will wash their sins away. These people also put the ashes and bodies of their dead loved ones in the Ganges, believing that by doing so their loved ones will be rewarded in their next life. If a faithful Hindu cannot make it to the shores of the Ganges before they die, they can purchase water taken from this dirty river and drink it. You can see why I call it the river of life and death.

The Bible tells us about a river that truly is a river of life. It's in heaven, and it flows from the throne of God. On each side of the river grows the tree of life. The branches meet over the river. This river gives life because it begins at the source of all life, Jesus.

Take a walk by a river sometime. Don't just walk by it, though; look closely into the water. In most cases you'll see life—fish, snails, plants, crayfish, water insects. As the seasons come and go, all life in all rivers here on earth eventually dies. In heaven, however, nothing will ever die. There will be an everlasting supply of eternal life that comes from living with God.

Did you know He wants us to start enjoying that eternal life right now? There will still be death on this earth until Jesus comes again, but we can be connected with the source of the river of life right now. Hold on to Jesus with all your might and taste of the Water of Life today.

Jim

Stickeen

Hold up my goings in thy paths, that my footsteps slip not. Psalm 17:5.

G o back!" the big man shouted to the little mutt that had insisted on following him from the Alaskan glacier-edged base camp. But the stubborn little dog refused, so John Muir, famous nineteenth-century American naturalist, let Stickeen follow him out on a glacier in gale force winds for a day's exploration.

In the afternoon's fading light and growing blizzard, Muir checked his compass before heading back toward camp. But they were stopped by a yawning 75-foot-wide crevasse. Only a skinny ice bridge connected the two sides about eight to 10 feet below the glacier's surface.

Stickeen nervously whined as Muir began digging support holes for his knees. Then the naturalist, leaning out over the crevasse, chiseled a foothold in the smooth side of the glacier. Painstakingly he chiseled another and another—with an extra little platform each time for the frightened Stickeen.

When Muir had worked his way down to the nearest end of the razorback bridge, he shaved a four-inch-wide path on top for Stickeen and then straddled it. Inch by inch Muir continued doing this across the entire bridge.

In the meantime, the terrified Stickeen stood on the last little foothold platform before the bridge crying pitifully.

"When I called to him," Muir later wrote, "he only cried the louder."

Finally Muir started off into the howling blizzard, but he returned one final time to plead with the little dog. Suddenly Stickeen stopped his yelping and carefully placed one paw on the top of the sliver-bridge. Then he slowly worked his way across the bridge before rushing up the ice footholds, past Muir, to the safety of the other side.*

Like John Muir and his ice ax, Jesus has made a way for us to cross the crevasse of sin. Will we be brave enough to trust Him to get us safely to the other side?

Carolyn

---

*Lisa Mighetto, editor, *Muir Among the Animals, The Wildlife Writings of John Muir* (Sierra Club Books, 1989), p. 92.

Your Goose Is Cooked!

Every day noisy flocks of geese on their way south passed over the farm of Mr. James. Whenever he heard them, Mr. James wandered outside to squint up into the sky and smile at the orderly procession.

One day as he watched, he heard a shot and saw one of the geese fall into his yard. He knew, without asking, that his neighbor was at it again, hunting just for fun. Mr. James hurried to the fallen goose and discovered that it was not dead. It had been shot in the wing. He carefully scooped up the injured bird, sheltering it in his jacket. In the barn he gently cleaned and dressed the wound and placed the squawking goose in an old rabbit hutch outside.

For several weeks Mr. James fed and cared for the restless goose. But it was hard. Each time he opened the hutch to feed the bird, it beat its wings against the wire and tried to escape. At last in mid-winter, Mr. James decided the wing was healed. He left the door of the hutch open, hoping the bird would take the chance and escape. Flocks of geese had been passing by overhead for several weeks now.

From inside the barn Mr. James quietly watched the goose. To his amazement the bird stuck its long neck out of the cage and bobbed its head. Then it squawked and withdrew back into the confines of the cage and made itself comfortable in its usual spot. The migratory season had passed, and with it the inner urgings of the bird's spirit.

The Bible tells us that the Holy Spirit doesn't urge us forever either. That's why **Proverbs 4:14** urges us not to make friends of the wrong people. **Do not set foot on the path of the wicked or walk in the way of evil men (NIV).** Eventually we won't have a conscience, and the things that once seemed so wrong will seem all right. When your goose is cooked, it means everything is done—it's as final as a dead, roasted goose.

Keep your conscience alive by listening to it! **Nancy**

This World Needs Some Flavor

You are the salt of the earth. Matthew 5:13, NIV.

I want you to think of the largest church you've ever been in. Now listen to this description and see how the biggest one you've been in compares to this church.

Its ceiling is 73 feet high, maybe eight or nine stories. This church took six years to build, and it seats nearly 5,000 people. Maybe some of you have been in a church this large, but probably none of you have ever been in a church like this one. For one thing, it's 800 feet deep inside a mountain. And for another, it's carved out of pure salt. That's right, salt! This church is in Zipaquira, Colombia. It's in a salt mine, and that 73-foot ceiling is held up by 73-foot pillars carved out of pure salt. But because it's buried in the earth, you could walk right by that church and never know it was there.

Maybe we're sometimes like that buried church. Do people know you love Jesus? Can they tell by the things you say and do that you are His faithful follower? Or can people go right by you and never know you're a Christian? Have you told anyone about Jesus lately?

Jesus said we are the salt *of* the earth. He didn't say we were the salt *in* the earth. We shouldn't hide the good news that our friends and neighbors need to know, the good news that says because Jesus died for our sins, we can be saved if we'll only accept His gift of salvation.

Salt makes food taste better if it's used at the right time and in the right amounts. Let everyone know by your words and actions that you love Jesus. Be the salt that gives the pleasant flavor that's needed in the lives of every man, woman, boy, and girl—the pleasant flavor that only Jesus can bring to a person's life. **Jim**

Flying Squirrels and Other Mothers

How often would I have gathered thy children together, even as a hen gathereth her chickens under her wings. Matthew 23:37.

Why would Jesus compare Himself to a chicken, of all things? Well, He didn't exactly. He was comparing His love for us to the protective, danger-wise love a mother hen has for her chicks. Let's take a look at what the amazing love of some nature "mommies" prompts them to do for their "kids."

Mothers protect their offspring. When Mrs. Squirrel senses an approaching bad storm, she'll sometimes abandon the hollow tree in which she's set up housekeeping. She carefully carries her babies by their stomach fur, one by one, to a more secure shelter.

Mama Bear will carry a cub—by its entire head!

Animal mothers sometimes give their young hard lessons in order that their "kids" will be able to survive in a tough world. Mother Seal sometimes pushes her baby off an iceberg into the sea for a crash course in swimming. Mrs. Otter might give a baby a watery ride on her back and then suddenly dive underwater, forcing it to paddle for itself.

When learning-to-glide day comes around, baby Flying Squirrel had better take the leap itself if it doesn't want Mom to push it out of the tree. Young kittens not paying attention to their first mouse-catching lesson may get their ears boxed by Mother Cat.

Yet, for all the rough lessons animal moms have to give their children, they will often put their own lives on the line for the babies. One naturalist watched a mother woodchuck turn around and start kicking up earthen barricades when a farm dog started digging in her family's burrow. The dog destroyed the barricades as fast as she could kick them up. The naturalist thought the mother would soon collapse, as the dog seemed to be gaining on her. But eventually the dog gave up.

This was the kind of protective mother-love Jesus said He had for His children. The kind that is willing to teach us hard lessons of trust so that we can survive our trip through a sinful world. And the kind that put His life on the line for us. **Carolyn** 247

Sep 1

The Apple of My Eye

Long, long ago, before medical doctors knew as much as they know now, it was thought that the pupil of the eye—that black dot in the very middle of your eye—was a solid thing. They called it the "apple of the eye." Warriors knew that if someone lost the "apple in his eye," he could not see, and that meant disaster. A blinded warrior couldn't go to war anymore. He would no doubt lose his family and have to beg for money on the streets, hoping somebody then would be honest enough to exchange the beggar's money for food. Being the apple of someone's eye still means that you are cherished. God thinks of His children as the apple of His eye. He doesn't want to lose you. And just as you enjoy giving gifts to the people you love, God says He likes giving gifts even more. Read His gentle words in **Matthew 7:11. "If you, then, though you are evil, know how to give good gifts to your children, how much more will your Father in heaven give good gifts to those who ask him!" (NIV).**

It's been said that "we can count the seeds in an apple, but only God can count the apples in a seed." And when God looks at you, He can see your true potential and wants to nurture you. God may not give you everything you ask for, but He gives you what you need. Maybe He will give you a letter from a friend when you're feeling lonely. Maybe it's the sudden insight into how an algebra problem is solved or finding the perfect reference for an English paper you're writing.

Today remember that you are the apple of God's eye—His very precious child.

Nancy

Sep 2

Fooled Again

There is a way that seems right to a man, but in the end it leads to death. Proverbs 14:12, NIV.

It was morning, and Jason was supposed to be up helping the family move to their new house. When his brother Ryan walked by his room and saw that he was still under the covers, he thought Jason probably needed more rest. A while later Jason's dad asked where he was. When Ryan said, "He's still sleeping," Dad said, "Go get him up right now."

Ryan slipped quietly into the room. As he crept closer to the bed he almost laughed at the thought of what he was going to do. Suddenly Ryan jumped on top of Jason, yelling as loud as he could, but something didn't feel right. Ryan whipped back the covers to find—only pillows. Just then Jason emerged from the shadows, laughing as hard as he could. He'd been waiting for half an hour for someone to try to wake him from his sleep.

Have you ever been fooled by something you thought was real, but wasn't? Samson thought he had found the real thing when he met Delilah. God had commanded Samson to marry a woman of Israel, someone who believed the same things about God that Samson did. But Samson didn't listen. He wanted his own way. Samson could have had all the good things that God had to offer him, but instead he disobeyed and went after Delilah. With his head shaved and his eyes gouged out, he ended up pushing a heavy grinding wheel.

Now, that doesn't mean that if you disobey your parents, the same thing will happen to you, but you may be sure there will be consequences for disobedience. They may not come for a while, but they will come.

God wants to bless you just as He wanted to bless Samson. If only Samson had followed God's plan, he would have been much happier. Ask God what His desire for your life is. Follow it, and be happy. **Jim**

Sep 3

Ridiculous Recipes

Bless the Lord . . . who satisfieth thy mouth with good things. Psalm 103:2-5.

A newspaper in Oregon features original recipes from first and second graders every Thanksgiving season. How many of the following recipes do you think you'd enjoy eating?

Green Salad
Ingredients:

20 carrots
30 heads of lettuce
Ranch dressing

Put 20 carrots in a bowl. Put 30 heads of lettuce in. Shake it up, then put dressing on (a little bit). Dressing should be from Wal-Mart. Time: 1 hour to make. Serves: 3.

Pumpkin Pie
Ingredients:

One crust
30-pound pumpkin

Scoop out seeds, then get gooey stuff out. Put pumpkin in oven for 30 seconds to cook it. Push it into piecrust. Cook it again. You don't want it gooey. If you want to, you can put sugar on it. Temperature: 100° F. Time: 20 seconds. Serves: 6.

Rice
Ingredients:

5 cups white rice

Wash rice with kitchen soap and then put in hot water. Cook 5 minutes. Add 1 gallon of pepper. It's ready to eat. Temperature: rolling water. Time: 5 minutes.*

"Yuck!" you might be saying. But hey, little kids aren't supposed to know what they're doing in the kitchen, right? But the Ultimate Chef, God, sure knew what He was doing when He made all kinds of fruits, vegetables, grains, and nuts for us to enjoy. He leaves it up to us as to how we put them together into pancake toppings, juices, roasts, casseroles, and desserts. Or how we season, sweeten, or just leave plain our heaven-provided tasty treats. Or how we boil, broil, nuke, fry, roast-over-a-campfire, or bake these wonderful foods that He's created.

Why? Simply because He loves us so much and wants us to be healthy—and especially happy.   **Carolyn**

---

*Grants Pass *Daily Courier*, Nov. 22, 1994.

Dance on the Razor's Edge

Many years ago an express package from England arrived in a South African town. The old man to whom the box was addressed refused to pay the delivery charges, since he hadn't ordered the box. Since there was no return address on the label, the young mailman was uncertain what he should do with the box. "Do you have any ideas?" he questioned the man.

"Take it back to the office and throw it away—or keep it, if you want to. I don't care," the man said in disgust, slamming the door shut.

With a shrug, the mailman took the box back to the post office. For many years he used the box as a footstool.

Then, more than 10 years later, the old man died. And only then, in memory of the old man, did the mailman decide to open the mysterious box. What he saw inside nearly made his own heart stop. Several thousand dollars were stacked neatly inside the box, each stack secured with rubber bands. Because the old man had refused to pay an insignificant amount of money in a delivery fee, he had missed out on receiving an incredible fortune. He didn't have the right attitude.

The people in Noah's day needed a change in attitude too. Read about them in **Matthew 24:38, 39. "For in the days before the flood, people were eating and drinking, marrying and giving in marriage, up to the day Noah entered the ark; and they knew nothing about what would happen until the flood came and took them all away" (NIV).** Could that same surprise happen to us today? It can if we don't listen to warnings from the Bible. What is your attitude about Jesus? Do you believe in a supernatural God? How else could something rise up out of the ground by an unseen force and burst open in dazzling colors, forming edible fruits from a diet of nothing but dirt and water? Incredible miracles like this happen every spring! And we take them for granted. But having seen them, do you believe there just could be a real heaven? Are you expecting to be there?

To doubt there is a God is like "dancing on the razor's edge." That means you think you're having fun, but you're actually hurting yourself and putting yourself in danger. It doesn't take a rocket scientist to know that "dancing on the razor's edge" is a bad idea. It can't hurt to believe in Jesus; but it hurts terribly *not* to believe. The decision is yours. **Nancy**

Sep 5

Secret Agent Christians

"Enable your servants to speak your word with great boldness."
Acts 4:29, NIV.

Did you ever want to be a secret agent? Wearing disguises, sneaking around, trying to catch bad guys, and being a hero always sounded exciting to me. As a secret agent you need to protect your identity. By changing costumes and speaking with different accents you can successfully keep others from finding out who you are.

Did you know there were secret agents in the Bible? That's right! Secret-agent Christians. There were quite a few, but today we'll talk about only three of them.

Agent Nicodemus really wanted to do what was right. He actually wanted to follow Jesus, but he didn't want anyone else to know about it. You see, he was on the Sanhedrin team, the agents who eventually put Jesus to death. To hide his identity, he didn't change costumes; he sneaked out at night so no one would see him.

Agent Peter followed Jesus for more than three years in broad daylight, so you might wonder how he could be a secret-agent Christian. When it came down to an interrogation by enemy agents, though, he snapped. He denied he even knew Jesus. Three times. He went undercover.

Agent Paul preached very openly, so why was he a secret agent Christian? Well, there are times when even God's most faithful messengers are called to go undercover. When enemy agents were after Paul, some friends lowered him over the city wall in a basket, and he escaped into the darkness.

Even though Nicodemus and Peter were not as faithful as God wanted them to be at certain times in their lives, Jesus didn't give up on them. Later they dropped the disguises and blew their cover. They became faithful out-in-the-open followers of Jesus.

Jesus won't give up on you either. Even if you've gone undercover when you shouldn't have, Jesus still wants you as one of His agents. So how about it? Are you ready to blow your cover and take your chances for Jesus?   **Jim**

Sep 6

Creature Courtesy

"Therefore all things whatsoever ye would that men should do to you, do ye even so to them." Matthew 7:12.

How little genuine courtesy for others we see anymore! On national television political candidates tear each other's reputations apart and advertisers try to show how inferior competitors' products are. How unlike God all this is! Why, even some of His little creatures practice the golden rule better than many human beings do.

One evening two naturalists were out walking in Pennsylvania. As they neared a log bridge over a creek, one of them pointed to a large raccoon that was starting to cross the bridge. The raccoon suddenly stopped and stared straight ahead, body tense. The naturalists soon understood why, for at the opposite end of the log bridge an opossum had just trotted up.

Would the raccoon become vicious? the naturalists wondered. When angry, a large raccoon will attack even a dog. The opossum continued toward the middle of the log, and the raccoon resumed advancing as well. Then the raccoon did the most amazing—and courteous—thing! When it looked as if its nose would have a head-on collision with the nose of the opossum, the raccoon suddenly put its arms around the skinny log and worked its way underneath. Hanging upside down, it clung to it until the opossum had had a chance to pass. Then the raccoon clambered back up on the log and continued its trip to the other side of the creek.

The Old Testament gives us several examples of people who loved God so much that they imitated His unselfish courtesy for others. Ruth chose to give up the rest of her young life to care for her aging mother-in-law in a foreign country. Abraham allowed his nephew Lot to have first choice as to where his enormous household would live—and Abraham took what was left. David courteously spared the life of King Saul—who had been trying to murder him. And what blessings eventually came back to these individuals who made their choices according to the golden rule!

Ruth became the wife of a famous man in Israel and an ancestor of Jesus. Abraham eventually became known as the founder of a whole nation. And David became the most famous king of Israel.

Oh, what we can learn from the example of courteous people—and courteous raccoons. **Carolyn**

253

Sep 7

Make the Hair Stand on End

I n October 1992 I read in the newspaper about an elderly woman who lived with her granddaughter in Seattle, Washington. One morning the granddaughter found her grandmother lying on the living room rug. It was cold in the room, and the old woman was cold, too. Her granddaughter shook her and shouted her name and tried to wake her up. When she didn't respond, the granddaughter quickly called 911.

The ambulance arrived within a few minutes and the paramedics tried CPR, but to no avail. Sadly they informed the granddaughter that there was no heartbeat; her grandmother was dead.

And so with a tearful goodbye the granddaughter watched as the ambulance attendants placed the old woman in a black zippered bag and took her to the funeral home on the other side of town.

When the funeral director unzipped the bag, the old woman was looking up at him, blinking her eyes in the bright ceiling lights. The funeral director's hair stood up on end! He guessed that the woman had actually never been dead at all, but had become so cold that her heart was beating slowly and weakly. Her trip in the body bag had warmed her up, so her heart began beating at a more normal rate, and she woke up!

When Jesus comes and wakes up all the sleeping people who have died, it may make our hair stand up on end at first. It seems incredible that it can really happen. But we can believe it will because God has already shown us that He has the power to do it. **1 Corinthians 15:20: But the fact is that Christ did actually rise from the dead, and has become the first of millions who will come back to life again someday (TLB).** That is the foundation of the Christian's faith—the incredible, believable power of God. **Nancy**

Bored to Sleep

Faith comes from hearing the message. Romans 10:17, NIV.

Boy, am I glad that's over!" exclaimed Joni as she walked through the church doors with her friend Ana.

"What do you mean?" questioned Ana.

"It's just that the pastor is so boring. I usually read or sleep during the sermon. I never listen."

"How do you know the sermon is boring if you never listen?" Ana mused.

"Well, I listened once a long time ago, and it was boring."

The Babylonians had surrounded Jerusalem and were waiting until the people ran out of food and gave up. Jeremiah told the people they should surrender to the Babylonians and live. Jeremiah was a prophet of God, and God was directing him to tell the people what would be best. But many who heard Jeremiah didn't like what he was preaching at all, so they went to King Zedekiah and told him they wanted to kill Jeremiah. The king gave his permission, and the people threw Jeremiah into a deep well filled with mud. They left him sinking in the mud, with no food, knowing he would eventually either drown or starve to death. That's pretty rough treatment for a pastor who gave a sermon the people didn't like!

Getting a blessing out of the sermon is as much your responsibility as it is the pastor's. If you would like to hear more stories, let your pastor know how much you enjoy it when he or she tells them. If you don't understand something that you heard in the sermon, after church ask your pastor what he or she meant. Not only will your pastor be pleasantly surprised and pleased that you were paying attention to the sermon, but I think you might even find he or she will start including the things you've asked for.

Pastors have an awesome responsibility given them from God. They can't always make their sermons "fun," because God often convicts them with the serious things of life. They have the job of helping us get ready for Jesus to come. So let your pastor know you're listening and interested in spiritual things. It'll do wonders for you both. **Jim**

Sep 9

Animals Just Wanna Have Fun!

Let the heavens be glad, and let the earth rejoice. . . . Let the sea roar, and . . . let the fields rejoice, and all that is therein. I Chronicles 16:32.

Oh, no! thought W. H. Hudson, as four huge pumas stealthily approached his sleeping bag. *They're going to kill and eat me   !*
        Camping under the starry skies of the Argentine pampas, the English naturalist waited in silence. Then one puma raced toward him, leaped, and landed on the other side of him before prancing like a kitten. The second one bounded over him and started tussling with the first. The huge felines continued to leap over him, playing hide-and-seek around his breathless form until they tired of the game and walked off into the darkness.

American naturalist Enos Mills once saw a black bear cub climb into an open barrel, tumble it over, and then roll himself down the mountain.

At the Amsterdam Zoo onlookers once watched a young hippo entertain himself for hours by swimming under a floating maple leaf and then blowing it into the air and watching it come back to the water.

African explorer Carl Akeley once watched a group of young elephants play "soccer" with a large ball of sun-baked mud for a distance of half a mile.

Sometimes flocks of rooks will fly high together, and then press their wings against their bodies and "skydive" toward the earth, opening their wings at the last minute to avoid a hard landing. Birdwatchers have seen this behavior time and again.

Seagull watchers at the Hudson River once observed a group of gulls sitting on a bridge railing, appearing to wait for small vessels to pass by. When one came, the gulls would land on it for a "free ride" under the bridge. Then—with much calling and excitement—they flew back up to the bridge railing to await a ship coming from the other direction.

And it's a known fact that deer play tag and hide-and-seek.

It seems that God gave animals a special desire to play and have fun. He certainly put that desire in us too, didn't He? So maybe that tells us a little bit more about what He's like—what do you think?   **Carolyn**

Lazy Man's Load

On the first day of the new year, Holly tore away the last December page with a large, self-satisfied smile. "This is going to be such a good year," she told her mother, "because each day I'm going to find at least one good thing to think about and enjoy. I'll make it the year in which each day has a bright spot."

Holly had learned a very important lesson. Her goal to have a good year was manageable when she broke it up into segments of evening and morning, a beginning and an end.

Each of your school assignments has a beginning and an end too. A research paper, for example, may have many beginnings and endings when you break it up into its many parts—research, note cards, first draft, second draft, and final copy. That's how God created the earth. Read about it in **Genesis 1:1-31. In the beginning God created the heavens and the earth. . . . And there was evening, and there was morning—the first day. . . . And there was evening, and there was morning—the second day. . . . God saw all that he had made, and it was very good. And there was evening, and there was morning—the sixth day (NIV).** God broke the job down into manageable parts, and when each part was finished, He said it was very good.

Lazy people don't like to make many trips, so they try to carry everything in one trip and make a mess of it. That's why "a lazy man's load" is considered to be a load that's too large to carry comfortably. Maybe you've taken a lazy man's load of laundry up to your room, dropping items along the way. Or if you wait until the night before a paper is due and try to do the whole thing then, you're taking a lazy man's load, and it's not likely you'll do very well.

Have a plan; know where you're going. Decide what your most pressing goal is for today; for your life. Write down the steps you can take, in order of importance, to achieve those goals and enjoy the feeling of satisfaction when you reach the ultimate goal at the end of the list.

Nancy

Sep 11

Don't Be a Big Shot

Sitting down, Jesus called the Twelve and said, "If anyone wants to be first, he must be the very last, and the servant of all." Mark 9:35, NIV.

Have you ever seen a person who was trying to be something they weren't? It may surprise you to know that animals sometimes try to be something they're not too. For instance, when a frog wants to appear big and scary to a snake that might eat it, it puffs up its throat with a lot of air and makes a loud croaking noise. When a bird wants to frighten an enemy, it puffs up its feathers. God gave these animals the instincts to put on such shows to protect themselves.

But what about people? Have you ever seen someone raise their voice or shake their fist at another person to scare them? Sometimes people try to make themselves seem bigger and more important than they are to impress or intimidate someone else. That might be OK for a bird, but do you think that's the way God wants us to operate? If Jesus is our example, and He became a servant, I think that's what He wants us to do also.

Yes, it's OK for animals to puff themselves up and look bigger than they really are to protect themselves. But Jesus created us to serve other people. That means that sometimes people will hurt us. Jesus says to trust in Him and become "the servant of all." That will be hard sometimes, because we all like to feel important, and how can you feel important if you're always doing things for other people? Here's how:

When we remember that we were important enough that Jesus, the King of the universe, came and died for us, we can feel very important. Besides, helping other people gives you a feeling of worth. So don't try to be a big shot. God created you just the way He wants you to be. In God's eyes, you are important enough to die for.   **Jim**

911! Meow! Arf-arf!

He shall call upon me, and I will answer him. Psalm 91:15.

R*-r-r-ing!* The phone at an emergency dispatch center in Florida rang insistently.

"Hello?" the operator said in a professional, no-nonsense voice.

"Meow," a voice answered at the other end of the line.

"Hello?" the perplexed operator asked again.

"Meow! Meow!" came the insistent response.

Quickly the operator dispatched the police to the traced address where there seemed to be a cat in trouble. Sure enough, Tipper, the cat, who was choking on his flea collar, had somehow hit the speed dial on his master's telephone. Police entered Tipper's home and quickly loosened the potentially deadly collar, saving Tipper's life. Tipper's owner, of course, was relieved to hear of the 911 rescue but stated, "I just hope he doesn't start dialing long-distance!" [1]

A dog named Lyric saved her owner's life. Because of a serious health problem Lyric's owner always sleeps with an oxygen mask. In March 1996 Lyric was awakened one night by an alarm that signaled a problem with the mask. In a burst of panic (but doing as she'd been trained) Lyric rushed to the telephone, lifted a front paw, and hit the speed-dial button. Soon paramedics were at Lyric's house, and the emergency was efficiently taken care of. [2]

If some animals have enough sense to call for help, how much more should we human beings do the same! God has set up a heavenly 911 emergency help line. But getting through to Him—and help—is even easier than hitting speed dial on a telephone. All we have to do is say "Dear God" or "Dear Jesus" (even just in our hearts) and *boom!* we're connected. Connected to the throne of our Father in heaven. He encourages us to "call upon me in the day of trouble: I will deliver thee, and thou shalt glorify me" (Ps. 50:15).   **Carolyn**

[1] *Guide,* Feb. 15, 1997, p. 32.
[2] *Guide,* Oct. 26, 1996, p. 32.

Sep 13

Give Him Enough Rope, and He'll Hang Himself

A small town near Seattle, Washington, had a big problem: an arsonist was on the loose, starting fires at different points all across the city. No one could catch him. After a while the fire chief began to suspect one of the volunteer firefighters was starting the fires. He was always the first one at the fire station to respond to the alarm. And he often had the fire engine started before the fire chief was even ready! But how could he prove it?

Five fires later someone reported seeing a man drop a lighted match near a field, then run to his car and speed off. The man was followed to the fire station. It was the volunteer. The fire chief had given him "enough rope to hang himself."

If you're on a tight leash or rope, you don't have much freedom. But if it hangs loose, you might trip on it and hurt yourself. So to give someone enough rope means you are in control of the situation—you hold onto the ends of the rope, but you let the other person have enough freedom so that they incriminate themselves. You don't have to tattle or get them into trouble—they do it themselves.

The Bible says we're all apt to get ourselves into trouble. The key is what we think about and what we wish for. Notice the two steps **James 1:14, 15** says to take when we get into trouble: **Temptation is the pull of man's own evil thoughts and wishes. These evil thoughts lead to evil actions and afterwards to the death penalty from God (TLB).** First we think about the sin. Then we take action. And if we repeat this sequence without stopping ourselves, we ruin our characters, and that leads to separation from God—eternal death—because we no longer want to be in His presence.

God gives us all enough rope, but He isn't trying to trip us. He just wants us to have choices. We can hang ourselves—or we can tighten the rope by staying close to God. It makes sense to move closer to Him.

Nancy

What Kind of Shape Are You In?

With joy you will draw water from the wells of salvation. Isaiah 12:3, NIV.

I looked out the window of the 727 jet, thinking how amazing it was that a huge hunk of metal like a passenger jet can fly. What keeps it from falling out of the sky? Well, I don't know too much about airplanes, but I know it has to do with at least two things. First, you need a lot of power to move something that big around in the sky. Second, it has to do with how the wind passes over the top and bottom of the wings. As the wings slice through the air, their shape causes air pressure to push up from the bottom and make the plane fly.

Did you know that the shape of your mouth can cause you to fly—or to crash? I'm talking about your attitude. You may think you don't have anything to be happy about, but think about this: Jesus, who lived in the most fantastic place you could imagine, came to this dirty sin-filled world. No, He didn't just come for a week's vacation. He stayed for 33 years. He wasn't treated very well either. In fact, some of the very men He came to save murdered Him.

Why did He leave heaven and all its glory? Because if He didn't, you and I would never have the opportunity to live in heaven with Him. Because He did come and live and die, you and I can spend eternity with Him.

Think about a place where there are no problems, where there's nothing to complain about or to be sad about. Think about spending the next few billion years there with Jesus, the one who died to save you. Now look in the mirror and watch the corners of your mouth turn up into a smile. It's true, you know; the shape of your mouth can keep you from crashing.

Jim

Sep 15

Christy, the Fake Watchdog

"Woe to you, . . . hypocrites! You are like whitewashed tombs, which look beautiful on the outside." Matthew 23:27, NIV.

N o, Christy, you're barking at the wrong people!" said my husband in a frustrated voice.

I didn't blame him for being upset. We'd gotten Christy at the Kampala Police Kennels in Uganda, Africa. We had big plans for the roly-poly, black, furry German shepherd pup. She'd grow into a playful, gentle family pet and would also become a responsible watchdog—scaring off midnight chicken thieves and other unwelcome intruders.

Poor Christy! As much as we loved and worked with her, she just couldn't seem to get it right. With teeth bared, she'd often bark ferociously at our friends, then let sinister-looking characters come right onto front porch late at night. One night I walked into the living room and was suddenly shaken when I realized four pairs of human eyes were lined up outside the window, staring at me. And where was our full-grown, muscular watchdog, Christy? She was sitting on the floor in front of the window, staring back at them!

When she was about 1 year old, Christy started hanging out with a huge stray dog, who taught her to kill chickens. We eventually had to tie her up so she wouldn't run off and attack local sheep and goats. Poor Christy! She *looked* like a responsible watchdog, but . . .

Some people are like Christy. On the inside they're not what they look like they are—or pretend to be—on the outside. Jesus called this kind of person a hypocrite. He told them, "On the outside you appear to people as righteous but on the inside you are full of hypocrisy and wickedness" (Matthew 23:28).

Like Christy, hypocrites are a big disappointment. They say God is love, but often they don't show God's love to those around them. Let's ask our heavenly Father to help us never be a whitewashed tomb, a fake watchdog, or any other kind of disappointment to someone who is looking for Jesus.

Carolyn

Knock the Spots Out

Many years ago hunters and marksmen made a game out of target practice. They would nail playing cards to a tree and attempt to shoot out the colored circles from a certain distance away. Any marksman who could "knock the spots" out of a card was considered highly skilled. Today if someone says you "knock the spots out" of any class you take, it means you excel in that class.

It obviously takes a lot of experience to knock the spots out of something. Some people have more experience with disappointment and anxiety than others. They learn, painfully, that disappointment has a lifespan. But guess what they end up with after a string of disappointments? They learn perseverance; they have an inner strength. The Bible promises this in **James 1:2, 3: Consider it pure joy, my brothers, whenever you face trials of many kinds, because you know that the testing of your faith develops perseverance (NIV).** If you have experienced trouble, you know this is true. People who survive hard times learn the valuable skill of pushing ahead anyway, knowing that everything comes to an end eventually. That's a comforting thought when things aren't going well. Unfortunately, it also works the other way: good things eventually come to an end, too. But that's not entirely bad news. One good thing may be replaced by another good thing.

A learned monk was asked by a student how he could find God. In response, the monk took the student to a deep watering trough and pushed the student's head under the water. Thrashing and fighting for air, the student tried to escape the teacher's hold, but he couldn't. At last, when the student gave up thrashing, the monk allowed him to come up for air.

As the student looked at the monk with shock and disbelief in his eyes, the monk said wisely, "When you desire God as much as you desired air, you will find Him."

That's the best thing about learning to knock the spots out of troubles. When the only sure thing in your life is that you want Jesus with you, you find a deep and meaningful relationship with Him.   **Nancy**

Sep 17

Attacked by a Shark!

He replied, . . . "If you have faith as small as a mustard seed, you can say to this mountain, 'Move from here to there' and it will move. Nothing will be impossible for you." Matthew 17:20, NIV.

There I was, relaxing on my air mattress with a box of frozen shrimp by my side (I was fishing, not eating). Now, it's important to realize that the Gulf of Mexico, on which my air mattress was floating, is full of interesting creatures. Big ones, small ones, colorful ones, but certainly no dangerous ones. At least that's what I thought.

As I drifted peacefully on my little mattress boat, I also drifted off to sleep. Suddenly my dreams were interrupted by an eruption about 20 feet in front of me. A large, gray, shark-shaped object leaped out of the water. All the safety precautions for protecting myself against a shark attack completely left my mind. I jumped off my air mattress and started running toward shore. Of course, no one can outrun a shark, but I wasn't stopping to think about that. I just wanted to get out of there.

As I headed toward shore, running as fast as I could in the waist-deep water, I noticed a family, laughing and pointing toward the spot where the shark had come out of the water. Why were they just standing there? Why weren't they escaping the jaws of death like I was? As I came closer, I heard the mother in the family say, "I've always wanted to see a dolphin close-up."

I turned around, looked closely, and sure enough, it was not a shark. There was Flipper, playfully entertaining beachgoers. How embarrassing! I had "made a mountain out of a molehill," as the old saying goes. Have you ever done that? Do you get yourself so worried that you panic? Well, our God can move mountains! He can take any problem we have and solve it. So don't make a shark out of a dolphin, just relax and trust Him to keep you safe.

Jim

Panic at Herring Creek

"You know the way to the place where I am going." John 14:5, NRSV.

The sun-reflecting granite walls on either side of me started closing in like a bad dream. The thick pine trees in my peripheral vision began whirling about, while the bass roar of Herring Creek behind me seemed to predict impending doom. I was overheated. I was panicked. But most of all, I was lost. Majorly lost!

Where's the path? I groaned inwardly. *Ah, there it is! No . . . it's that opening back into the forest over there. Wait a minute; didn't I come through sort of a rock alley before I arrived at the creek? Help! How do I find my way?*

The previous week someone had told me that the trail to Herring Creek was "beautiful and easy to follow." Everything in my gut told me to go into the forest, but that put the sun in the wrong place for getting back to the trailhead and campground.

Ah! The compass—and the map! Why had it taken me so long to remember them? Quickly I pulled them out of my daypack. Trying to swallow my panic and think with a clear head, I decided to go where the map and compass were pointing me, although it didn't "feel" right. Within five minutes I was recognizing familiar landmarks and was headed safely back to the trailhead.

I'm not the only person in history to have panicked when I didn't know which way to go. Jesus was talking about heaven once, and His disciple Thomas, perhaps afraid of being left behind, blurted out, "How can we know the way?" (John 14:5, NRSV).

Jesus answered, "I am the way" (verse 6). In other words, if Thomas stayed close to Jesus in everyday choices, in thought, and in prayer, Jesus would be a "compass" for him, showing him the way. Thomas would always know where he was going and how to get there—no matter how confusing everything else around him seemed.

Jesus wants to be our compass too.   **Carolyn**

Sep 19

Pie in the Sky

We all want others to think that things are going well in our families. Sometimes people fake it so others will think everything's OK. Is it "pie in the sky" to want a happy family?

To be searching for "pie in the sky" means you're looking for something sweet—but you can never get it because it's always out of reach. Pie in the sky is something you'll never be able to have. Do happy families exist, or is belonging to a happy family a pie-in-the-sky idea?

How do you know if your family is healthy? Do you think a healthy family never argues with each other? No, sometimes a healthy family does argue. Does a healthy family never get angry at each other? No, healthy families get angry at each other sometimes. Does a healthy family always want to be together? No, sometimes kids from healthy families want to get away from their parents and other members of their families for a while.

So how do you know if your family is healthy? Read the Bible's description in **James 3:17: The wisdom that comes from heaven is first of all pure and full of quiet gentleness. Then it is peace-loving and courteous. It allows discussion and is willing to yield to others; it is full of mercy and good deeds. It is wholehearted and straightforward and sincere (TLB).**

Families in trouble don't talk to each other respectfully about their feelings. In these families nobody talks about anything but the weather. They avoid each other. If they're angry, they hurt each other by acting out instead of trying to come to an understanding and apologizing to each other. A family like this needs help.

If you think your family needs help, don't be afraid of "ruining the family's reputation." Talk to a trusted adult friend—maybe your pastor or school counselor. They don't judge. They are there to help you bear your burdens.

A happy family is not "pie in the sky." It's reachable with help and with everyone working together. With help, your family can become people who like to be together, who support each other in their safe, sweet place called "home."   **Nancy**

On Top of the World

There were shepherds living out in the fields nearby, keeping watch over their flocks at night. Luke 2:8, NIV.

What would you like to become when you grow up? A doctor, teacher, carpenter, lawyer, or a shepherd? Now, how much fun could it be to be a shepherd? I don't know about you, but I've always thought being a shepherd would be pretty boring. That is, until I heard about some shepherds in France.

There is a part of France called the Landes district. The problem with being a shepherd in this part of France is that much of the land is partially covered with water. It's pretty hard to keep up with your sheep when you're trying to wade through swamps. So these French sheepherders have come up with an ingenious way to get around. Here's how they do it. Each shepherd walks on stilts and uses a long walking stick to help him keep his balance. When the shepherds need to stop and rest, they use the walking stick as a seat, which makes these guys look like camera tripods!

That makes me think of some other shepherds I've heard about. They were the shepherds who received the good news that Jesus would be born. They weren't on tripods, but if they had been, they would have fallen right off from surprise! A bright light appeared in the sky and hovered over them. (If such a thing happened now, people would say it was a UFO.) But the shepherds knew it was angels, and they were afraid. The angels told them not to be frightened, because they were bringing great news, the best news of all time: Jesus the Saviour was born, and they were the ones to hear it first!

I must admit I've never wanted to be a shepherd, but I sure would like to have been one that day. God could have told the king that Jesus was to be born. So why did He bring the good news about Jesus to shepherds? I think He knew they would listen. Are you listening for Him today? You never know what great news He has for you!   **Jim**

Crazy Caleb

The Lord is my portion, . . . therefore I will hope in him. Lamentations 3:24.

"C aleb's crazy!" shouted a little camper to the lifeguard. "He's been trying to choke me under the water!"

"I'm so sorry, Caleb," I told the 10-year-old an hour later. "We've given you so many chances this week. But this time I'm afraid I'll have to take you back home."

"Don't care—hate everybody anyway!" he spat out.

I knew Caleb's father was in prison for mistreating family members, and I knew Caleb lived in poverty. The bitter unfairness of sin had left this boy angry and deeply disturbed. On the way home Caleb talked endlessly about people he knew, his words laced with hatred.

Toward evening I asked, "Hungry?"

He nodded.

"Never been in a restaurant before," said Caleb almost shyly a few minutes later when we pulled up to a fast-food café beside a dusty stretch of highway. We sat at one of the indoor picnic tables and looked out across the two-lane highway at a rundown motel. What an ugly place!

When Caleb finished his sandwich, french fries, and milk shake, I ordered him more fries and another shake. He kept gazing at the dumpy dwelling across the highway. Then, without turning his head, he said, "That must be what Paradise looks like," and sighed contentedly.

I looked at the two rusty cars parked in the weeds.

"Paradise must look like *that* place—with the pretty flowers in front and all the trees and blue sky. It's quiet in Paradise, and no one gets beat up. Not with God up there, they don't. Hope I go there."

"Oh, Caleb," I said slowly, "I hope we *both* go there."

"That food was good," he said suddenly. Twisting his head back toward the counter he asked, "Want another napkin?"

"Sure," I answered.

"Hey!" he called loudly from the napkin dispenser, "Use toothpicks? I'll bring ya one."

Caleb seemed to have lost his anger, at least for the time being. I'm not sure why. Perhaps it was because he'd caught a little glimpse of Paradise.

Carolyn

Read Between the Lines

When the letter arrived, Janet tore it open eagerly. She hadn't heard from Natalie since her family moved away. The letter was newsy, but Janet noticed something rather odd about the sentences. Some of them went clear across the page, and others ended halfway across, continuing on the next line:

"Dear Janet,
    "We had a lovely trip
        coming across the miles to
    our new home.
    Your house soon
        became a memory, although I'm making new friends.
    I'll call you sometime
        and maybe we can talk,
    before we see each other again.
                    "Love, Natalie."

The phone call came that evening. Natalie laughed delightedly at Janet's confusion with the odd letter. She said, "It's obvious you haven't learned to read between the lines."

"I know what reading between the lines means," Janet said defensively. "It means figuring out the difference between what someone says and what they really mean."

"But originally it meant to read every other line," Natalie said. "Start with the second line, and just read every other one."

Janet picked up the letter. Beginning with the second line, she read, "'Coming across the miles to your house soon. I'll call you sometime before we see each other again.'" Now it made sense!

There are hidden messages in the Bible that leap out at us, too, depending on our understanding. Some of them lay buried until some experience casts a new slant on the old stories. That's why it's important never to stop reading the Bible. What does **James 1:25** say about that? If **anyone keeps looking steadily into God's law for free men, he will not only remember it but he will do what it says, and God will greatly bless him in everything he does (TLB).** **Nancy**

269

Sep 23

Sherpa

"If anyone would come after me, he must deny himself and take up his cross daily and follow me." Luke 9:23, NIV.

At more than 29,000 feet (that's more than five miles!), Mount Everest is the tallest mountain in the world. If you've ever visited a high mountain area, such as the Rocky Mountains in the United States, you've discovered that it's difficult to breathe at high altitudes. The higher you climb in the earth's atmosphere, the thinner the air gets. Your body tells you that you're not getting enough oxygen and says, "Breathe faster!" You may get a headache, feel sick to your stomach, and become totally exhausted, all because of thin air.

Now back to Everest. If you lived around this mammoth mountain, your body would get used to living in thin air. There are a group of people called Sherpas who live around the 13,000-foot level. Not that many people knew about these hardy folks until 1922, when a man named G. C. Bruce and a group of other climbers ascended Mount Everest. The Sherpas helped the team by guiding them up the mountain and cheerfully carrying their supplies. Without complaining, the sturdy Sherpas have led hundreds of expeditions up the highest mountain in the world. Some of them have even given their lives on this dangerous mountain helping strangers find their way.

When Jesus asked us to follow Him, He knew the way would be rough at times. Some faithful individuals have even given their lives to follow Jesus. So how is it that we can be happy following Him, when it isn't always easy? Jesus gives us peace and strength. He helps us find our way through rough times and rocky roads. Best of all, He's promised us an eternity with Him.

The men and women who have climbed Mount Everest have done it with one thing in mind: they wanted to reach the top. But they didn't all get there. We can be confident that if we put our trust in Jesus and give our lives fully to Him, we will reach the top and spend eternity with Him.

Jim

God Has No Trojan Horse Virus

It is impossible for God to tell a lie. Hebrews 6:18, TLB.

Everywhere we turn, it seems, someone is trying to deceive us. Earlier this year a TV news magazine ran a behind-the-scenes exposé on magazine modeling. Skin tones and arm and leg widths are electronically altered to make models appear "better" than possible.

Then there's deceit on the Internet. A local newspaper* recently carried a warning from the U.S. Department of Energy. It warned Internet surfers about what is called a computer Trojan horse virus named AOL4Free. A Trojan horse is a seemingly useful computer program that contains concealed instructions that when activated destroy files. So people who opened that "file" thought they were going to get an America Online account for free. Instead, they got a devastating surprise. The fake file destroyed everything on the users' hard drives. But guess what? There really *is* a Macintosh program named AOL4Free.

To make things even *more* confusing, *another* message circulating on the Internet warned that an "AOL4Free virus-infected e-mail message" could destroy a system when a user read the message. But—get this—that warning was a *fake* warning and did not apply to the destructive virus. So the U.S. Department of Energy had to issue a warning about a fake warning!

Another deception is quietly surfacing these days in some children's Bible story books (of all places). For example, a writer may tell the Creation story but leave out the part about God resting on the seventh day and setting it apart as special. Other children's books don't repeat all the Ten Commandments as Moses recorded them from God in Exodus 20.

In the midst of all this world's deception, isn't it a relief to know a very important secret God told us about Himself? The secret is this: It's *impossible* for God to lie. God has no Trojan horses.

Why? Because deceit doesn't exist in His character or in His great heart of love. A good friend will always tell you the truth. That must make God our best friend of all!   **Carolyn**

---

*Associated Press, "'Trojan Horse' Virus Lurking on the Internet," Hagerstown, Maryland, *Herald Mail*, Apr. 23, 1997.

Sep 25

Get Up Steam

There's something really bizarre that happens to students when they have tons of homework to do: they become paralyzed. Often they can't even lift their heads off the couch to sit up, much less walk to a desk! One of the main causes of this terrible affliction is that they don't know where to begin. And unless they do begin, they'll never "get up steam" to complete the job.

As you may have guessed, the expression "get up steam" comes from the old days of steam engines. Before a train or steamboat could get moving, someone had to start a fire under the boiler. After a time the water was hot enough to generate enough steam, which, when vented through a pipe, turned the engine.

When I think of "getting up steam," I think of a process. What comes first? Starting the fire. How do you "start a fire" when it comes to your homework? You sit at your desk and open your books to start your shortest assignment. Why the shortest? Because success breeds success. After you've finished the shortest assignment, you begin another one. If you then give yourself a time limit in which to finish that one, you "get up steam" and can really fly!

The Bible is a practical book of advice. What does it say about work? **Ecclesiastes 7:8: Finishing is better than starting! (TLB).** Being warmed up and finishing the job is better than starting the fire, and it feels better too. You might surprise yourself! Writer Robert Benchley says, "It took me 15 years to discover I had no talent for writing, but I couldn't give it up because by that time I was too famous." His engines were in high gear.

Just see where your gears take you when you get up steam! The next time you sit down with your textbooks, take the attitude that you're working up steam. It will get better once the wheels have started rolling.

Nancy

I Don't Shine Shoes

Now that I, your Lord and Teacher, have washed your feet, you also should wash one another's feet. John 13:14, NIV.

Hsu Chu came from a very wealthy Chinese family. When his family needed something done, they paid for someone to do it. Hsu Chu dressed well, spoke well, and settled for only the best.

Hsu Chu chose a medical career and entered the China Inland Mission Hospital for his training. He determined to do his very best, study hard, and become someone people would take note of.

One day the superintendent of the hospital asked Hsu Chu to clean and polish some shoes. Hsu Chu looked at the superintendent and said, "No gentleman or scholar would do such lowly work." Hsu Chu was not about to put himself on the floor to clean someone's shoes. A wealthy scholar should not be asked to do such trivial work, he thought.

Quietly the superintendent took the shoes and shined them himself. Then he asked Hsu Chu to come with him. He asked Hsu Chu to sit down while he read to him the thirteenth chapter of John. Hsu Chu listened in amazement to how Jesus, the Master of the universe, treated His disciples. Tears welled up in Hsu Chu's eyes as the superintendent read the verse that says, "Now that I, your Lord and Teacher, have washed your feet, you also should wash one another's feet." Hsu Chu cried as he prayed for his Lord and Master to forgive him.

Hsu Chu didn't just pray, however; he did something. Whenever there were jobs to do, such as washing dishes, cleaning floors, or polishing shoes, he did them well, and he did them cheerfully. If Jesus was willing to wash His disciples' feet, shouldn't we be willing to polish someone else's shoes?

Sometimes we're tempted to think that certain things aren't good enough for us, that we should settle for only the best. Well, you're right. We should settle for only the best. We should settle for following the example of Jesus, who served the very people He created with humility and gladness.   **Jim**

Sep 27

Peeping Mugenzi

Let thine eyes look right on, and let thine eyelids look straight before thee. Proverbs 4:25.

Where we permit our eyes to look will often determine where we permit our feet to wander. A person whom I will call Mugenzi taught me that lesson in a most painful way.

One evening while living in Africa, I decided to get a drink of water before heading up the hill to school to participate in the Saturday night program with the students. I hurried down the hallway and rounded the sharp corner into the kitchen and flipped on the light.

There, with its nose almost pressed through the windowpane, was the huge face of a man, staring down at my sinkful of dirty dishes. I don't know who was more startled—he or I. But I do know who yelled the loudest. My scream sent him scurrying off into the blackness of the night.

When my family and I returned from the Saturday night program, we once again went into the kitchen for a drink of water. Our sink had been emptied of dishes! The window had been pried open, and everything that could be fitted through the metal grid on the window had been stolen! That man's wandering eyes had led his feet back to our window and into our house to commit a robbery.

You may think things like that happen mostly in faraway places like Africa. But rising teen shoplifting statistics show that the same type of thing happens in our own country as well. Unfortunately, some kids who would never *think* of shoplifting might get into someone else's locker at school or "borrow" items from a classmate's lunch, never intending to return or replace them.

King Solomon talked about situations in which looking at the wrong things can actually lead us to commit sin. In Proverbs 4:25 he counseled, "Let thine eyes look right on, and let thine eyelids look straight before thee." In the next verse (verse 26) he cautions us to "ponder" or think about the direction we will take next. This writer made it clear that keeping our eyes in the right places will keep us walking in the right paths (verse 27).

Carolyn

Ugly Duckling

No doubt you've heard the classic story by Hans Christian Andersen about the ugly duckling. In case you haven't, I'll refresh your memory with a paraphrased version of my own.

Shortly after hatching from his egg, a little swan finds himself alone. He tries to make friends with a family of ducks, but they make fun of him because he doesn't look like them—he's much bigger and very awkward. He doesn't know how to quack, and his feathers aren't golden yellow. The ducks call him ugly, and he's sure they're right.

The weeks pass, and the lonely little swan floats downstream, still looking for someplace to fit in. At last he rounds a bend in the stream, surprising a family of white swans, who consider him to be the most beautiful white swan on the lake. Suddenly the homely baby swan realizes he has developed into a respectable adult.

The swan looked odd when he tried to be a duck, but when he gave up trying to be something he wasn't, he fit right in. The Bible speaks to this. Read **Matthew 10:39. "If you cling to your life, you will lose it; but if you give it up for me, you will save it" (TLB).** We don't fit in with this world of greed, immorality, and selfishness. If we give up our selfishness and live by God's rules, we'll find a satisfaction we've never known before.

You've been giving up things for a long time already. You gave up bottles for real food. You gave up crawling for walking. You traded in your tricycle for a bike. You gave up dependence for independence. Eventually you'll learn how to make your own money and get your own job so you can live by yourself. You will have given up a tremendous number of things, but think how much you will have gained in return!

As you give up craving the things of this world and begin to focus on a life with Jesus, you change from being an ugly duckling as your life is transformed into a swan.
Nancy

275

Undercover Duke

"The Holy Spirit will teach you at that time what you should say."
Luke 12:12, NIV.

If you think you're shy, I want to tell you about the fifth duke of Cavendish, who lived in England during the 1800s. He developed one of the most beautiful greenhouses in all of England. It seems as though he got along better with flowers than he did with people.

His real name was William John Cavendish Bentinck Scott. He was royalty and was expected to meet and greet people and take his place in the government. William, however, was just too shy. He quit the government at a young age and decided to work in his greenhouse.

After a while he decided he didn't even want to see his servants, so he closed himself in one corner of his mansion so that he would have no contact with his servants or guests. If anyone wanted to contact him, they had to place a message in a message box on the outside of his door. The duke would then write a reply and place it in the box for pickup. If he happened to meet any servants when he took his daily walk, they were told to look away.

As time went on, Sir William became even more withdrawn. He had some local miners dig tunnels from his mansion to his greenhouses and other buildings. When he wanted to go out, he actually went under the ground into his tunnels, where he could walk unseen to various parts of his property.

The Bible says we are to go to all the nations and tell them the good news about Jesus, His offer of salvation, and His second coming. To do that we're going to have to talk to people. Don't be like Sir William. People need to know what you already know. Don't be afraid to tell them. God's own Holy Spirit will give you the words to speak.   **Jim**

Sep 30

Mudslide

[There is] a time to laugh. Ecclesiastes 3:4, NIV.

I had no idea that day in a remote part of Zaire that I was headed for the worst, most public embarrassment of my life. Our school's director had invited us to "go shopping." I'd dressed as I would in the United States for a shopping trip to a nice mall—medium-heeled sandals, a neat skirt, with a pale yellow sweater to match. As I'd soon learn, I had a *lot* to learn about "going shopping" in Africa!

I was not prepared for the thick mass of humanity that came into view as our van pulled over the last ridge and halted by a short mud-slimed trail that led down to the vast expanse of the open-air market. Recent torrential downpours had made the market area look like a soupy football field on a rainy Super Bowl Sunday.

A hush fell over the assembly as we foreigners emerged from the van. I wasn't used to being the focus of 4,000 eyes. I got up courage to smile at the huge crowd and then decided to play it cool by taking very casual steps down the steep trail leading to the market.

Suddenly the word "mudslide" took on a whole new meaning as my sandaled feet flew out from under me and my whole right side literally hit the trail. Three seconds later I arrived in the marketplace as if I were trying to beat the shortstop's throw to second base. As the air filled with 2,000 voices screaming out thunderous waves of laughter, I somehow unsuctioned my big leather handbag from the inches-thick muddy slime and struggled to my feet.

The Bible tells us that God has evidently set aside "a time to laugh." So I suppose I should be glad if I helped 2,000 people have a good laugh and a lot more chuckles as I walked around with caked mud drying on my whole right side.

From that experience, though, I learned this valuable lesson: in those times God has set aside for laughter there will certainly be those moments when the best thing we can possibly do is laugh at ourselves.

Carolyn

Oct 1

Hallmark

On a public television station not long ago I was fascinated by a program on how to make antique furniture. The craftsman showed how to put together chests of drawers and kitchen cabinets in the style of early American times. And then he spent 10 minutes on a demonstration of how to make the new furniture look old, or what he called "distressed." He pounded nails here and there and pulled them out, filed away a corner or two, chipped off an edge, gouged a hole, and even dragged a screwdriver across the top to make it look scratched. When he was done it did indeed look like a 100-year-old piece of furniture.

Not long ago an Oriental rug importer tried a similar thing. He tied brand-new rugs to the back of a car and dragged them down the street so they would look worn. Then they were hung in a room filled with cigarette smoke. Brown water was smudged here and there. When he was finished, they were sold as antique Oriental carpets for exorbitant sums of money.

He fooled a lot of people! Sometimes it's easy to be fooled if you don't know what to look for. People who deal with gold and silver coins know to look for the hallmark, the official stamp of quality that's impossible to forge. "Hallmark" comes from a company in England called Goldsmiths' Hall. Every coin from this manufacturer bore the "Hall mark" that indicated its authenticity and grade of purity. So trustworthy was the Hall mark that "hallmark" has come to represent something genuinely superior.

Anyone who is a true friend of Jesus is given His hallmark. You can recognize it in their sensitivity and caring spirit. Sometimes people who don't understand that hallmark make fun of Christians. The kindness of Christians is sometimes misinterpreted as stupidity. That's OK. Jesus predicted it. **John 17:14** says, **"I have given them your word and the world has hated them, for they are not of the world any more than I am of the world" (NIV).** Someday Jesus will take us to heaven, where everyone is kind. That may be the first place many of us are fully understood. It's going to be wonderful! **Nancy**

Caution, Slippery Path

The Lord will guide you always. Isaiah 58:11, NIV.

I live in Colorado, where you're a little out of place if you don't ski. About once a year almost everyone at my school packs up their skis, puts on their gloves and hats, and heads to the slopes for a day of frozen fun. If you were to go with us, this is what you'd have to do.

Once on the slope, you hop on this moving chair that hangs from a suspended metal cable and are whisked to the top of the mountain. After you successfully get off the moving chair, you stand at the top of the mountain, looking at all the possible routes to take. You then proceed to ski down the hill at a high rate of speed.

Of course, there are several things you must look for on your way down the hill. In addition to keeping your balance, slowing down at the right time, and stopping, you must also look out for people on the slope. Some go slower, and you'll have to pass them, making sure you don't turn the same way they do. Otherwise, a collision may take place. Very messy.

Why do people ski? Because it's fun! The benefits far outweigh the troubles. Life is a lot like that. Sometimes it's difficult, and things get in your way. Sometimes you may feel as though you're hanging far above stable ground and wonder if you'll fall. Sometimes the way is very slippery, and you wonder if you'll ever make it.

When I go skiing, I never go alone. I always go with someone who knows the mountain—a personal guide. That way I don't get lost and my guide is with me if I get in trouble. It isn't as lonely, either.

Let Jesus be your life's guide. He'll lead you down the right path. If you find yourself in trouble, He'll help. Even if you feel like you're hanging by a thread, don't give up; Jesus will hold you. The road may not always be easy, but because you've trusted in Jesus, the True Guide, you'll arrive safely home. **Jim**

$O_c t$ 3

Messy Manicure

There is laid up for me a crown of righteousness, which the Lord, the righteous judge, shall give me at that day: and not to me only, but unto all them also that love his appearing. 2 Timothy 4:8.

Mom won't be back for a little while, I thought, looking at the four pairs of Sabbath shoes she'd asked me to polish an hour before sundown that Friday afternoon. Polishing the family's shoes for Sabbath was not my favorite job. But I'd hauled them out to the garage, set them on newspaper spread on the cement floor, and got the right color polishes down from the shelf.

"Cordovan" was the shade for my dad's size 11 shoes. I pulled the little puffball that was attached to the lid out of the bottle and put a drop on my index finger. H'mmm, I thought, that brown has a lot of red in it—kinda looks like nail polish. Sure wish Mom would let me paint my nails!

Then I had an idea. I painted two nails cordovan brown and held out my hand. That looks quite glamorous, I thought, keeping the mop-up rag handy in case I heard Mother coming out the back door. When I'd finished the nails on one hand, I started on the other one.

And that's why I had eight fingernails polished instead of eight shoes when I heard Mother's unexpected gasp. "Young lady, what do you think you're doing?" She could see exactly what I'd been doing—and hadn't been doing. It was too late to save myself.

Do you think I "loved" the sudden "appearing" of my mother that afternoon in the garage? No way! She was the last person I wanted to see! Why? Because instead of doing the job she'd left me to do, I was doing something else.

It will be the same way when Jesus comes back to this earth. Jesus told us He has a special gift for all those who "love his appearing." If we're busy at the job He left us to do, we will love His appearing! But if we're doing something else, He'll be the last person we want to see.

If you aren't feeling real excited about Christ's second coming right now, you might want to take a closer look at your nails—er, I mean your—choices.

Carolyn

Heap Coals of Fire on Someone's Head

Arnie was different from everyone else in his class. He was tall for his age, and his hair grew faster than everyone else's (or maybe it just got cut less often). His greasy brown locks often hung in his eyes or got stuck on his eyelashes. His most annoying action was a never-ending jerk of his head to fling the offending hair from his eyes. But what was worst of all was the constant grin on his face.

The kids called him names and laughed at him when he read out loud in class, stumbling over the simplest words. When they graded each other's papers and announced how many math problems he got wrong, Arnie kept on smiling. Jack was the worst one for teasing Arnie. It was always Jack's idea if the other students picked Arnie last for their team or chose not to play with Arnie on the playground.

Then Mrs. Campbell assigned Jack and Arnie to be science project partners. Jack fussed when he learned about it, but Mrs. Campbell was firm. If the boys didn't work together, they both would fail.

Weeks passed. Imagine their surprise when Jack and Arnie unveiled their intricate display. It was a complicated engineering feat that began with a marble in a chute. When the marble fell into a water-filled cup, the cup tipped over, spilling the water and the marble into a glass below. The weight of the glass, resting on a seesaw, flipped the other end of the seesaw into the air, bumping a light switch that turned on a reading lamp on a table.

Jack and Arnie's display won the grand prize. And though Arnie had thought up most of it, he told everyone it was Jack's idea. Arnie's whole life changed because of his kindness to Jack.

In **Proverbs 25:21, 22,** wise King Solomon wrote, **If thine enemy be hungry, give him bread to eat; and if he be thirsty, give him water to drink: for thou shalt heap coals of fire upon his head, and the Lord shall reward thee.** Your kindness will melt the iciness in the other person and heat them up as much as if you literally poured fire on their head. The most fun is seeing their struggle to keep on being mean while you're being so kind.

Nancy

Oct 5

The Tallest Snowman

Declare his glory among the nations. Psalm 96:3, NIV.

Snowmen are cool! Actually, they're more than cool; they're cold! I think the biggest snowman I ever built was about six or eight feet tall. Pretty tall. But Prince William, the tallest-ever snowman, was built in Alaska in 1992. It was 76 feet 2 inches tall, about as tall as a six- or seven-story building!

Some people who lived a long time ago tried to build the highest-ever tower, the Tower of Babel. You can read all about it in Genesis 11. Now, there's nothing wrong with constructing a tall building, unless you're building it for the wrong reasons. These people were definitely building this tower for the wrong reasons. You see, they thought they could outsmart God and become famous. They thought that if God sent another flood, they'd just climb up their tower and outrun the rising water. They wanted to be known as the people who outsmarted God. They figured that everyone would know who they were if they beat God at His own game. But playing those kinds of games with God is danger-ous. He is a Father who will discipline us for our own good, and He dis-ciplined those ancient tower builders.

While they were in the middle of construction, He changed all their languages. Friends had no idea what their buddies were saying. They all had to live in separate areas, grouping themselves with people whose language they could understand. I hope some of those people were hum-bled enough to ask God to forgive them.

God wants us to give honor and glory to Him. He doesn't want us to build huge houses and have fancy cars and be famous just so that we can get people to pay attention to us. He wants us to use whatever He's given us to bring glory to Him. Are you building any Towers of Babel in your life? If you are, why don't you come on down and point people to Jesus?

Jim

Shut the Door!

The prince of this world cometh, and hath nothing in me. John 14:30.

Tara was awakened abruptly in the night by the sound of scuffling feet outside her bedroom window. Still half asleep, she heard what sounded like a can being tossed into the street, some muffled laughter, and a heavy object rolling away.

Paralyzed by fear, she finally got up the courage to kneel at the head of her bed and look out the high window. It was so dark she couldn't tell if the garage door was open or closed. But Dad shut it every night. She stared hard into the murky blackness. Yes, the big door appeared to be open, but she couldn't see the family car!

"Daddy!" she whispered a moment later by her parents' bed. "Wake up! I think the car's been stolen!"

Dad took a flashlight and stumbled out the front door toward the garage. Twenty seconds later he came flying back into the house, fully awake. "I'm calling the police!" he shouted. "The car's gone!"

A few minutes later a tall police officer sat at the kitchen table with Dad. "The chances of ever finding your car again are very slim," said the officer soberly. "It's probably on its way to Mexico already."

"Oh, if only I'd made sure that the door was shut!" groaned Dad.

Jesus told His disciples that *He'd* closed the garage door. Well, not exactly in *those* words. What He actually said was that Satan had wanted to get hold of Him, but He'd not left anything in His life "open" to sin. That's how Jesus was able to stay safe from the devil's power.

It's the same with us. We can close the obvious doors by avoiding things like drugs, corrupt videos, music with foul lyrics, and dirty literature so Satan can't get a foothold. But you can read about other "doors" through which he can sneak in and steal our souls in texts such as Ephesians 4:26, 27, and Galations 5:19-21. God will help us "shut" those doors and keep our souls safe for eternity.

By the way, about noon the day after the car theft Tara's dad found the family car at the bottom of the hill!   **Carolyn**

Oct 7

You Can't Have Your Cake and Eat It Too

"You can't have your cake and eat it too." I'm a little embarrassed to admit this, but it wasn't until a few years ago that I really understood what that meant. I was thinking of the statement in two steps: first, being handed my cake, and then eating it. It seemed very logical that I could eat my cake after it was handed to me. So when people said I couldn't have it and then eat it, it didn't make sense.

But just recently I learned that through the years the phrase somehow got turned from its first usage. It used to be said "You can't eat your cake and have it too." In other words, you can't expect to eat your cake and still have it available. You can't spend money without lowering your bank account. You can't spend your life seeking worldly pleasures and expect to draw closer to Jesus. You can't expect to break the law and live without a guilty conscience. You can't eat your cake and have it too.

Every decision you make either strengthens or weakens your connection to God and, ultimately, the direction of your life. If you stop to think about what you do day after day you begin to understand what's important to you. What do you spend most of your time thinking about? Getting rich, or knowing God better? Getting an A in math, or thinking up ways to cheat for that grade? Do you value the approval of your friends over what you know to be right? Are you more interested in what you can have on earth than in what's waiting for you in heaven? The Bible tells us where to put our treasures. It's in **Matthew 6:20: "Store up for yourselves treasures in heaven" (NIV).** You do that by believing in God and living a life of kindness and honesty.

One of the horrors of facing death is the realization that you have misspent your life. Christians don't suffer that horror. A good life is a rewarding one, and it leads to an even more rewarding life in heaven.

Nancy

284

King of Gold

Don't let the excitement of being young cause you to forget about your Creator. Honor him in your youth. . . . Fear God and obey his commandments, for this is the entire duty of man. Ecclesiastes 12:1-13, TLB.

I remember hearing the story of King Midas when I was a kid. As I recall, the story says everything King Midas touched turned to gold. How would you like to be able to do that? Well, that story is just made up, but there is a true story about a real King Midas. Oh, things didn't actually turn to gold when he touched them, but when you read about all the riches he had, it seems like everything was turning to gold.

This king's name was Solomon. In 1 Kings 10 the Living Bible says that each year Solomon received gold worth about $20 million, and that didn't even include what he received in taxes and trade. This guy had so much gold he made armor and shields for his soldiers out of gold. He also had a giant throne made of ivory, overlaid with pure gold. Even his drinking cups were made of gold. He had horses and chariots and ships. You name it, he had it. He was richer than all the kings on earth.

Do you know how he got all those riches? God gave them to him. Actually, God gave them to him because he didn't ask for them. He asked for wisdom to rule his people. God thought that was the wisest choice he could have made, so God also gave Solomon everything else he could dream of.

But guess what? Pretty soon Solomon started concentrating on all the riches God had given him. He started marrying foreign wives who worshipped idols, and soon Solomon forgot all about God. Solomon tried it all. He had riches and pleasure galore. He also experienced a lot of pain. But after experiencing everything that this world has to offer, Solomon came to this conclusion: it's all meaningless without God. Take Solomon's advice. Keep your eyes focused on Jesus. Don't wait until you're old to serve God. **Jim**

O_{ct} 9

Laddie and Boy

No servant can serve two masters: for either he will hate the one, and love the other; or else he will hold to the one, and despise the other. Luke 16:13.

Laddie and Boy were two drug-detector dogs working with a police force in England. After a drug bust in the Midlands, the two dogs were ordered by one of their police officer masters to lie down and wait for further instructions. The officers wanted to interrogate two of the suspects before deciding whether or not to arrest them.

Since it was a cold night, the officers questioned the suspects in front of the fireplace. While they were being questioned, the suspects stroked and patted Laddie and Boy until the canine pair drifted into dreamland. The suspects evidently said something that led the policemen to believe they were guilty, and one of the officers quickly rose to arrest them. The suspects stopped stroking the dozing dogs, and one of them raised his head and growled at his master, while the other one actually jumped up and sank his teeth into the police officer's leg!*

Boy and Laddie had a problem deciding whom they wanted to be their masters. Obviously, they couldn't be loyal to both the police and the suspects. Just like those police dogs, you and I can't be faithful to both Jesus and what the world has to offer. We have to make a choice.

When Jesus told His disciples "No servant can serve two masters," some Pharisees—overhearing His words—began to sneer. But Jesus knew their hearts. He knew they were greedy and stacking up riches for themselves at the expense of the poor. He reminded them—and His disciples—that what this world holds as being of great value is really nothing in the eyes of God.

That's a good reminder for us, too—especially when we, like Boy and Laddie, start thinking we can serve two masters.   **Carolyn**

---

*Stephen Pile, *The Incomplete Book of Failures* (New York: E. P. Dutton, 1979), p. 63.

Feel the Pinch

Mike and Billy, both 12 years old, lived near a beautiful lake. During the winter Mike's mother drove the boys to school. But come spring, when the weather was warm and sunny, they walked to school. It always took them longer, but one day it took them extra long. They had to walk past the lake. Well, actually, they didn't *have* to walk past the lake, but they chose to, so they could stop and do a little fishing before school.

The time flew by. When Mike finally looked at his watch, he realized to his horror that it was 10:30. "I can't believe this!" he said. "My dad's going to kill me!"

Billy said, "We've got to come up with a good reason we're late, and then it'll be OK." Both boys thought about this as they hurriedly packed up their fishing gear and hid it under a bush. Then they ran toward the school. By the time they faced the teacher, they had the perfect excuse.

"My mom's car had a flat tire, and she couldn't change it, so we had to run the rest of the way here," Mike lied.

The teacher nodded solemnly. "All right," she said. "Take out a piece of paper and take your chairs to opposite corners of the room." When the boys were settled far away from each other, the teacher said, "Now write the answer to this question: Which tire was flat?"

Needless to say, both Mike and Billy "felt the pinch." Everyone who has ever done something sneaky and gotten found out knows what they felt like right then. They didn't like themselves very much. What does **Proverbs 14:9** tell us about guilt? **The common bond of rebels is their guilt. The common bond of godly people is good will (TLB).**

Every one of us has choices to make that will result in either "feeling the pinch" of a guilty conscience, or feeling good. Sometimes you have to choose a clear conscience over, say, a friendship. That's a wise, but often difficult, choice. At the moment it may not feel very good, but when you realize that you did the right thing, you'll like yourself.

Do you want to know how to have good feelings? Good feelings come from being responsible. **Nancy**

Oct 11

Put Up Your Guard!

Carry each other's burdens, and in this way you will fulfill the law of Christ. Galatians 6:2, NIV.

My son has a hedgehog named Spike. Hedgehogs are cool animals who have little spikes sticking out all over their bodies. But they're shy, and it takes them a while to decide whether you are friendly or not. Whenever they need to defend themselves, they stick those little spikes up straight, and believe me, they're sharp. I can't pick up Spike without getting stuck. My son can, though. I think it's because he spends more time with the little guy, and Spike knows that Christopher is friendly.

Some people are like hedgehogs. Whenever people get close to them, they stick up their "spikes." Sometimes they seem mean or stuck-up. But do you know what the problem really is many times? Sometimes people have hurt them before. They're afraid someone else (like you) might hurt them again.

So should you give up on these hedgehog-like people? No way! Jesus was always helping hurting people. It takes a lot of patience, and sometimes you might even get *your* feelings hurt. Jesus had His feelings hurt when He helped some people too, didn't He? But it's worth it when that hurting person finally smiles back at you, or when they say thank you for being a friend. Even if they don't, though, there is someone smiling at you. God, from His home in heaven, is smiling the biggest smile you can imagine when you help those hurting people.

Do you know who is hurting? Maybe they aren't very well liked. Maybe it's one of your classmates at school. You can even start by practicing kindness in your own home. It may not be easy, but God can help you get the job done. Get down on your knees right now, and ask Him to help you bring joy into a hurting person's life. **Jim**

Abandoned!

The angels are . . . spirit-messengers sent out to help and care for those who are to receive his salvation. Hebrews 1:14, TLB.

Mom, I can't see a thing—it's pitch-black!" gasped 9-year-old Troy as he watched the bus disappear into the African night. "Where are we? Why did the driver just push us out?"

"I don't know, darling," answered Mother, trying to keep the panic out of her voice.

Mother and Troy had been returning from a long one-day trip to visit Matthias, a discouraged student, who was studying at a seminary up the coast. After an afternoon of visiting, prayer, and a little sight-seeing walk with the student, Mother and Troy had climbed back into a bus for the four-hour return trip.

"Mom, is the driver drinking beer again?" Troy asked at one of the many stops the bus made.

"I'm afraid he is," answered Mother.

As the bus neared Mombasa, the intoxicated driver jammed on the brakes, opened the door, and ordered, "Get out here!" and then literally pushed Troy and Mother off the bus.

In the pale light coming from the door of the bus, Mother and Troy seemed to be standing beside an endless orchard of some type.

"We can't see anything," whimpered Troy.

"But our guardian angels can," answered Mother. "Let's pray and then just start walking."

Fifteen minutes later, as Troy and Mother were carefully shuffling along in the humid darkness, a small car whizzed by. Then another one. Soon they came back. Both cars were carrying a very large Indian family.

"Are you in trouble?" asked the father. "Don't you know how dangerous it is out here at night?"

When Mother named the rural hotel where she and Troy were staying, one of the children said, "Why, that's exactly where we're going right now for supper!"

"Our guardian angels sure knew which road to lead us onto, didn't they?" exclaimed Troy after a thank-You and good-night prayer.

"They surely did!" answered Mother.   **Carolyn**

Oct 13

Make Fish of One and Fowl of Another

A few years ago I attended a nurses' conference. When I filled out my registration form, I had specified "no meat" for the catered lunch. I expected to get a salad or meatless manicotti. So I was surprised when they set before me a plate of poached fish and rice. That wasn't meatless to me!

I have since learned that meats are divided into the categories of fish, flesh, and fowl. Red meat (or flesh) is another term for beef—it is red before you cook it. White meat might mean it's chicken or pork. And seafood isn't considered meat at all, because it doesn't have blood vessels in it.

To "make fish of one and fowl of another" means to discriminate between things that are basically similar, such as fish and fowl. It means we approve or disapprove of something based on the *label* we give it, not on what it *really* is.

People do that to food, and too often we do that to each other. Students are divided into "gifted" and "challenged" and are stereotyped by their achievements. Unfair distinctions are too often made between the wonderful diversity of races and cultures that exist in our world. One race or culture assumes they somehow have different rights than another. Sometimes we assume that uneducated villagers in another part of the world don't have the capacity to feel the same love toward their families as we do, as though it doesn't hurt them as much when a loved one dies as it would hurt us.

But we are all humans. And we are here on this earth together to be the hands and hearts of Jesus to each other. Jesus said in **Matthew 25:40, "I tell you the truth, whatever you did for one of the least of these brothers of mine, you did for me" (NIV).** Let's not look at our differences. Rather, let's look at what we share with each other. Do you see the kid that everyone laughs at? Imagine how he or she feels and stick up for them whenever possible. The new kid in school? Invite them into your group. That's how we show our love for God.   **Nancy**

Saved From the Grip of Death

The Lord knows how to rescue godly men from trials. 2 Peter 2:9, NIV.

The sun was shining as George sat down on the porch swing in the backyard. Out of the corner of his eye he noticed some movement in the grass. He walked over to the spot and found a baby squirrel struggling to survive. Its eyes were closed, it was gasping for breath, and looked as if it would die within a very short time. *What can I do?* thought George. *There must be a better way of putting the squirrel out of its misery.*

"I know," George said out loud. "I'll take him to Lonnie." Lonnie had a very large python. The python had to eat, and this squirrel was going to die, so it seemed like the best thing to do.

George went to the garage and put on some gloves. He walked back to the squirrel and picked it up. It was barely moving now, so he took it to Lonnie, who put it in the python's house. George didn't really want to see the python eat the squirrel, so he left.

The next day Jonathan came over to visit. "Hey, George!" Jonathan shouted as he rode up to the yard on his bike. "Guess what? I've got a new baby squirrel!"

"Where'd you get him?" questioned George.

"Well, I was visiting Lonnie yesterday, and I saw this cute little baby squirrel in with his python. I told Lonnie he couldn't kill that squirrel, so he gave him to me."

"Oh," said George. "Do you think he'll live?"

"Well, I fed him some milk with an eyedropper, and he's already looking better."

I don't know if you've thought about it, but without Jesus we'd be like that little squirrel—caught in Satan's grip. But God came down and rescued us so we could spend eternity with a Father who loves and cares for us. **Jim**

Oct 15

Why God Turned Off the Radio

"Indeed, the very hairs of your head are all numbered." Luke 12:7, NIV.

Spooked by the slightest rustle of wind in the tall branches above me, I quietly made my way through the damp waist-high elephant grass to the rendezvous place—a rocky outcropping where several dormitory girls had asked me to meet them in the predawn darkness for Bible studies.

With the help of my flashflight I located the rocks and sat down on their cold damp surface. Just as I saw the girls' kerosene lantern bobbing its way down the hillside, a most irritating sound sliced through the air. It was that of an out-of-tune guitar, backed up by a totally out-of-tune foreign band. Someone in a little hut down in the draw had just turned on their transistor radio for the day—and turned it on *loud!*

"Oh, God," I sighed, "do we have to put up with *that* distracting noise?" An immediate silence descended on the hillside.

"Bonjour, madame," whispered the girls as they approached. After praying together, we opened our Bibles and, in the light of the kerosene lamp, began to read. "Indeed, the very hairs of your head are all numbered."

"Does that mean," asked one of the girls, "that God knows everything about us? About what I want and what I need?"

"I guess so," answered the other one, "if the number of hairs on our heads are important to Him."

Yes, God knew about the hard times in the future of those students. He knew the strong faith they'd need to have in Him when their country, Rwanda, would soon be plunged into an unspeakably brutal civil war. He knew the comfort of prayer the girls would need to face death or a deathlike existence in a refugee camp or a lonely life after friends and loved ones had been killed.

Yes, the very God who knew the exact number of hairs on my students' heads also knew they needed those early mornings of quiet time—without distraction—to begin making Him their best friend.

And *that's* why I believe God turned that radio off for two years!

Carolyn

Poke Holes in Something

I t was a brand-new coat I had purchased at Costco—brilliant teal, with a purple and teal plaid lining. I was quite proud of the thing because it was such a change from the dull gray herringbone wool coat I had worn for 8 years. Unfortunately, I left it hanging over the back of a chair one evening while our little rabbit was out of its cage.

I didn't notice anything when I put it on the next morning. In fact, not until I sat down at a very respectable restaurant that evening to have dinner with friends did I notice the little hole the rabbit had nibbled in one of the sleeves. As I brought my dinner roll daintily to my mouth, I was stunned to see the tattered hole screaming out at everyone. The rabbit had "poked holes" in my appearance, and there was no way I could appear sophisticated as long as I wore that tattered sleeve.

To "poke holes" in someone's argument means you destroy their logic or reasoning so that their argument "doesn't hold water" because of all the holes. You destroy their credibility.

There's another argument that goes around that needs some holes poked into it. That's the argument that because you did something wrong, or because you don't go to Sabbath school every week, God is disappointed in you and can't love you, and that your future in heaven is impossible. Nonsense! God loves you because He made you. He no doubt feels sad if you don't enjoy going to church. He intends for church to remind us how much He does love us. He's sorry when we make choices that aren't right. But that doesn't mean He doesn't love you.

Don't you feel proud when you create something of your own—a picture or a poem or cookies? Of course! And God is proud of you too, because He created you to look like Him. **Genesis 1:27** says, **God created man in his own image, in the image of God he created him; male and female he created them (NIV).** Not only do you look like Him, you also like to create things—just as He does. You were created by God. That's why He loves you so much. And that's what makes you special, no matter what you do. **Nancy**

Oct 17

Just Ask

"Whoever enters through me will be saved." John 10:9, NIV.

There I was, standing on a stool by the anesthesiologist, looking into the open chest cavity of a heart patient. The doctors were performing open heart surgery. I had seen the scalpel open the skin on the chest of the patient. Then they used a small saw to cut the sternum (breast bone) in half. A special tool opened up the chest, more cuts were made, and there it was—the heart. What a wondrous creation God has made!

I'll never forget what happened next. The doctors actually stopped the heart and hooked the patient's arteries and veins to a heart/lung machine. The machine did the work of the heart, which was packed with ice and stopped so the doctors could do the necessary repairs.

I'm not a doctor or a nurse. I don't even work in a hospital. So how did I get into an operating room to watch open heart surgery? I asked! There was a time I thought I wanted to be a doctor. I had always wanted to see an operation, and I knew the nurse who scheduled the surgeries. I guess most people don't get the chance to see open heart surgery. So I feel pretty lucky. Well, I guess it wasn't really luck; it was because of who I knew.

Some people think they have to be lucky to be saved. No way! You get to heaven the same way I got in the operating room—you need to ask the right Person. It's who you know.

Do you know Jesus? He just asks that you come to Him. I never would have made it into the operating room if I hadn't walked through the doors. Come to Jesus today; ask Him to save you. And guess what? He will!

Jim

Living in Fantasyland!

Commit everything you do to the Lord. Trust him to help you do it and he will. Psalm 37:5, TLB.

A recent study shows that more and more teenagers are not living in the real world. Because of school, home, and friend problems, kids are "retreating" into their bedrooms to form a new "family." The members of this new family are the telephone, the computer, and the television. Many adults seem driven to live in Fantasyland too.

One such adult was a king named Ludwig II. About the time of the American Civil War, various European wars were also in full swing. King Ludwig II of Germany decided not to live in the real world. Maybe running a kingdom was just too stressful for him. So he chose to live in a fantasy from the past—about 600 years in the past, to be exact.

How did he do this? Well, so fascinated was he by life in the Middle Ages that he began pouring everything from his bank accounts into the building of medieval castles. When he'd used up all of his personal money, he started spending the government's money on his castles. By and by, King Ludwig II had built three huge castles. (Neuschwanstein, the most famous, is the one after which the Fantasyland castle at Disneyland is modeled.)

But sooner or later, reality caught up with Ludwig, as it does with all of us. Ludwig's wasteful castle-building proved to his subjects that he was no longer fit to be their king. Germany needed a king who lived in the real world, and Ludwig couldn't deal with reality. His wacky building program caused the downfall of his kingdom.

Like King Ludwig, we can retreat into Fantasyland for only so long. We can hope our fantasy life will go on forever, but make-believe castles will eventually crumble. One day we will have to look life squarely in the face.

When times are tough, the safest family we can surround ourselves with is God, our Father, and Jesus, our Brother. God has promised that if we will just trust Him with reality, He will show us how to deal with it.

Carolyn

Oct 19

Back-Seat Driver

B ack-seat drivers. "Look out!" they scream as you back up the car. "Slow down!" they hiss as you round a corner. It's as though they're trying to drive the car from the back seat with a steady stream of unsolicited advice.

Many people of Jesus' day found the words of **Matthew 19:30** very difficult to understand. **"Many who are first will be last, and many who are last will be first" (NIV).** The people in high positions, who were first, didn't want to be told they would be last. But what Jesus meant was that the things people strive for on this earth aren't always the things that count toward eternal life. People who are in the "back seat" of life—the people who are anxious and dependent on others, will someday be honored by Jesus.

There was once a bus driver who hated his job because at a certain point in his run he had to wait for seven minutes beside an ugly littered area of town. He often wished someone would do something about the unsightly mess. Then one day he decided he would use his seven-minute wait to pick up as many tin cans and as much paper trash as he could. Within a few days the place was looking better. He began to look forward to his seven-minute delay.

When spring came, he was so enthusiastic about his project he decided to scatter flower seeds around. By the end of the summer many of his passengers had heard about his project and rode with him to the end of his run just to see how how beautiful the area had become. His silent works ended up bringing him recognition. He was moved from the "back seat" to the "front seat," the way all of those who trust Jesus will eventually move. Don't let anyone tell you that Christianity doesn't get you anywhere. It does: straight up.   **Nancy**

Teach and Learn

I pray that you may be active in sharing your faith, so that you will have a full understanding of every good thing we have in Christ. Philemon 6, NIV.

I want you to find a Bible, open it quickly, and find a short verse that you've never seen before. Now, on a sheet of paper write the verse you've found. Next, everyone should spend a couple minutes teaching the rest of the group their verse. Go over it several times to make sure everybody knows the verse. Last, ask each person to recite all their new verses.

OK, here's the big question: Which verse did everyone know best? Probably the one they chose. There's something about teaching something that causes the teacher to learn best of all. You may have repeated all the other verses correctly, but the one you know best is most likely your own.

The things you share you understand better yourself. Any teacher will tell you the one who learns the most in the classroom is the teacher. And that's what Paul was saying to Philemon and his friends when he said that sharing their faith would give them a full understanding of the good things about Jesus. Have you shared your faith lately? An amazing thing happens when you do. You'll be the one who learns most.

So don't wait until you think you know everything in the Bible to tell someone else about Jesus. When Jesus healed people, all some of them knew was that they were healed. They knew nothing more about Jesus than that. But that didn't stop them from telling others about what Jesus had done for them. Just tell what you know, even if you know only a little bit. You'll learn more about Jesus than you thought you ever could simply by sharing with someone else. **Jim**

Oct 21

Good Dog!

An evil man is snared by his own sin, but a righteous one can sing and be glad. Proverbs 29:6, NIV.

Police officers in a Detroit, Michigan, precinct rushed to the scene of a burglary. But they could find no clues as to the identity of the burglar—just a nondescript dog wandering about the premises. The dog seemed friendly enough and enjoyed the officers' company as they checked for fingerprints, out-of-place objects, and any other sign that might reveal the identity and whereabouts of the burglar.

"I don't know what else we can do here," sighed one investigator. "We've checked everything we can think of."

Another officer leaned over to pat the friendly dog. Then he straightened up and looked thoughtfully into the distance. He looked down at the dog again. "You know," he said to the group, "this hunch may be totally off the wall, but you never know unless you try." He looked at the dog sitting at his feet. Suddenly he commanded, "Home, boy!"

The dog immediately came to attention, turned on his heel, and trotted purposefully down the street.

"Let's follow the dog!" the officer yelled.

Sure enough, the obedient dog led the police officers straight to the home of its master—the very burglar who had committed the robbery the police were investigating!

People in authority are always thinking of ways to trap lawbreakers. But in the case of sin, the person who continues in a known sin—without repenting of it and allowing God to help him change their behavior—will eventually trap himself. Just as the dog's burglar-master did.

The Bible says, "An evil man is snared by his own sin, but a righteous one can sing and be glad." Gaining God's victory over a stubborn sin is certainly something to be glad about! And knowing that that sin has lost its power over our life—and can't trip us up again—is *really* something to sing about!

Carolyn

---

*Taken from Stephen Pile, *The Incomplete Book of Failures* (New York: E. P. Dutton, 1979), p. 62.

Button of the Cap

I'm told that in China it used to be considered mandatory to compliment others while sort of putting yourself down. A polite conversation might go something like this: "Hello, my most treasured friend! And how are your beautiful children?" To which the friend would reply, "My ugly little brats are at home with my ugly wife. I am supposed to invite you to my small and dirty home for an evening of your most stimulating conversation."

Perhaps this cultural rule against speaking highly of yourself is the reason the Mandarin Chinese used a system of buttons on their caps to denote their social class. That way new acquaintances could tell just by looking at their cap how much respect a person deserved. Certainly the "polite" conversation wouldn't reveal much.

Today, if someone says they're "the button on someone's cap," it means they're "on top." Their friendship is a status symbol. Isn't it too bad that some people collect friends for what those friends can do for *them*, instead of what they can do for those *friends*? What's more, isn't it too bad those people don't think much of themselves unless a certain person spends time with them?

Galatians 3:28 says that we are all buttons on God's cap. **There is neither Jew nor Greek, slave nor free, male nor female, for you are all one in Christ Jesus (NIV).** God doesn't see us in colors or social classes or IQs. Paul advises us to look past our differences and become one family in Christ. Christians aren't prejudiced against races. They may have differences with certain individuals who are a different race than they are, but it isn't fair to dislike a whole race of people because of how they look or because of the actions of one person of that race. God wants us to give up our stereotypes and get to know people as kindred spirits, who have feelings just as we do. We're happiest when we accept others and practice the golden rule.

Nancy

Oct 23

I See It, I See It!

Let him who boasts boast about this: that he understands and knows me. Jeremiah 9:24, NIV.

Aren't the stars amazing? There are so many stars no one has been able to count them all. The bigger stars are actually planets that you can see through a small telescope you can buy at some department stores. I love to look at the moon. Even with binoculars the mountains and craters on its surface are visible.

One of the largest telescopes in the world is found in Russia's Caucasus Mountains. It's an unbelievable 80 feet long and weighs 935 tons. What's so amazing about this telescope is not its size, but what it can see! If you were to light a candle and drive 15,000 miles away, you could still see the candle with this Russian telescope!

You see, those big telescopes have huge mirrors that collect light from the night sky and direct that light through the lenses so that you can see a planet or star more clearly. It makes sense. If the lights are out in your room, you can't see what is in your room very well. Your eyeballs can collect only so much light. If you turn the lights on, you suddenly see all kinds of objects around you. It's the same with the night sky. We can't see some of the planets with the naked eye because they are so far away, and their light is so dim. If you have a telescope with a big mirror collecting every bit of light it can, you begin to see the planet you couldn't see with only your eyes. It's like opening a whole new world.

God can open the eyes of your understanding, too. He can help you see that He's taking care of you. Even when the light of hope is dim, God can help you know that your life is in His hands. **Jim**

Flour Before Candy

"Martha, Martha," the Lord answered, . . . "only one thing is needed. Mary has chosen what is better, and it will not be taken away from her." Luke 10:41, 42, NIV.

Grandmother had just entrusted $5 and a short grocery list to my little brother and me. "If there's any money left over *after* you get the groceries, you can each get yourself a candy bar," she said.

We pulled our little red wagon to the store and got everything on Grandma's list. But we mistakenly got two 10-pound bags of flour instead of two five-pound bags. Then we got everything else on the list. Right before going to the checkout clerk, my brother chose a Hershey's chocolate bar, and I dropped a Rocky Road into the cart.

"I'm sorry, but you don't have enough money here to pay for all these groceries," the clerk at the checkout counter informed us. This news stunned us, and we realized that we needed to start making some choices.

Grandma had said she was going to make a cake with the flour, so of course the sugar had to stay. We pulled other items out of our cart—eggs, oil, veggies, milk—until the clerk stopped shaking her head. After a quick mental calculation she suggested we trade one of our big flour sacks for a smaller one, and then smilingly checked us through. We arrived home with 15 pounds of flour and five pounds of sugar. (The two candy bars were in our stomachs.)

"What on earth were you two thinking of?" gasped Grandma in disbelief.

In spite of our tears, she sent us back to the store with a note to the clerk, a new list, and a chance to make new choices. But what about the already-eaten candy bars, you ask? Well, we had to pay for *that* choice out of our allowance.

Once Martha complained to Jesus that her sister Mary, who was listening to Jesus, was not choosing to help her in the kitchen.

"But Martha," Jesus said, "Mary has made the best choice possible." Jesus was trying to teach Martha what our grandmother taught my brother and me. Veggies before candy bars—and Jesus before everything.

Carolyn

Oct 25

Raise an Eyebrow

Have you heard that scientists have looked forward to this date for hundreds of years? What's that? You haven't heard? What did your eyebrows just do when you heard that first sentence? Did they rise? To be honest, scientists don't care what today is; I just wanted you to raise your eyebrows about something.

Many times we do things with our bodies that communicate messages that are as good as words, if not better. You wave at a friend without saying a word, and your friend knows you are glad to see her. And when someone tells you something you find surprising, you usually raise your eyebrows in disbelief.

Sometimes, when I read the Old Testament stories of God sending out His people to kill other people in neighboring towns and villages, my eyebrows go up. I can't believe that a loving God would do that. It's sort of like the bits and pieces of a story I heard on the news a few years ago about a man in Mexico who cut off a girl's legs. He just went right into her house and cut off her legs while the neighbors cheered.

"How cruel!" you say with a gasp.

Yes, it might have been cruel—if the girl hadn't been trapped in her home after an earthquake and the man was a rescuer with no other way to get her out of the rubble. She was grateful, for it was the only way she could get out alive.

When you read the Old Testament stories about people dying because they didn't obey God, it sounds as though God is mean. Hold on. Don't raise your eyebrows. There is a lot we don't know about Old Testament times. God will give us explanations when we watch the "videos" of our histories with Him. Don't let anyone make you mistrust God. God isn't a mean supernatural tyrant. God is love. Read **Jonah 4:2** to see what Jonah said about God. **I knew that you are a gracious and compassionate God, slow to anger and abounding in love, a God who relents from sending calamity (NIV).** Just be patient; it will all make sense.

Nancy

302

Time for a Test

I have hidden your word in my heart that I might not sin against you. Psalm 119:11, NIV.

You may not like it, but tests are a fact of life. You have to take a test to get your driver's license, and you have to take tests to pass your classes. If you want to become a lawyer or a doctor or even a licensed plumber, you have to take a test. You even have to take a test to go to college.

The most unusual college entrance exam may be the one at Al Azhar University in Cairo, Egypt, where many people are Muslim. The Koran is the holy book of the Muslim worshiper, and it's almost as long as the New Testament of the Bible. In order to qualify to attend Al Azhar, each student must memorize and recite the entire Koran—which takes three entire days. Now that's a lot of work! You might think not very many make it into this famous university. Not so! In fact, at one time it was the world's largest university. Of its approximately 20,000 students, all of them have passed the entrance exam. Every single student has memorized and recited the entire Koran.

How much of God's Word do you know? I'm sure you know many verses already. Memorizing God's Word helps you keep your eyes on Jesus all throughout the day, and it helps you to stay away from sin.

Why don't you memorize some of the Bible today, and add another verse tomorrow? Pretty soon you may find that you know a whole chapter, or even more. It's a wonderful way to get to know your best friend Jesus even better. When He comes again, He'll be looking for those He knows. If you've gotten to know Him through His Word, you'll be one of those He'll smile at and say, "Come, I know you." **Jim**

Oct 27

One Fat Cat!

The Lord make you to increase and abound in love one toward another. I Thessalonians 3:12.

What do you call an older man with a lot of money? A fat cat. So then, what do you call an older *cat* with a lot of money? I suppose "fat cat" would work for that too. If so, then Flat Nose, who lived in Chicago, Illinois, was one fat cat!

Flat Nose was one of five cats belonging to Mrs. Margaret Montgomery at the time she died. In her will she stipulated that her entire estate ($24,000) go to her cats. Of the five felines, Fat Cat—er, I mean, Flat Nose—survived the longest.

The late Mrs. Montgomery's employee cared for the cats and, according to the requirements of the will, made the animals home-cooked meals that included regular servings of pot roast. Flat Nose didn't die until he was 20 years old!

Once a man whose name no one seems to remember left his inheritance to a cat hospital. And not for better medicine or equipment, either. No, the unknown cat lover dictated that his inheritance pay for an accordian and the salary of hospital employees who would play that instrument in an area where all the sick cats could hear it. "Play it continuously—day and night," the will stated. The unknown benefactor felt that the sound of an accordian is close to that of a human voice and would comfort the sick animals.

Someone who has written a book about cats states that in California cat owners can find the following for their pets: an acupuncturist, a cat resort, a cat department store, a feline rest home, a rent-a-cat agency, cat psychiatrists, cat acting coaches, and an annual meowing contest.

The "fattest" cats I've ever heard about were owned by a man in San Diego, California. Upon his death his two cats inherited $415,000.

It is wonderful when people place a high value on animals that God has created. But it's far better when people place a high value on each other. For not only does God create people, He values them. He values you so much He gave His very own Son to die so that you can live with Him forever. **Carolyn**

Taken from Leonore Fleischer, *The Cat's Pajamas* (New York: Harper and Row, 1982), pp. 49-51.

Scarce as Hen's Teeth

Have you ever looked in a chicken's mouth? If so, did you notice whether or not they have teeth? We had a chicken coop in our backyard when I was a little girl, and many times I was sure those hens had teeth when I nudged them off their nests so I could collect the eggs. They pecked so hard sometimes that it felt like teeth were biting me. I looked many a chicken in the eye—and in the mouth—but I never saw a tooth.

The fact is, chickens don't have teeth. If anyone should ever find a chicken with even one tooth, it would definitely be world record material. So if someone tells you something is as "scarce as hen's teeth," it means you'd be extremely lucky to find it.

In our fast-paced lives today, quiet time alone is often as scarce as hen's teeth. And yet quietness is where we find God. Read what **Psalm 46:10** says about it: **Stand silent! Know that I am God! I will be honored by every nation in the world! (TLB).**

Remember those times you've found God? Sitting on velvet grass in the gentle sun beside a quiet lake . . . hearing the birds sing and the wind playing in the trees . . . the sound of a canoe paddle slicing the water . . . feeling peaceful, as though everything was right in the world . . .

Every living thing is proof enough that God is real. He is the unseen force that holds our universe together. And whether we acknowledge Him or not, He just keeps on being there, lending His power to gardens in the spring, keeping each star in its special place.

Take two minutes to be silent and study God's handiwork. He cares about *you!*

Nancy

Oct 29

At Just the Right Time

Like newborn babies, crave pure spiritual milk, so that by it you may grow up in your salvation, now that you have tasted that the Lord is good. I Peter 2:2, 3, NIV.

At what time of year would you guess most mammal babies are born? If you guessed spring, you're right. Why do you think most mammal babies are born in the springtime? Well, God planned for most mammal babies to be born at this time of the year so they would survive. If they were born during any other season, storms, cold, and other harsh weather would kill most of them. God knew these fragile little babies would need plenty of warm sunshine and fresh food to help them survive the first few months of life. He also knew they would need the long summer to learn how to fly, run, swim, or crawl. What good care God takes of all His creatures!

Sometimes young people may worry they aren't good enough for God's standards. You may have been tempted to think that you can't live up to His expectations. Actually, you can't. None of us can. But forgiveness is available, and God can change us. God knows you are a growing Christian and that it will take your entire life to become what He wants you to be.

Baby birds can't fly when they first enter the world; the legs of a foal are so wobbly you might wonder if it'll ever run. God also knows and understands that you are a young Christian with many years of growing ahead of you.

So what can you do to grow as God's child? Just as each baby animal depends on its parents for food, shelter, and the lessons of life, you and I need to depend on God, our heavenly parent. If we keep our attention fixed on Jesus, He will give us all the strength we need to grow up into mature Christians. Jesus will walk with us every step of the way, at just the right time.   **Jim**

Damon's Denial

Whosoever will come after me, let him deny himself, and take up his cross, and follow me. Mark 8:34.

I used to do drugs a lot," said Damon,* a distant relative we hadn't seen since he was small. "And I do mean . . . a *lot* of drugs. But I don't do them anymore."

"Was it hard to break the habit?" asked Mother.

"Not for me," Damon said with a careless wave of his hand. "I can take 'em or leave 'em. Excuse me a minute." Damon disappeared outside and didn't return for a long time. This was only the first of such "disappearances" during his visit.

We began noticing other bizarre behavior patterns too. He didn't shower; he dropped his dirty clothes in piles around the house. Once when he and I went shopping for Mom, Damon stood on the curb in front of the grocery store and started waving to strangers in passing cars. He'd call out, "Hey! Great to see you again!" "When are you coming over?" "Yep, it's me! Back in town!" Our rising suspicions proved true. From other relatives we learned that Damon was still on drugs but was continuing to live in a state of complete denial.

A couple years later Damon came to visit my parents again. "It was so sad—and weird," my mother told me over the phone after he'd left. "All he was wearing were hiking shorts, sockless tennis shoes, and an ankle-length Batman cape. He's still in denial about drugs."

Before we point an accusing finger at Damon, however, let's remember it's easy to "be in denial" about a bad temper, gossiping, or an overeating problem. We can be "addicted" to certain kinds of music, video games, or even TV shows. It's especially easy to deny that *we* might be partly responsible for situations like bad grades or broken friendships.

Jesus told us that the only thing He wants us to deny is ourselves—deny those sinful cravings for things, activities, or behaviors that harm us. Why not ask Jesus to help us look for any areas of denial in our lives? He wants to help us deny ourselves and follow His wholesome, healthy, happy example. **Carolyn**

---

*Not his real name.

Oct 31

Another Lie Nailed to the Counter

In a creaky general store that smelled of sweet soap and dusty flour, a tradition was once started in the name of crime prevention. On the wooden counter beside the cash register were several coins nailed to the counter.

One day a customer, who was new to the town, inquired about the history of the coins. "Why are they nailed down?" he asked.

The store owner twitched his mustache and hitched up his pants. "Those are counterfeit coins," he informed the man. "And they're nailed there so that you and I both know that I can tell a counterfeit from a real coin. You hand me one of those counterfeits, and I nail it to the counter and call the sheriff! Then you go with him to our local jail for a bread and water diet. Do I make myself clear?"

The customer nodded nervously and made his purchase quickly—in real money.

When we say there's been "another lie nailed to the counter," we mean another scam or coverup has been exposed. It's a warning to future con artists that we're on to them. There's another lie that needs to be nailed to the counter—the lie that we have to be "good" before Jesus loves us. It's true that eventually God will have to destroy those who do not repent, but it's also true that God wants all of us to recognize what we're doing and turn to Him. He wants us to pull Him close to our hearts and get to know Him. That's what will save us. You see, God doesn't condemn us—that's the lie that must be nailed to the counter. We condemn ourselves. **John 3:17** says, **God sent not his Son into the world to condemn the world; but that the world through him might be saved.** If we persist in doing the same sins over and over, on purpose, with no regard for others, eventually we singe our consciences and don't care about anyone but ourselves anymore. That's called the unpardonable sin, the sin that will keep us out of heaven. But if we keep on listening to the Holy Spirit and trying to make good choices, we stay close to God. His arms are open to us!

Nancy

Tune It Up

By faith Enoch was taken from this life. Hebrews 11:5, NIV.

A tuning fork looks a little like a fork you eat with, but it has only two prongs and is much thicker. Piano tuners and some musicians use them to tune their instruments. When you tap the tuning fork on a wooden surface and then hold the handle on a table or board, you hear a unique musical note.

Musical notes vibrate at a certain rate, and that vibration is what gives the note its particular tone. For instance, middle C vibrates 264 times per second. The piano tuner listens to middle C on the piano, then he or she listens to the tuning fork to see if they are both vibrating 264 times per second. When they are, the middle C key on the piano is in tune.

It's important for the Christian to be in tune with Jesus. When we live in tune with Him, we'll live the happiest lives possible. Enoch lived in tune with God. The Bible says Enoch walked with God. He was so close, in fact, that he was taken to heaven to live with God permanently.

Living in tune with God isn't always so easy though, is it? There are many things to distract us. We need to make an appointment with God each day—and keep it. The more we get to know Him, the easier we'll be able to tell if our heart is in tune with His.

Without a tuning fork, most piano tuners wouldn't know if the instrument was in tune or not. It might sound OK, but unless they compared it with the tuning fork, they'd never really know for sure. Unless you and I spend time with Jesus every day, we'll never really know for sure if we're in tune with Him or not. So take your tuning forks—God's Word and time in prayer—and let Him make a beautiful song with your life.　　**Jim**

No Ambulances in Heaven

Blessed are the dead which die in the Lord. Revelation 14:13.

The siren nearly broke my eardrums. My 7-year-old brother and I exchanged frightened glances as we sat beside the ambulance gurney holding our bruised and bleeding mother. She kept trying to smile at us despite the apple-sized purple welt on the side of her face. We were all in shock as the ambulance raced us toward the hospital.

"There's Donovan's house!" my brother exclaimed, suddenly coming to life. "He'd be surprised if they knew *we* were in this ambulance!"

Donovan, a classmate of mine, was 9½, just a little younger than I.

"Our car was broadsided by a drunk driver at a country intersection," Mother told the doctor at the hospital as he checked her over. She had a broken collarbone and a badly bruised shoulder. My brother and I had some ugly bruises, but that was all. Dad was well enough to ride to the hospital in a police car.

I finally had the courage to ask, "How is Grandma?"

No one answered my question. She'd been in the back seat with my brother and me. But when we'd all been thrown out (those were the days before seat belts), she, being heavier than us kids, had fallen into the ditch. Then our crumpled car had rolled on top of her.

A couple hours later a family friend broke the news to my brother and me. "Your sweet grandma is dead. She was killed instantly and never knew what happened. But she's asleep in Jesus now, so she can never feel pain again."

The next few days we all hurt so bad. Dad kept saying, "Time will heal our hurt." Mom kept saying, "Jesus will make Grandma live again someday."

Well, I hurt *real bad* for a while. I missed my grandma so much—she'd lived with our family since before I was born. But Dad was right—after some time passed, I *didn't* hurt so much.

But most important, Mom was right. Jesus *will* come back to resurrect Grandma, who died loving Him with all her heart. When angels bring her up out of her grave, I'm going to be the first one running into her arms (that is, if my little brother doesn't get a head start).

Something else that makes me as glad is this: God won't need any ambulances in heaven.   **Carolyn**

Grist for the Mill

H e'd been in three schools in one year. Neil seemed to be on a downward spiral as far as his school life was going. Every time he was asked to leave a school, it was the same. "Neil has a behavior problem," his parents were told. "He doesn't stay in his seat, he talks out of turn, he is disruptive in the classroom, and we just can't operate a positive learning environment with him here. I'm sorry. We don't have any special education classes he can attend, so we feel it's best for the other students if you find another school for your son."

At last Neil's parents chose a school near their home. Imagine their happiness when Neil's school counselor told them Neil's behavior could possibly be helped by medication. They were referred to a psychiatrist who specialized in attention deficit disorder, or ADD. She explained that some people need medication to keep the metabolism in the brain "hot" enough so that they can sit still and concentrate without having to invent stimuli, such as moving around the room or shaking a leg or something else that their brain instinctively makes them do.

In a short time Neil's behavior improved, not only at school, but also at home as his emotional outbursts became less often and less intense. At last Neil began to enjoy learning and began to believe he was a good kid after all. All his bad experiences in school had been "grist for the mill" in helping his school counselor and the doctor diagnose his problem.

Grist is grain that's waiting to be ground into flour. It may seem somewhat worthless compared to flour that has many more uses. Although it may seem worthless now, eventually it will be turned into something of value. Every decision you make can be grist for the mill of your life. Every honest thing you do strengthens your character. Read **John 3:21: Whoever lives by the truth comes into the light, so that it may be seen plainly that what he has done has been done through God (NIV).** Everything that happens to you—the good, the bad, and the ugly—can be grist for the mill if you take the attitude that "I can learn something from this."   **Nancy**

TV on the Brain

Whatever is true, whatever is noble, . . . whatever is pure . . . think about such things. Philippians 4:8, NIV.

When I was a kid my favorite television show was *Lost in Space*. It was about a family who explored other worlds and became lost in space. They traveled from planet to planet, encountering monsters and aliens of all kinds. I still remember all the characters, including the robot, who was smarter than everyone on board the ship. Unless his circuits were damaged he would always give the right instructions to the human crew. I can even remember some of the episodes.

That was 30 years ago. Why do I remember all that? Because it's etched on my brain. God created us with brains that are made to lock information in permanently. That's a good thing. Unfortunately, when we make decisions to put bad information into our brains, that's locked in permanently too. Whether it's something we see on TV or read in a book or a joke we hear, it's liable to come rushing back into our memory when we least want it there.

The best solution is to make good choices about what we put into our brains. Not because someone told us we should, but because God knows what He's doing. He wants to keep us from sin for our own happiness. There will always be times when we have the opportunity to put something into our brains, when no one is looking, when our parents or teachers will never find out. Of course God knows. And you'll never forget it.

God created your brain to be able to do that. Put in the good stuff. That's how the Owner's Manual, God's Word, says you'll get the best results from that wonderful piece of equipment God put in your head.

Jim

Jo Jo

Come unto me, all ye that labour and are heavy laden, and I will give you rest. Matthew 11:28.

J o Jo,* a Labrador retriever, was trotting down a Kentucky road, minding his own business. He was never sure what happened. Perhaps he strayed out too far into the road. Perhaps the person operating the oncoming vehicle was driving under the influence of alcohol. All Jo Jo knew was that when he heard the screech of brakes, he immediately felt a tremendous impact that sent him flying through the air.

Landing in a heap, Jo Jo heard the vehicle rush off down the road. The retriever tried to raise his head, but every effort brought him immense pain. Then from somewhere in the depths of his canine brain, Jo Jo remembered a warm place that smelled of friendly humans and cats and dogs. After many attempts, Jo Jo finally held up his head, and then struggled to his feet. Incredibly, Jo Jo dragged himself for one mile down the road to the place he had seen in his mind—an animal hospital! There Jo Jo "checked" himself in. Soon the veterinarian and his staff were hard at work examining and caring for Jo Jo.

How did Jo Jo know about the animal hospital? Well, that's where his master boarded him while he was away on trips. That's where Jo Jo received attention, good care, and a lot of love.

As automatically as Jo Jo found the animal hospital when he was in pain, Jesus wants us to come to a hospital when we're desperate, too. Jesus tells us where the hospital is. He says, "Come unto me . . . and I will give you rest." Our loving Saviour has all the right remedies for any hurt we might ever have. Like Jo Jo, who found help by going to the animal hospital, we can always find help by going to our "hospital," Jesus.

Carolyn

_____
*_Guide_, Aug. 9, 1997, p. 32.

Nᴏᴠ 6

Strike While the Iron Is Hot

Maybe you've watched a blacksmith pulling on the bellows to heat up the coals, checking his piece of iron that glows red-hot in the fire. At some precise time known only to him, the smithy removes the iron from the fire and begins striking it with a special mallet to form it into what he needs.

If you've ever seen a blacksmith at work, you know he doesn't stop and cross his arms to chat with you after he pulls the iron from the fire. The iron cools very quickly. He knows he has to "strike while the iron is hot" and keep working while it's soft enough to mold.

To "strike while the iron is hot" means to do things while you have the chance. Right now, while you're young, is the time to begin practicing Christian values that will result in a good adult character. The Bible tells us how in **Psalm 119:9: How can a young man stay pure? By reading your Word and following its rules (TLB).** Some Bible rules worth following are honesty, kindness, and purity in thoughts and language. You may find yourself in a situation where you have an opportunity to practice one of the rules of the Bible. Strike while the iron is hot and put the rule into practice immediately. Maybe it will be the opportunity to be kind when friends are gossiping unkindly about someone in your class.

Religion involves more than just avoiding sin or covering it up after it happens. Religion involves a change in your attitude toward sin to the point that it doesn't even seem attractive to you. Religion also involves repeated decisions for right. Strike while the iron is hot and make good decisions. Many chances to do good come only once, and they come suddenly. Take the attitude that you will capture every chance you can find to do good. **Nancy**

314

The Wrong Commandment

We do not use deception, nor do we distort the word of God.
2 Corinthians 4:2, NIV.

Kristen was just a little girl, but even when you're only 3 years old you can learn to follow the rules of the house. She knew she wasn't supposed to eat in the living room. She was supposed to take her shoes off at the door, and she was never to jump on the bed. Kristen's mom and dad wanted her to learn these lessons early so they wouldn't have a problem when she was older.

One day when Kristen's parents were doing some work around the house, they noticed that Kristen had wandered off. They quickly went to look for her, because a 3-year-old can find all kinds of things to get into. As they walked down the hall, at the other end of the house they heard a squeaking noise. Entering their bedroom, they discovered Kristen jumping up and down on their bed. At first Kristen looked as if she didn't know what to say, but soon she blurted, "And Jesus said, 'Thou shalt jump on the bed.' Matthew 6:44."

Of course there is no verse in the Bible about jumping on a bed. Kristen was just looking for an excuse. But that's pretty quick thinking for a 3-year-old.

Instead of searching the Scriptures to discover what the Bible says, many look for verses to support what they *want* to believe. There have even been people who used the Bible to persuade others that they were Jesus. Many hundreds have taken their lives because their so-called Jesus told them to.

Open your Bible and ask God to show you what He wants you to know. Let God know that you'll accept and obey whatever He wants to teach you. It may not always be comfortable following God's instructions, but you'll have confidence in knowing that you're following God's pure untwisted Word. **Jim**

Holdup!

O thou that savest by thy right hand them which put their trust in thee from those that rise up against them. Psalm 17:7.

"We're in trouble now!" shouted Pierre, the mission truck driver, slamming on the brakes.

"Do government soldiers always point bayonets at you like that?" gulped Jon, the student missionary in the front seat beside him.

"Those aren't government soldiers, son," answered Etienne on the other side of him. "Those are rebel soldiers."

"What are they going to do?" asked Jon.

"You never know," answered Pierre, "but I'm going to pray that they *don't* find all that money the treasurer just got from the bank to pay all the mission workers. But there's really no place back there to hide it!"

"Out!" ordered a big angry-looking man dressed in camouflage fatigues, his bayonet almost in Pierre's face.

"Faster!" commanded another at the rear of the truck, where several rebels took turns prodding workers with their bayonets as the frightened men jumped to the ground from the canvas-draped back of the truck.

"Just a little inspection," said the head rebel. "Nobody'll get hurt if you follow orders."

"Need to see everybody's ID!" shouted a soldier from the back.

Jon reached for his passport. But no one seemed interested in it. The rebels were busy emptying the workers' wallets. *Dear God,* prayed Jon, *please don't let them find the mission salary money!*

Two soldiers jumped into the back of the truck and ran their hands around the insides of some spare tires. Another searched the cab. Then the leader ordered everyone back onto the truck and sent them on their way.

A knocking on the cab window made Jon turn around. Through the small pane of glass between the cab and the back of the truck he saw the beaming face of the mission treasurer, who was holding up a pouch full of money!

"Thank You, Lord!" the three front-seat riders said almost in unison.

Back at the mission the treasurer explained, "Just before jumping down I threw the pouch into one of the spare tires. God must have kept that rebel's hand from touching it!"

Carolyn

Backing the Wrong Horse

Back when DeLorean automobiles first came out, there was the usual excitement, because they were new and different. I was fascinated with DeLoreans because their doors opened in a unique way. Instead of having a hinge at the front of the door, the hinge was at the top, so that the door lifted up, much like a bird lifts its wings, and the rider climbed under the "wing," pulling it down to close himself or herself safely inside.

In the beginning it was a prestigious thing to own a DeLorean. They were unique—made of stainless steel. And they were owned by unique people. Some thought a new trend in car design had been born. As it turned out, they were "backing the wrong horse." The DeLorean company went bankrupt. The dream died.

The expression "back the wrong horse" comes from the sport of horse racing. Players gamble on which horse they think will win the race. If their horse doesn't win, it is said that they backed the wrong horse. It also means that someone is supporting a losing cause.

The Bible warns us that just before Jesus comes, the world is going to be in chaos. We already have seen earthquakes, floods, famines, riots, wars, disasters of the week, and murders on a daily basis. Even so, there are those who say that we who believe Jesus is coming again are backing the wrong horse. Don't believe it! You may be one of the people who sees Jesus coming in the clouds. If your life is a struggle right now, hold on! Jesus is coming again. Whenever you get scared, repeat the words of **Psalm 23:4: Even though I walk through the valley of the shadow of death, I will fear no evil, for you are with me; your rod and your staff, they comfort me (NIV).**   **Nancy**

Look at Me!

Pride goes before destruction, a haughty spirit before a fall. Proverbs 16:18, NIV.

It's hard being a younger brother or sister. You want to do what the older kids in the family do, but you're not tall enough or strong enough or mom and dad won't let you. It's an exciting moment when you finally catch up and can do what your older brothers and sisters are doing.

It was like that for my sister. She wanted to do what I was doing, but being almost two years younger than I, she was always just a little behind. Finally the time came when she could ride a bicycle too, but I was still ahead of her. You see, I could ride with one hand, and Kay couldn't. She'd practice by taking her hand off for just a second. She didn't want me to see her, so she'd go out on her bike when she thought I wasn't looking.

Finally the day came when she was going to show me that she could ride with one hand, just like me. I was sitting on the front porch as she rode down the street. She turned her bike around and headed down the sidewalk. As she came to our house she shouted, "Hey, look at me!" As I looked up she rode one-handed past the front of our house.

What Kay didn't notice was the neighbor's huge mail truck that was parked with its back end hanging over the sidewalk. I was so busy watching as my proud sister rode with one hand that it was too late when I noticed where she was headed.

Even though my sister and I argued from time to time, I didn't laugh at what happened next. Kay's bike went under the back end of the mail truck while her body smashed into the big vehicle. Ouch!

Sometimes we want everyone to look at us. We want to be recognized and appreciated, but it's best to look for God's approval rather than other people's. That way we don't have to go around shouting, "Hey, look at me!"

Jim

The Egotist's Valentine

These six things doth the Lord hate: yea, seven are an abomination unto him: a proud look, a lying tongue, and hands that shed innocent blood, an heart that deviseth wicked imaginations, feet that be swift in running to mischief, a false witness that speaketh lies, and he that soweth discord among brethren. Proverbs 6:16-18.

Oh, who will be my valentine? Just you wait and see.
It's someone with a high IQ (Who looks a lot like me).
A face to launch a thousand ships . . . The latest new hairdo . . .
Who qualifies on all these counts? I do! I do! I do!

Oh, who fulfills my every dream, sits on my highest shelf?
This special one takes all my time (If I do say so myself!).
So if you're wondering who I'll choose to be my valentine
Watch as I whisper in my mirror: "Be mine! Be mine! Be mine!"

To be perfectly honest, I've never heard of anyone giving themselves a valentine, especially one that sounded as self-centered as this one does. But I have known people who couldn't walk by a mirror without looking at themselves.

Egotistical people are hard to be around. Even God says that "a proud look" is disgusting to Him. In fact, of seven things the Lord refers to as abominations, a proud (or egotistical) attitude heads the list.

I'm not sure why. Maybe it's because it was pride that caused Lucifer's downfall and caused him to brag, "I will be like the most High" (Isaiah 14:14). Maybe it was because it was pride that caused Eve to want to be as intelligent as God, causing her to believe the lies of the serpent in the Garden of Eden. (See Genesis 3:5.)

How different from proud sinners was Jesus when He lived on this earth! Although He had every reason in the universe to be proud, He "humbled himself, and became obedient unto death, even the death of the cross" (Philippians 2:8).

When we ask Him, He will help us have His own sweet, loving attitude. Now *that's* an attitude that attracts valentine cards!   **Carolyn**

Don't Take Any Wooden Nickels

Wooden nickels, once quite popular in some of the general stores in America, were simply discs of wood with a picture of someone, often an American Indian, branded on one side, and the name of the store branded on the other side. Customers were given a certain number of wooden nickels for each purchase they made in that store. Certain items in the store could be exchanged for a certain number of that store's wooden nickels.

It took quite some time to collect enough wooden nickels to equal anything of value. And what many customers didn't realize was that everything in the "wooden nickel" stores was priced higher than anywhere else. Still, customers thought they were getting something for nothing, and many of them shopped nowhere else. Eventually the word got out that the wooden nickel scam benefited nobody but the store owner. People were warned not to take any wooden nickels.

And that's good advice for us, too. Don't blindly follow the crowd, because the crowd doesn't always know what's best. A crowd can get you into trouble. One of the tasks of growing up is to learn to be smart enough to make smart decisions, even though no one else may think as you do. It took one person to see through the wooden nickel scam. That person took the time to think it through and shared their insight with someone else. The news was passed along, and soon most everyone was wise and making good decisions. The result was that wooden nickels weren't used much anymore.

It takes courage to think for yourself. But it takes only one person to turn things around for many others. Many an adult credits their child for helping them decide to go to church or to conquer a bad habit. Read what **1 Timothy 4:12** says about that: **Don't let anyone look down on you because you are young, but set an example for the believers in speech, in life, in love, in faith and in purity (NIV).**

Presidents of big corporations and presidents of the United States—anyone in a position of responsibility—got there because they have learned how to make responsible decisions. **Nancy**

Warning, Warning!

In your anger do not sin. Ephesians 4:26, NIV.

August 27, 1883. The people of the islands of Indonesia were going about their business as usual, when the volcano of Krakatoa blew into the sky with the force of what some scientists estimate as 26 large atomic bombs. Volcanic debris and ash were everywhere. When it was all over, 36,000 people on the nearby islands of Java and Sumatra had been killed by the huge tidal waves it had triggered.

A volcano erupts when the pressure underneath the surface of the earth becomes too great for the earth to hold back. The process may take many years, but when it can be held back no longer, lava and steam spew from the top of the mountain, sometimes without warning.

Anger can be a lot like a volcano. Sometimes it's been building for a long time. There are times when people seem to lose their temper for no particular reason at all. But there is a reason. It's found below the surface of their lives. Sometimes people have been hurt by other people, and they blow up at the first person who crosses them.

Being angry is not a sin by itself. The Bible says "In your anger do not sin." It's what you do with your anger that can be sin. Do you use anger to hurl insults and say rude things to people? When we're angry because someone did something wrong to us, it's an act of selfishness. We need to ask God to help us love the other person and pray for them. But God wants us to be angry when people are treated unfairly. When someone else is hurt by another person, use your anger to stand up for that person. While you should never be cruel to the people who have hurt you or someone else, you should let them know, in love, that what they've done is wrong. I think that's what Jesus was doing with the people who were desecrating His Father's temple when He drove the money changers out.

We all experience anger. Ask God to help you direct yours to help others. **Jim**

Nov 14

Toads and Other Heroes

Happy is the man that findeth wisdom, and the man that getteth understanding. Proverbs 3:13.

You oughtta see this big toad out here," said my uncle as I joined him and my aunt on the front patio of their home one hot summer evening. "Comes out at night when the porch light's on and just snags them bugs."

I looked at the huge wart-covered creature and shuddered. Then I let out a little scream as two small somethings flew from behind my chair and landed just in front of my bare toes.

My aunt and uncle laughed at me, and my uncle drawled, "Them's just little toads, hangin' 'round their big hero, watchin' how he catches bugs."

My aunt added, "Night after night we've watched his stomach hang lower and lower till we think he can't hold any more."

"Yep," continued my uncle. "Then a lightnin' bug or a big June bug comes crawlin' up, and you can just see the big dude eyein' him and sayin' to himself, 'Can I get 'im down, or can't I?' Then he snags 'im, and the wings is half hangin' outta his mouth. And you see him stretch a front leg, or hunch a shoulder forward, tryin' to make room for the rest of that thing."

"Then he's full and hops off," said my aunt.

"Yep," said Uncle. "And all them little guys move in and start snaggin' mosquitoes. They've been learning from their hero."

Little frogs hang out with big frogs and learn a lot from them. We learn a lot from our heroes too. Whether we realize it or not, our heroes—entertainment stars, sports celebrities, or friends from school— are always giving us lessons about how to live life. And sooner or later our heroes influence our choices.

The Bible tells us we become like those on whom we focus. Our heroes can either lead us closer to God or down the road to self-destruction. It all depends on whom we choose as heroes.

And just in case you forgot, having Jesus as our number one hero is the only guarantee to making right choices and having a happy life—forever.

Carolyn

He's His Own Worst Enemy

The czar of Russia once offered a $30,000 prize for the best portrait of himself. More than 1,000 artists competed for the prize. A few days before the judging was to begin, the committee was passing through the gallery where the pictures were to be hung and noticed that the task was almost completed. All, that is, except for one picture that was leaning against a wall that was already covered with pictures. With a quick glance at the portrait, the committee members agreed that it wasn't really anything that spectacular, and perhaps no one would notice if that particular portrait wasn't displayed.

Their comments were overheard by none other than the artist himself, who rushed over to defend his work. "Begging your pardon," he interrupted them, "but I have every right to display my painting. I suggest you keep an open mind and let me have it hung at just the right height with just the right light, and then you pass judgment upon it under the right circumstances."

Reluctantly the committee members agreed. And—you guessed it—when the vote was counted, this artist's portrait was the one selected as the very best. When viewed in the right light, it was wonderful!

Have you ever been told that you aren't going to amount to anything? Sometimes teens hear that from their friends or from their teachers or families, and they mistakenly believe it. They become their own worst enemy because they put themselves down again and again. Many of us admire someone else's talent and think that the things we're good at aren't as important. That doesn't mean we're a failure. The important thing is to recognize what we do well and improve on it, as **Ephesians 4:1** seems to say. **I urge you to live a life worthy of the calling you have received (NIV).**

Maybe you don't look like you're going anywhere right now. Don't give up on yourself. Don't be your own worst enemy! Think positively! Keep on doing your best. And at the right time, in just the right light, you will shine. Everyone has at least one gift hidden away inside, and you can find yours. **Nancy**

Nov 16

Don't Try This at Home

Do not fear, for I am with you; do not be dismayed, for I am your God. Isaiah 41:10, NIV.

Can you float on your back? With some air in the lungs, and the correct positioning, almost anyone can do it. Floating on your back is no miracle, of course, but what about walking on water? With all your weight on your two feet, it's impossible, as a Hindu yogi named Rao found out in 1966 when he tried to walk on water.

The crowd, who had paid to see this amazing feat (no pun intended), waited in hushed silence as yogi Rao prayed at the edge of the five-foot deep pond. With his prayer finished and his yogi robes swishing in the breeze, Rao stepped with confidence into five feet of water—and quickly sank to the bottom, his yogi robes no longer swishing in the breeze.

But there were two men who *did* walk on the water. Jesus and Peter. Here's how it came about. One windy night Jesus sent the disciples ahead in a boat on the Sea of Galilee while He stayed behind to pray. I suppose the disciples thought Jesus would find another boat, but Jesus didn't feel like using a boat that night. When He got to the water's edge, He just kept walking—on top of the water! The disciples thought He was a ghost.

When Jesus came a little closer, He told them not to be afraid. "If that's really You, Jesus, let me walk out to You," Peter called out.

So Jesus said, "Come."

And guess what? Peter walked on the water too! That is, until he became afraid of the wind and sank.

It's pretty easy to be afraid of things, isn't it? But remember this: Jesus is in charge of everything. So the next time you become afraid of something in your life, pray, and know that if Jesus can walk on water, He can certainly solve your problems.

Jim

Pack Rats and All!

Better a little with reverence for God, than great treasure and trouble with it. Proverbs 15:16, TLB.

First I heard it scurrying across the floor," said my dad, "then I felt some little tugs on the blanket, and the little guy ran across my legs."

"Ooooh, yuck!" I groaned.

"Next I heard the pack rat start dragging one of my shoes away."

"Where were you again?" I wanted to know.

"In Minnesota, recruiting students for the Christian school where I taught. I'll never forget those families up in remote northern Minnesota. They lived in one-room log cabins with maybe a suspended curtain or two separating tiny portions of the house into bedroom spaces for privacy."

"Were the houses dirty—you know—" I asked delicately. "With the rats and everything?"

"Oh, no, they were clean, but the people just couldn't afford insulation. And that night, after sharing what little food they had with me, they pointed out the curtained-off space where I'd be sleeping—and warned me not to leave my shoes on the floor."

"Why?" I wanted to know.

"I guess the salt from perspiration in the socks and shoe leather attracted the rats. Well, hearing all this kind of spooked me, especially when I started hearing rats a bit after we'd all retired. Of course, when I heard one of my shoes being dragged off, I dived for both of them, then locked them in my suitcase until morning."

"Did the kids from that family ever come to your school?" I wanted to know.

"Yes, they certainly did. But they were so poor those girls had just three dresses apiece for summer *and* winter. But they were the neatest-looking dressers in the school. They'd wash one of their dresses every night and iron it and always looked just fine, in spite of their being so poor. And know what else?" asked my dad. "They were the happiest kids in school. I guess, like the apostle Paul, they'd learned the secret of being happy. They chose to be very thankful for what they *did* have—pack rats and all," nodded Dad with a chuckle. **Carolyn**

Keep Up With the Joneses

Y ou know how it is when your friends all wear the same things, and you want to have it too. Maybe they can afford $50 jeans, but your family struggles just to keep you in church school, so you have to wear hand-me-downs or nonlabel jeans. Sometimes it's hard not to be able to "keep up with the Joneses."

When my husband was in college, we lived in a tiny little apartment called the Vets' Apartments at Walla Walla College in Washington State. We didn't think of ourselves as poor, although we didn't really have much money, but we knew that someday we'd live better. It was quite easy to "keep up with the Joneses," because all our neighbors were poor too.

Our first Thanksgiving there I realized how poor we must have seemed to the local church members, because the Pathfinders came to our door, handing out food baskets. I had handed out food baskets when I was a little girl, but I never thought I would ever be poor enough to receive one! It made me happy, and it made me cry. It also made me realize how much a little thing like a food basket and a caring smile can mean to someone who doesn't have very much.

If you have a classmate who's having a hard time trying to keep up with the Joneses—and the Joneses are you—try not to notice. Better yet, tell your friend you don't care what anyone wears; it's what's inside that counts. **Proverbs 14:21** gives advice on how to treat the poor. **He who despises his neighbor sins, but blessed is he who is kind to the needy (NIV).**

Nancy

Safely Hidden

I long to dwell in your tent forever and take refuge in the shelter of your wings. Psalm 61:4, NIV.

Charles was sitting in his house by an open window enjoying the sunshine and fresh breeze, looking at his garden below. He looked forward to this time of peace and solitude away from the cares of the world. Then out of the corner of his eye he noticed some movement. A small bird darted frantically back and forth. The sharp eyes of a hawk were trained on the little sparrow, its talons poised to attach themselves to the smaller bird's body.

By now Charles was focused on the battle. He stood up to get a better view of what was about to happen. As the two birds moved closer, the small sparrow quickly darted toward the open window. Flying directly at Charles, the little bird disappeared into the folds of his coat. Looking somewhat confused, the hawk turned and flew off into the beautiful morning sky.

Charles Wesley, the man who watched that minibattle, was a famous preacher and songwriter. Those two birds reminded him of the struggle we often have in life. Satan, our enemy, is out to get us, but we have a God who will protect us in the folds of His love. Charles wrote the song "Jesus, Lover of My Soul" because of what he saw that morning. Thousands have sung that song with the assurance that Jesus is always standing near to protect and hide us from the cruelties of this world and from Satan's claws.

It's true that we are in a battle, a battle that's just as real as the one that hawk and sparrow were fighting that day. But we have a place to hide, a shelter that will protect us. That shelter is Jesus. Run to Him and hide today.   **Jim**

"Will Eat You Alive!"

Do not give dogs what is sacred; do not throw your pearls to pigs. Matthew 7:6, NIV.

Let's see what's on your menu for breakfast," said the just-back-from-vacation veterinarian's assistant. She reached for the cat's medical chart as the yellow-eyed animal purred on the other side of the cage bars. There, scrawled across the top page, was this warning in big red letters: "Will eat you alive!"

The woman looked from the chart to the beautiful gray cat, purring contentedly. "Surely this note can't be about you! All animals love me. How about a little rub behind your ears?" She opened the cage door a crack and reached a finger behind Maisie's right ear. With lightning speed the cat sank 10 claws and a set of teeth into the woman's hand.

"Yeow!" she screamed.

The cat, back arched and eyes dilated, growled at her from a cage corner.

"Good morning," called the veterinarian in a cheery voice. "Welcome back from—" He stopped short when he saw the torn hand of his shocked assistant. "I see you've met The Shredder," he said. "You just can't trust her."

A cat psychiatrist might have diagnosed Maisie as "socially unbalanced." Since kittenhood she had never let anyone but her owner touch her. When guests came over, Maisie would lounge in their midst, tempting someone to pet her. She'd even rub up against people's legs and purr. She was never dangerous—until someone trusted her enough to reach out. Then she'd attack when least expected.

Like Maisie, gossipers, exaggerators, and liars have a way of suddenly turning on others who reach out to them. In Matthew 7:6 Jesus warned against trusting ourselves to those who might turn on us. But even if we can't trust certain people with our secrets, we can always pray for those individuals.

By the way, if we want to be like Jesus, we'll take care not to be a Maisie, either.

Carolyn

Keep Your Head Above Water

The one thing that spells disaster when you fall into the water is going under and not getting your head back up. You have to admire a person who's struggling in the water, but keeping their head up in spite of everything. When we're going through rough times, we sometimes say, "I'm barely keeping my head above water."

A drowning person should keep their head up above water, not only so they can get air, but also so they can see the shore and head toward it. They can hear any directions someone may need to give them, such as where a dangerous current may be, or from which direction a lifeboat is coming.

Sometimes our lives may become so complicated and busy that we think the pressure is going to kill us. Papers are due, tests are coming up, friends don't understand our intentions, parents tell us no, TV programs tempt us, we have a bad hair day—all of this can make us feel as though we want to stay in bed and pull the covers up over our heads and disappear. But we have to keep on putting one foot in front of the other, taking one task at a time, keeping our heads above water.

Sometimes our lives are so busy we don't have time for Jesus anymore. Jesus hasn't changed—but we have. If you've come to that point, beware. You're not keeping your head above water spiritually. What does **Romans 12:2** say about that? **Do not conform any longer to the pattern of this world, but be transformed by the renewing of your mind (NIV).** You become what you think about. You are transformed by renewing your mind. That might be as simple as saying to your overwhelmed self, "Just for today, there's nothing that God and I can't handle together." Then take life's challenges one at a time, from the most urgent to the not so important. By leaning on God, you'll keep your head above water. **Nancy**

Wilbur Knew Where to Go

Jesus answered, "I am the way and the truth and the life. No one comes to the Father except through me." John 14:6, NIV.

Wilbur was an English box turtle. And while it's true that a turtle can't do much, Mrs. F's class loved Wilbur. They believed that Wilbur knew who they were and loved them back. Each day different students would bring Wilbur pieces of fruit and vegetables, and Wilbur seemed quite content in his big aquarium with all the food he could eat.

One day Darla asked Mrs. F if she could take Wilbur out for recess. "Please," begged Darla, "I promise to take good care of him and always watch him carefully."

With a little bit of worry in her voice, Mrs. F said yes and watched Darla take Wilbur out the door and into the school yard. When it was time to come in from recess, the children lined up as Mrs. F called them. Everyone quietly filed into the classroom and sat down for their math lesson. After a few moments of silent work everyone heard an "Oh, no!" from the back of the room. Then Darla burst into tears and said, "I forgot Wilbur outside!" Everyone gasped.

"Quickly!" Mrs. F said. "Let's all go outside and search for Wilbur."

After 15 minutes of frantic searching, Wilbur was still lost. Crying children gathered around Mrs. F. Their best little buddy was gone. What would they do? It was then that Christina asked, "Why don't we ask Jesus to help us?" So they all knelt down on the playground and asked Jesus to help them find Wilbur. Mrs. F told the children to hold hands and walk across the playground, and on the first trip across the yard Darla spotted Wilbur. They all thought Wilbur was lost, but Wilbur knew just where he was going—straight toward the pond on the other side of the fence.

You and I won't ever get lost in this world as long as we head toward Jesus. Wilbur was headed for a safe place, and Jesus is the safest place I know for you and me.

Jim

Tubular Trouble

A wise son heareth his father's instruction. Proverbs 13:1.

M y dad must think we're real wimps!" exclaimed Kurt. "First he makes us put on these stupid life jackets, and then he says we have to get out at the first bridge and wait for him to pick us up."

Nicky dipped his head back into the river water and looked up at the nearly cloudless sky turning in slow circles as he paddled his inner tube. "Yeah, Dad *did* seem kind of paranoid."

"He could have at least let us go until the third bridge," complained Kurt, settling down in his inner tube.

"Well, we can have a good time until the first bridge at least," said Nicky, trying to get his friend in a better mood.

But at the first bridge Kurt called out, "I'm going on!"

"Wait! What about your dad?" asked Nicky nervously.

"We'll get out at the second bridge and walk back."

But the current picked up, and the boys couldn't get to shore at the second bridge or the third bridge.

"Oh, man, we're dead meat now!" cried Kurt, clinging to Nicky's tube as the third bridge passed quickly overhead.

Nicky said, "I don't want to spend the next two months floating through northern California, or have my life end when I go over a waterfall somewhere."

"Oh, man, I never *thought* about that," Kurt said, his voice catching.

"Well, I think your dad did, and that's why the first bridge was such a big deal to him."

"A bridge! A bridge!" called Nicky after what had seemed like miles of floating and hours of cooking under the summer sun. "Look at all the first-aid equipment and stuff. Must have been an accident—or a drowning!"

"I don't care. Let's head for shore," shouted Kurt as he flopped over on his stomach and began madly paddling. "It's our last chance!"

A search-and-rescue team, a sheriff, and Kurt's relieved—but very distressed—father met the wayward inner-tubers at the base of the bridge.

"A wise son heareth his father's instruction," states the Bible. And after his tubular trouble, Kurt resolved to do a *lot* more listening to his father's instruction than he'd done in the past. **Carolyn**

It Goes Without Saying

The English language is a funny one. Often we make a statement that contradicts what we really mean. Take "it goes without saying," for example. We say something doesn't need to be said, and then we say it anyway.

There are many things that don't need saying. You don't need your friend to say he or she likes you; you just know you care about each other. And a person doesn't need a busload of friends to be happy. Studies show that the average number of "good friends" each person has is three. The Greek philosopher Aristotle once asked, "What is a friend?" then answered his own question with "A friend is a single soul dwelling in two bodies."

It goes without saying that God loves us. He is our friend, and His love is huge. Before you read about it in today's text, see if you can say **John 3:16** from memory. **For God so loved the world, that he gave his only begotten Son, that whosoever believeth in him should not perish, but have everlasting life.** When God loves, He loves a world. And when He gives us something, it is His one and only—His one and only Son. God loves you. It's obvious and doesn't really need saying, but we like to hear it anyway.

In the following sentence, insert the name of each person sitting with you and say it aloud: God loves _____. Now believe it. Christianity is an attitude, the attitude that you are loved by God.   **Nancy**

The Most Powerful Wind

The wind blows wherever it pleases. You hear its sound, but you cannot tell where it comes from or where it is going. So it is with everyone born of the Spirit. John 3:8, NIV.

Two hundred thirty-one miles per hour sounds like the speed of a winning race car. Actually, it's the speed of the highest wind ever recorded on earth. It happened on Mount Washington in the state of New Hampshire in 1934. Mount Washington can be a very deadly place to be when the wind kicks up.

The wind is a powerful force, but it can also be very relaxing if you're sitting in the shade of a large tree on a sunny summer afternoon while it blows gently across your face.

Is it any wonder Jesus used the wind to represent the Holy Spirit? The wind can be quiet, just as the Holy Sprit can be a "still small voice." The wind can be powerful, just as the Holy Spirit came upon Samson and caused him to have the strength to kill a lion with his bare hands. The wind is always moving somewhere, just as the Holy Spirit is always working in the lives of people to lead them to Jesus.

We sometimes forget about the Holy Spirit. The wind is invisible, and in many of our conversations the Holy Spirit is invisible too, but He's just as much God as are the Father and His Son, Jesus Christ. The Holy Spirit does so many important things for us. We need to think and talk about Him more often. He guides us, He helps us pray, He comforts us, and He gives us power to speak for Jesus in difficult situations.

The Holy Spirit, although invisible, is our friend and guide. When Jesus left this earth, He sent the Spirit to be our special helper. Thank You, Jesus, for not leaving us alone, but for sending us the Holy Spirit to be our special assistant here on earth. **Jim**

Bug Zapper!

Forsake the foolish, and live. Proverbs 9:6.

W hoa! That was a big one!" exclaimed Kim. He and Jeff were standing on either side of a huge "bug zapper" lantern hanging in Lori's front yard. All the kids had been dropped off for supper, vespers, and marshmallow roasting at Lori's house.

Zap! Sizzle! Crisp! Plunge! Another charred bug dropped onto the growing pile of insect remains collecting at the base of two wire screens surrounding the brilliant—but deadly—bulb.

"They're crazy!" said Jeff. "Most just follow the crowd and die."

"Look at these guys over here," said Kim, pointing. "They sit in this outer fence-screen thing, watching all the others kill themselves. Then they do the same thing!"

Caroline thought about some temptation "lanterns" in her own life—and about Mom and Dad's too-frequent warnings about MTV watching, or her hanging with "the wrong crowd."

Cut me some slack! she thought. *Sometimes being around my parents is like being in prison! Like I'm gonna do something really dumb and get hurt. No way!*

"Then there are these bugs over here," laughed Kim, "all flying as close as they can—they want to be near the action, but still think they won't get hurt. Sooner or later, they can't help flying closer and closer . . . until they finally get zapped too."

"I can't believe this!" Jeff pointed to a large bug caught in a wisp of spiderweb clinging to the outside screen of the lantern. "It's struggling to get out of the web so it can fly *toward* the light. The web is actually *saving* its life, but it's too dumb to see it!"

Kind of like me not wanting to take my parents' advice sometimes, Caroline reluctantly admitted to herself.

"Did you have a good time at vespers?" asked Dad, when he and Mom arrived later to pick up Caroline.

"Yep," she answered. "Watched a lot of bugs get fried."

"What? Is that *all* you did?" laughed Mom.

"No," answered Caroline. "But maybe it was the most *important* thing I did. Thanks, you guys."

Carolyn

Can't See the Forest for the Trees

Question: How far can you walk into the woods?

Answer: Halfway. Any farther and you begin walking out. It's easy, when you're in the woods, to have no idea where the middle is. You feel like a small ant that's surrounded by towering trees. If you get lost, you try to know those trees by individual characteristics so you can tell if you're walking around in circles or not. Some people make marks in the bark of trees they walk by; others put rocks in the elbow of a low branch. Still other people choose the best idea—staying put and "hugging a tree" until they are found.

It's OK to get to know trees individually. But what "not seeing the forest for the trees" means is that if a person focuses too much on the details of something, they miss the bigger picture. For example, when he or she preaches, does your pastor stand behind a podium or walk around with a little lapel microphone? There are some people who worry so much about whether or not the pastor walks around or stands still (the "trees") that they can't concentrate on his sermon (the "forest"). Too often it's these little things that make people so angry they don't want to come to church anymore. What does **Song of Solomon 2:15** say about little things? **Catch us the foxes, the little foxes that spoil the vines, for our vines have tender grapes (NKJV).** It's not the big foxes—the big things—that make a difference; sometimes it's the little foxes. It's too bad that people miss out on fellowship with others who believe in Jesus because they worry about where the pastor stands to talk to them.

What's most important at church is saying something encouraging to someone else, because that's what being a Christian is all about. And that's part of the reason we go to church: to encourage each other.

Remember, people who can't see the forest for the trees are only going to hurt themselves. Don't let them hurt you, too.　　　　**Nancy**

NOV 28

A Cooling Love

For this cause I obtained mercy, that in me first Jesus Christ might shew forth all longsuffering, for a pattern to them which should hereafter believe on him to life everlasting. I Timothy 1:16.

The weather can do all kinds of strange things. Did you know that the highest temperature ever recorded in the shade was 136°F, in the country of Libya? Virtually no rain falls in Chile's Atacama Desert, although several times a *century* a squall may strike a small area of it.

One of the most amazing stories in weather history happened in the town of Spearfish, South Dakota, in January 1943. At 7:30 a.m., after a night of subfreezing temperatures, it was still −4°F. Two minutes later it was a balmy 45°F—a rise of 49°F! That's one degree every two and one-half seconds!

There was a man in the Bible whose temper once rose about that fast. It happened in the Garden of Gethsemane almost 2,000 years ago. When Peter saw that armed guards were taking Jesus prisoner, his anger boiled over the rim. He took out his sword and chopped off a man's ear. Now, I don't think for one minute that Peter meant to cut off that man's ear. I think he had more serious damage in mind for the man's skull.

Yes, Peter had quite a temper. He was known for his quick harsh words and actions. And yet, when we look at his life later on, we see a humble servant of Jesus Christ. How did it happen? What changed Peter's life? I believe it was the way Jesus treated him. Later, when Jesus was being sentenced to death, Peter denied that he even knew Jesus. Jesus simply looked at Peter with eyes full of sadness and forgiving love. That was it! No harsh words for Peter. No glaring looks. Only a glance that said, "Peter, I love you."

Today Jesus offers forgiveness to you, too, for all that you've ever done. Accept His offer and follow Him. The change in you will be more amazing than the temperature change in Spearfish, South Dakota.

Jim

Scary Safari

Be sober, be vigilant; because your adversary the devil, as a roaring lion, walketh about, seeking whom he may devour. I Peter 5:8.

Lion to the right of us!" called the African safari guide, who was riding in the back of the small Japanese pickup truck. Also in the back of the pickup were 10-year-old Simon and his cousin, Ted, and Uncle Joe, who were visiting from America.

Inside the cab Simon's father, a missionary, jammed on the brakes and cut the engine. Simon heard Mother say, "Wow! Look at that magnificent mane! He's right out here in the open too."

"Look! He's standing up in that tall grass!" whispered Simon to Ted.

"And he's yawning," observed Ted.

"No, I think he's making those growling sounds we hear," said Uncle Joe.

Suddenly Simon swung himself around and through Dad's open window, followed closely by Ted.

Dad turned the key in the ignition. "Maybe we'd better move on now—since there's not enough room in the cab for all of us—and the lion has started coming our way!"

He pressed the starter. Nothing happened.

"Won't it start?" Mother asked in sudden alarm.

"The engine won't even turn over."

Ted and Simon exchanged frightened glances. "Let's pray!" Simon suggested.

Dad kept his eyes closed just a little longer after Simon said amen, then turned the key again. The motor made no sound—but something amazing started to happen. The little pickup began to roll forward—not fast and not far . . . just far enough to reach a little slope in the dirt road. Once on that slope Dad was able to pull out the clutch, jump-start the engine, press down on the gas pedal, and leave that stalking lion in a big cloud of yellow dust.

The Bible tells us that Satan is like a roaring lion, roaming everywhere to see whom he can devour. God answered Simon's prayer in order to provide a way of escape for his family from the African lion. God is even *more* ready to answer *any* prayer to Him in order to help us escape from the most dangerous lion of all, the devil.   **Carolyn**

Blood Is Thicker Than Water

Charles Manson, a convicted murderer with a swastika tattooed in the middle of his forehead, is an avowed satanist, an evil man. In 1975, one of his followers, Lynette "Squeaky" Fromme, tried to assassinate then-president Gerald Ford. She was arrested and jailed.

Lynette's parents were afraid of her, even though she was their daughter. In an interview not long after the arrest, Lynette's mother recalled hearing that her daughter had told someone she had finally come to the place where she could kill her parents. Her mother said, "And yet, as hard as I try to steel myself against caring about her, I can't stop caring. It hurts so badly. No matter what, you can't get rid of the blood that flows there in that girl. It's mine."

To say that "blood is thicker than water" means that people stick up for their relatives and are loyal to their relatives, no matter what kind of people their relatives might be.

The Bible tells us that we are related to God. Christians are "children of God." That means we are relatives of God—brothers and sisters of Jesus. And when the judgment day comes, and we stand before the Judge, blood will be thicker than water. Read what **John 5:22** says about the judgment. **"The Father judges no one, but has entrusted all judgment to the Son" (NIV).**

In his book *Contact: The First Four Minutes,* Leonard Zunin, M.D., tells a story about the Babema tribes of southern Africa. Their approach to dealing with antisocial behavior is for the whole tribe to gather in a circle around the offender. Then each member of the tribe relates, in great detail, every good thing that person has ever done. Everyone takes part, including the children. No good thing is left unsaid. Sometimes several days may pass, but at the end there is a joyful celebration as the person is welcomed back into the tribe. That's how families support each other.

It's reassuring to know that our final judge is a family member. No matter what we've done, we don't have to worry about an outsider judging us harshly. When our judge looks at our lives, it will be with love and mercy, because blood is thicker than water.
Nancy

You Can't Judge a Book by Its Cover

The Lord said unto Samuel, Look not on his countenance, or on the height of his stature; because I have refused him: for the Lord seeth not as man seeth; for man looketh on the outward appearance, but the Lord looketh on the heart. I Samuel 16:7.

There are some amazing little gems in the little town of Herkimer, New York. Oh, you can't see them by looking casually. In fact, most people would pass them right by if they didn't know they were there. They're called Herkimer diamonds, but they aren't really diamonds. Actually, they're quartz, and normally you can't see them. You've got to dig and pick and pry to find them.

For some reason, God formed these little "diamonds" into perfect tiny crystals that look like a jeweler has cut them that way. Finding them is difficult, though, because they're hidden in ugly limestone. You might have to break open hundreds of pounds of limestone before you find that perfect crystal. It's almost like someone pulled the limestone apart, placed the quartz inside, and glued the limestone back together again. You'd never know they were there unless someone told you.

Thousands of years ago there was a boy who was like a Herkimer diamond. David didn't look like a king on the outside. He was young, small, and a shepherd. How could a shepherd be the king? Well, God had great things in mind for David, and he did become not only a king, but a man after God's own heart. God knew David was the man for Him, because God looks on the inside of a person, not the outside.

God has great things in mind for you, too! Maybe those around you can't see it, because they can look only on the outside. And just as Herkimer diamonds are embedded in plain-looking limestone, God sees very precious material inside of you and knows how to get those diamonds out. Everyone who saw David saw a shepherd boy, but God saw a king. And when God looks at you, He sees all kinds of valuables to be used for His kingdom. Let Him take your life and reveal the treasures within.

Jim

Dec 2

Heads Up!

As birds flying, so will the Lord of hosts defend Jerusalem; defending also he will deliver it; and passing over he will preserve it. Isaiah 31:5.

I'd just started shelling peas on the back steps under the eucalyptus trees when the huge black-and-white crow appeared out of nowhere and lighted on a branch above me. I could hear the crow hopping from branch to branch overhead.

Then *crash!* A long twig suddenly smashed on the step just below my sandaled feet.

The crow must have dislodged a dead twig, I thought.

Crash! Another twig. It seemed to have come right from the vicinity of the crow. I moved way over to the right of the step and resumed my work. Almost immediately another sharp twig hit between my shoulder blades.

No way! I thought. *Surely that crow isn't intentionally bombarding me!* I moved three steps down—and watched the crow. Sure enough! He playfully hopped forward until he was directly overhead. Then he loosened a twig and . . . bombs away! Perfect hit! Directly into my bowl of peas.

Well, then it turned into a wonderful game, with me moving up and down the long row of stairs, and the crow changing perches to stay directly above me. Every time I'd let out a little scream or laugh, he'd caw gleefully and bob his head up and down.

Then, just as quickly as he'd come, he took flight, and I never saw him again.

God's deliverance will come as quickly as that crow came out of nowhere to play with me. Jesus told us to watch for signs of His second coming. He told His disciples, "When these things begin to come to pass, then look up, and lift up your heads; for your redemption draweth nigh" (Luke 21:28).

Maybe God said to "look up" so that every time we see a bird flying swiftly overhead, we will remember that soon He will save us with that same swift speed.

Carolyn

Ride the Gravy Train

A s I write this, computer billionaire Bill Gates has just announced his engagement to one of his employees, a computer programmer by the name of Melinda. I don't know what Melinda's financial status is currently, but after she becomes Mrs. Bill Gates she will be a billionaire, sharing her husband's vast fortune. You could say she'll be riding the gravy train.

In the old days, during a cattle roundup, there was one person who was in charge of the cooking. All the food supplies were carried in his wagon. He never had to worry about being hungry, because he always had food handy. He rode the gravy train, which meant he had everything he needed to make himself comfortable.

Most teenagers don't realize it, but until they leave home and get their own jobs and apartments, they are riding a gravy train. They don't have to worry where their next meal is coming from, or whether they'll have a coat next winter, or shoes, or clothes. Their parents take care of all that. They take care of those needs because they love their children and have made a promise to be responsible for them.

Being responsible and caring for someone means you try to help them avoid painful mistakes. When your parents say no, they aren't trying to interfere in your life; they are trying to help you avoid trouble. Your parents are like God in a sense. They are not the enemy; they are your friends. The next time your parents tell you no, don't argue. Take a big breath and remind yourself that your parents are people you can trust. If you ask them you'll probably find they have a very good reason that centers around your well-being.

Most of all, if you follow your Christian parents' advice, you will have no reason to be afraid to meet God. **1 John 2:28 says, And now, my little children, stay in happy fellowship with the Lord so that when he comes you will be sure that all is well, and will not have to be ashamed and shrink back from meeting him (TLB).** If you have gravy today, remember to thank God for your Christian parents, who love you more than any other human on earth.   **Nancy**

Dec 4

You Can Run, but You Cannot Hide

He that covereth his sins shall not prosper: but whoso confesseth and forsaketh them shall have mercy. Proverbs 28:13.

Rocky and Barco are two sergeant majors who proudly wear their uniform each day they are on duty. They aren't ordinary officers—they're dogs! Their job is patrolling for drugs in the Rio Grande Valley along the Texas border. In 1988 alone these valuable hounds "sniffed out" $182 million dollars' worth of drugs. Nobody can hide drugs from their incredible noses. They're so good that Mexican drug dealers put a $30,000 price tag on their heads.

Remember Jonah? I don't know what he was thinking, but he thought he'd get away from God by hiding in a ship going the opposite direction from Ninevah. So God sent a special fish-shaped boat to pick up Jonah. He learned that you can't hide from God!

But stop right there! Why would anyone want to hide from God anyway? All He's offering is love and forgiveness and compassion. That's pretty scary, huh? Actually, the only thing to be afraid of is *not* being on God's side. Drug smugglers can't hide from Rocky and Barco. We can't hide our sins from God. Confess your sins to Him, and let Him show you His forgiveness. There's no need to hide!   **Jim**

Pick It Small!

I am small . . . yet do not I forget thy precepts. Psalm 119:141.

Brand-new, my mandolin cost $300. But the sound it puts out is worth nothing unless I use my 75-cent pick to play it. Here's a story my grandmother used to tell me about something little bringing value to something big.

That little "something" was a small Dutch boy who used to walk to school along a large dike that kept the sea from flooding his village at high tide. Coming home one evening from school, the boy noticed a small hole in the dike through which a thin but steady stream of water was spurting.

The quick-thinking boy shoved one of his skinny fingers into the hole and said to his younger sister, "Quick! Go tell the men of the village the dike has sprung a leak."

Almost as soon as his sister disappeared in the direction of the village, the little boy had to push another finger into the hole. Then another finger, and another. Then his fist and, finally, his whole arm up to his elbow.

Even though darkness fell, that brave little boy stood his ground, supplying the needed strength to keep the huge dike from cracking and letting the high tide pour in to sweep away the village.

When the village men eventually arrived with sandbags, they found the unconscious little boy hanging by the shoulder from the hole in the dike—and not one drop of water was getting through. Needless to say, from that day on the little Dutch boy was always greeted as a hero in his hometown.

God often chooses little things to do big jobs. Five loaves of bread and two small fish fed more than 5,000 hungry listeners. A little captive maid brought God to the army general Naaman. Two tiny coins from a poor widow's purse were worth more to the kingdom of heaven than all the gold and silver given by the arrogant rich.

If you happen to be feeling small, simple, or weak, better hold on to your hat. For God probably has something really *big* planned for you!

Carolyn

Dec 6

Don't Bark up the Wrong Tree

It is an old rule of raccoon hunting that the hunt take place at night. You can imagine the scene: moonlight, men on horseback with rifles slung over their shoulders, a frightened raccoon scurrying across the hills in advance of the dog pack.

Lucky for the raccoon, it can go one certain place the dogs can't: up a tree. If a raccoon stays in the first tree it climbs, the dogs will eventually circle the tree, barking loudly, until their masters catch up with them. The raccoon will be shot, and one of the men will begin making plans for a new fur hat.

But sometimes a smart raccoon runs up one tree, then jumps into another tree before the dogs know about it. While the dogs proudly stand guard at what they think is the tree with the raccoon in it, the raccoon is happily scampering away in safety.

To "bark up the wrong tree" means to believe something that isn't true, or to pursue something that can never happen. There are those who bark up the wrong tree by saying old people don't care to be around children. I know a group of young people who spent a whole day at a senior citizens' home as part of an adopt-a-grandparent program. Each one of them adopted a resident for the day. At the start of the day the residents sat in a circle in their wheelchairs, and the recreational director introduced everybody. There was an awkward moment after that when one of the young boys turned to a nurse nearby and asked, "What do we *do* with them?"

The nurse whispered quietly, "What they miss most is the touch of a human hand. Hold their hands and ask them questions, or just tell them about yourself and your family."

By the end of the afternoon they had enjoyed several games of Bingo, sang songs around the piano, and had a talent show of sorts that was wildly applauded by the residents. As the young people left, one of the residents, with tears in her eyes, held the hand of her adopted grandchild and kissed it. "Read **Matthew 8:3**," she said. Here's what that verse says: **Jesus put forth His hand, and touched him.**

Someone needs the caring touch of your hand today too.   **Nancy**

344

Fright in the Night

This is the record, that God hath given to us eternal life, and this life is in his Son. He that hath the Son hath life; and he that hath not the Son of God hath not life. 1 John 5:11, 12.

One warm summer evening in northern Michigan my friends and I sat on the dock by the lake at Camp Au Sable, looking into the night sky, full of sparkling lights. What an awesome sight! Then we turned our attention to the moon, whose light shimmered on the lake before us. Slowly, almost without notice, a small cloud, about the size and shape of a man's hand, began to move in front of the moon. I wondered if my buddies were thinking the same thing I was. What if this was the moment Jesus was to come back? The cloud got closer and brighter as the light from the moon shone through it. Was this it? Was Jesus coming? I didn't feel ready—I felt scared! I started to pray, thinking that maybe if all my sins weren't forgiven I could do it quickly before He came. Maybe then I'd be ready.

We continued to watch the cloud. Of course, Jesus didn't come that night, and it turned out that my friends were thinking the same thing I was, and none of them felt ready for Jesus to come either.

How is it with you? Do you feel ready for Jesus to come? Why is it that so many people say no to that question? Maybe it's because we have misunderstood what being a Christian is all about. Does it really have to be this scary? The answer is no, it doesn't!

When you have a parent who really loves you, nothing can break that connection. You might make mistakes, but does that mean you are no longer their son or daughter? Of course not! They might not be pleased with what you did, and they might even punish you. But you are still their child.

It's the same with God. When you accept Jesus into your heart, you are His child. You still will make mistakes, but forgiveness is yours, and you still belong to Him. When Jesus does break through the clouds to take us home, you'll be there to meet Him. So keep looking up, not with fear, but with confidence! **Jim**

Dec 8

"I Could Eat a Horse!"

Be content with such things as ye have. Hebrews 13:5.

Three cowboys were once out on the range herding cattle.* The job took most of the day, and the cowboys always had to be on the alert so that none of the cows strayed or got lost. This left no time for even a quick sack lunch in the saddle.

When the most grueling part of the job was over and things were calming down for the day, the three cowboys finally had a chance to talk. As you might guess, the subject that kept coming up was food.

"I'm so hungry," said the first one, "that when we get back to town tonight, I'm going to be able to eat a horse!"

"But that's not even half of what I'm going to be eating!" exclaimed the second cowboy. The two continued discussing what and how much they would consume—if they could ever get to a restaurant.

Then one of the cowboys looked at the third, a Navajo, and said, "Aren't you even hungry?"

The third cowboy looked off into the distance and said, "No."

His companions looked at each other in astonishment, and then shook their heads in disbelief. The three finally finished their day's work and were able to go into town, where all three ordered vast quantities of food at the nearest restaurant. When the server brought the food, the first two cowboys watched in amazement as the Navajo inhaled his gigantic meal.

"Hey!" one of them finally said. "Just an hour or so ago you said you weren't even hungry. What gives?"

"An hour or so ago," answered the Navajo, "it wouldn't have been *wise* to be hungry because there was no food."

A very wise man once gave some friends this good advice: "Be content with such things as ye have." Because, Paul continued in his letter to the Hebrews, God said, "I will never leave thee, nor forsake thee."

Maybe the Navajo cowboy's wisdom came from knowing that when he had God in his life, he had everything he'd ever need.

Carolyn

---

*HealthWise, April 1997, p. 8.

346

No Rest for the Wicked

After a rash of arson fires in eastern Washington a few years ago the police suspected they were all related but couldn't seem to find their suspect. It turned out to be a 28-year-old woman in town. When she finally confessed, those who had met her said she was always very fidgety and restless and hard to get to know. The police asked her why she had confessed. Her answer? She turned herself in because she was afraid she was going to hurt someone unless she was stopped. She was tired of looking over her shoulder all the time, worrying if the police were going to find her, worrying about dropping hints at work, worrying that the people she worked with would be unkind to her if they knew what she was doing on her time off. She said that being in jail was much better and more peaceful than running around with a guilty conscience.

The Bible tells us in **Isaiah 57:21** about the life of the wicked: **There is no peace, saith my God, to the wicked.** A guilty conscience is never quiet. Criminals say they do the things they do because they don't intend to obey anyone else's rules; they make their own. Such a foolish excuse! They end up with even less freedom than anyone. And in jail they have to follow more rules than ever before.

Often people who have been mistreated by someone in authority (a parent or a teacher or other respected adult) get themselves in trouble because their anger makes them disrespect *all* authority. If you don't learn which adults you can trust, you may also find it difficult to trust God. If you feel this way, please talk to someone you trust.

God wants you to have peace. He is a person who can always be trusted to be fair.   **Nancy**

Dec 10

The Little Boy
Who Couldn't Sing

I can do all things through Christ which strengtheneth me.
Philippians 4:13.

Almost everyone dreams of being world-famous, whether it's a baseball player, a musician, or maybe an author. Nearly everyone has dreamed of being the best at something. Many years ago there was such a boy in the country of Italy. He wished that he could be a singer. He didn't have much hope, though, because even as a boy he worked many long hours in a factory to help the family make ends meet.

When he was 10 years old, he had saved enough money to take his first voice lesson, but the results were not what he had hoped for. His teacher said emphatically, "You can't sing. You haven't any voice at all. Your voice sounds like the wind in the shutters." What a disappointment!

But there was someone else who believed in little Enrico. It was his mother. She believed that one day he would be a great singer, and she told him that she would make any sacrifice to pay for his voice lessons.

Satan would like you to believe you are worth nothing at all. That you'll never amount to anything. That God couldn't love you, because your sins are too great. But just as Enrico's mother believed in him, there is Someone who thinks you are very valuable. And I guess He should know, because He made you. His name is Jesus! He has all the strength you need to do incredible things for Him. And just like Enrico's mother, He's done everything necessary to pay the price for your future. He's put so much value on your life that He gave His own life for you. Imagine! The God of the universe was willing to die for you and me! What a great God He is!

What became of Enrico? The little boy who couldn't sing became one of the greatest singers the world has ever known. His name was Enrico Caruso. Jesus sees infinite possibilities for you. He sees you living forever with Him. Now that's the kind of fame and fortune I want! **Jim**

Dec 11

Dragon's Breath

The dragon was wroth [angry] with the woman, and went to make war with the remnant of her seed, which keep the commandments of God, and have the testimony of Jesus Christ. Revelation 12:17.

Andrew is an excellent caver. One Sunday he and some of his friends rappelled part way down a cave known as Dragon's Breath. Then Andrew volunteered to be the first one to go the rest of the way.

Almost as soon as his feet touched the slippery cavern floor, Andrew realized he felt light-headed, as if he couldn't think clearly. Pulling matches out of his little pack, he lit the wick of a candle stub. The flame quickly turned from yellow to blue and almost died out.

Although Andrew's mind wasn't working as quickly as normal, Andrew understood the situation.

"Bad air!" Andrew called to his caving buddies 50 feet above. "I'm gonna try to come up!" Feeling like a chunk of lead, Andrew clipped his harness onto the main rope. Several times during the ascent he vomited and nearly passed out.

His friends, waiting up where the air was still good, helped Andrew climb the last 100 feet to the mouth of the cave. An hour later doctors in the nearest emergency room had an oxygen mask clamped over Andrew's face. Today he is back to his normal healthy caving self.

Just as surely as the bad air in Dragon's Breath threatened the life of Andrew, a *real* dragon is roaming this earth in pursuit of us. That dragon is Satan. We breathe his poisonous breath every time we watch, listen to, talk about, or allow our minds to dwell on anything that is unholy. How he loves to contaminate God's "oxygen" in our minds with impure CDs, movies, magazines, jokes, TV shows, or even off-color conversation.

Unless we, with God's help, climb up out of the devil's foul atmosphere and breathe our Father's pure air, that dragon's breath will lead us to guaranteed pain and certain death.

In Genesis 3:15 God promised He's eventually going to slay the dragon (also known as the serpent) who so relentlessly pursues us. I want to stay close to the Dragon Slayer, don't you?   **Carolyn**

Dec 12

Argus-eyed

There's a newspaper in our town that's called the Hillsboro *Argus*. I always wondered where the name came from and why anyone would choose that name for a newspaper.

Then a friend told me about a character in Greek mythology named Argus. Argus was deformed, no doubt about it. He had 100 eyes. And not all those 100 eyes would sleep at once. Now we all know why a newspaper would call itself *Argus*—because its reporters never sleep; they're always on the lookout for news.

Read **James 4:7: Submit yourselves, then, to God. Resist the devil, and he will flee from you (NIV).** What does the devil do? He flees! A fleeing person doesn't take their time. A fleeing person gets away as fast as they can. That's a wonderful promise, but notice that attached to the promise is a responsibility for us: we submit to God and resist the devil, and then he flees.

Before we can resist the devil, we have to recognize who he is. We have to be Argus-eyed when it comes to resisting temptation. The Bible tells us that if something doesn't agree with the Bible, it's false information. Something may be of the devil if doing it results in bad feelings and secrecy. The devil's goal is to rob us of our integrity—the feeling that we are doing what is right and have nothing to hide.

The best way to recognize the devil is by submitting to God. Before you overeat, ask God to give you the strength to resist. Then leave the kitchen. Before you do something with your friends that you know you shouldn't do, ask God for the strength to resist. Then stop yourself. Do some fleeing of your own, if necessary.

If you're in the habit of doing things God's way, it doesn't take long to know when you're on dangerous ground. When you call on Jesus, you send the devil packing. You can resist the devil, and he will flee from you. That's the power of God in you.   **Nancy**

The Seven-Year Nap

The Lord himself shall descend from heaven with a shout, with the voice of the archangel, and with the trump of God: and the dead in Christ shall rise first. 1 Thessalonians 4:16.

Gary Dockery was a police officer. One day in 1988, while serving citizens of Tennessee, he was shot in the head and rushed to the hospital. His condition was very serious, and soon he slipped into a trancelike state. He lay in his hospital bed day after day, month after month, year after year, until finally his family discussed removing him from life support.

Then one February day, more than *seven years* later, Gary just woke up. Quickly his family rushed to his side. Gary started to talk nonstop. (I guess you might too, if you'd been asleep for seven years.) Gary talked to his loved ones, called his brother on the phone, and caught up on what he'd missed during his seven-year nap. He talked for 18 hours straight.

The day after Gary woke up, he had to have surgery for a serious case of pneumonia. His doctors were afraid the anesthesia would cause Gary to slip back into a coma, maybe permanently. You'd think his family would be terribly upset, but Gary's brother, Dennis, said that even if his brother were to slip back into a coma for good, he was grateful he'd been able to tell him that he loved him.

Have you ever wondered what it will be like when Jesus comes again? What joy we'll experience when we see our loved ones! I think we'll have a lot to catch up on. We'll probably feel like talking nonstop. But we won't. Soon after we see our loved ones for the first time, someone else will catch our attention. Our focus will be riveted on the face of our Saviour. Jesus will be the great physician who will open our eyes and rid our bodies and minds of sin's cruel infection. What a day that will be! God brought Gary Dockery back to his family, and Jesus will bring us into God's family when He comes again. And by the way, we'll have plenty of time to tell our friends that we love them. In fact, we'll have forever! **Jim**

Dec 14

Give Me a Break!

Their sins and their iniquities will I remember no more. Hebrews 8:12.

I hopped onto the Nordictrack in my new third-story apartment. *Stride-stride-stride.*

Bang-bang-bang! Something like a broomstick handle started thumping on the ceiling below. Soon someone was pounding on my door.

"You too noisy!" said the large woman at the door who identified herself as Hilda, the neighbor living below me.

I apologized and to show I'd meant no harm, I gave Hilda my phone number. Big mistake! A week later, when I tried to practice saxophone and banjo, Hilda phoned. When some of my French students came over to prepare *la cuisine française* [French food], Hilda phoned to ask if we were dancing in the kitchen. (We weren't.) Then when neighbors across the hall banged something and turned their CD player up full blast, I started the countdown. This time Hilda didn't phone. Instead she came storming upstairs, knocking on *my* door to demand sternly, "You dropping heavy furniture up here?"

"No, Hilda," I answered, "I've been sitting at my table paying bills for the past two hours."

She eyed me suspiciously. I then told Hilda everything I'd done to minimize my "noise." I'd stored my Nordictrack and joined a gym for exercise instead. I did no unnecessary *walking* in the apartment after 9:30 p.m. I practiced music only in the bathroom, with a ceiling fan whirring. I stuffed a dish towel in the saxophone to muffle the sound. Two clothespins silenced the vibrating banjo bridge. I wanted to say, "Hilda, give me a break!"

Even four years after I stopped making noise above Hilda, nothing I did or said ever convinced her that I was anything other than a noisy person. She always remembered my noise from those first two weeks.

I'm so glad God isn't like Hilda. Even though our sins caused His Son to die, our heavenly Father promises to forgive and *forget* them when we ask forgiveness (Psalm 103:10-12)!

If God—forgetting our earlier sins and mistakes—allows us to develop into "brand-new" people, can't we allow the same for each other?

Carolyn

Win the Battle, Lose the War

A pedestrian paused on an overpass to watch construction crews working on the street below. The construction foreman called out to him from a utility truck. "Sir, you'll need to move, please, or you might be injured there."

"I'll leave when I decide to," the stubborn man replied. "I have a right to stand on a public street as long as I want."

A few minutes later an iron rod unexpectedly fell from a crane, and the man was injured. He sued the company but lost his case because he'd been warned. He had "won the battle but lost the war." He'd won the argument of where he could or couldn't stand, but was injured.

In a real war a battalion may capture a town here and there, but that doesn't mean anything unless they win the war. The war is what counts.

As you go through life, you may think you're winning many battles. Some people compromise their purity, thinking it will make them popular. Others cheat on exams, thinking they're winning a battle over grades. But these folks aren't winning the war; they're losing! They lose the greatest war of all—the struggle to maintain integrity, that sense that you have nothing to be ashamed of.

Solomon learned too late that he had won many battles, but he had lost the war. He counsels us to enjoy the desires of our hearts, but to be careful, because someday we will reap the rewards of our choices. He wrote in **Ecclesiastes 11:9, Follow the ways of your heart and whatever your eyes see, but know that for all these things God will bring you to judgment (NIV).** What choices are you making? Are your choices creating for you a future filled with happiness or heartache? You are choosing your future with every choice you make today. **Nancy**

Dec 16

Out With the Old, In With the New!

If anyone is in Christ, he is a new creation; the old is gone, the new has come. 2 Corinthians 5:17, NIV.

One day I discovered there were tiny eggs on the underside of the milkweed plants growing in the field beyond our backyard. I picked one of the plants and placed it in a large jar in my room. I used a hammer and nail to punch holes in the lid, then fastened it securely on the jar and waited expectantly to see what would happen next.

About two weeks later a dozen tiny caterpillars with brilliant yellow, orange, black, and white stripes were crawling around my jar. I added fresh milkweed leaves to the jar each day and watched their little bodies swell. The caterpillars grew rapidly and were soon as big around as my thumb.

One morning I looked in the jar to see what my fat little friends were up to. Nothing moved. Had they escaped? I looked around the room, but found nothing. I looked in the jar again, this time a little more closely, and was amazed to see several bright green chrysalises with tiny golden zippers. They were beautiful! During the next few weeks I watched them change from bright green in color to transparent. Soon the brightly colored wings of a monarch butterfly were visible within each chrysalis. What an amazing transformation!

But that's nothing compared to the transformation Jesus can make in your life. He can clean out your heart and get rid of bad habits. Don't spend your time trying to do that yourself; frustration will take over and you'll give up. We can't just change ourselves. Instead, spend your time with Jesus. Read His Word each day and get to know Him.

I was overjoyed when my "pet" monarchs emerged from their cocoons, beautiful silky-winged expressions of God's love. You'll be even more amazed at the new life God can give you when you look to Him each day.

Jim

Just Say "Ah-h-h-h"

God loves a cheerful giver. 2 Corinthians 9:7, NIV.

"O-o-o-oh!" I groaned as I woke up one morning in Africa. "My tooth is *killing* me!"

"I heard there's a French dentist in Ruhengeri," said my neighbor. "That's six hours by bus, but he could probably help you."

Six *miserable* hours later I worked my way past two women holding chickens and staggered off the bus. At the other end of town, outside a tiny clinic, I took the last place in the patient line. Soon I would find relief for my screaming tooth.

"Just say 'Ah-h-h-h!'" ordered the tall blond dentist in a dingy white coat. "Your dental work is primitive and looks horrible!" he exclaimed. "Like something they'd do over in America."

"Excuse *me!*" I felt like saying. Instead, I started explaining that my dental work had been done by a highly respected and professionally trained relative of mine, but the dentist cut me off.

"Yep, I can sure tell *you're* American by that 'cowboy' accent you're trying to speak French with. What an ugly-sounding language you people speak over there!"

Now, I'd come to this dentist because I believed he would help me. And he did—with my filling. But he certainly made the time I spent with him most miserable. His attitude was anything but cheerful, and to this day I must admit I did not fully appreciate the dental help he gave me.

Only one kind of service is pleasing to God. Do you know what kind that is? It's *cheerful* service. Even if we're doing something good for others, a bad attitude on our part can take away from the good we're doing.

But you and I can ask God to share *His* joy with us. Then we can choose to *act* cheerful, and He will take care of the rest.

Even though my tooth was killing me and the dentist was helping me, I came away resenting both him and the country he represented. With God's cheerfulness in our lives, people will appreciate both us and the heavenly Father we represent.

Carolyn

Dec 18

Muddy the Water

A man traveling through a very small town stopped for gas at a country store and noticed this sign in the window: "This store closed on May 28 because of the weather." Since it was only May 13, the man asked the owner how he knew what the weather would be like so far in advance.

"Well," said the old man, scratching his scruffy beard, "if she rains light, I'm going fishing. If she rains heavy, I'm going to stay home and work on my tackle."

"But how do you know it's going to rain?" persisted the man.

"Don't care if it rains or not," explained the proprietor. "If it's sunny, I'll go fishing or work on my tackle anyway. All depends on the weather."

He was "muddying the water," confusing things with unnecessary information. It would have been much more understandable if he had simply announced that the store would be closed May 28.

The phrase "to muddy the water" is thought to have originated when a fisherman hollered at someone crossing upstream, stirring up the mud so he couldn't see the fish anymore. Sometimes people muddy the water when they talk about their understanding of God. Some may say that "God doesn't love people who smoke." Others may say that you have to be a "good" person before you can be a Christian or come to church. Both are wrong. **John 15:13, 14** is like a love letter from Jesus. **The greatest love is shown when a person lays down his life for his friends; and you are my friends if you obey me (TLB).** Jesus says He loves you, no strings attached. And when you follow His advice and obey Him, it shows everyone that you are His friend. **Nancy**

What? No Toilet Paper?

But as it is written, Eye hath not seen, nor ear heard, neither have entered into the heart of man, the things which God hath prepared for them that love him. I Corinthians 2:9.

A few years ago I visited Russia. Soon after I landed in Moscow, it was obvious that if I was looking for a luxury vacation spot, this was not the place. I can remember thinking, *These people have so little; I'm glad I don't live here.*

But my thoughts began to change soon after I met a few of my Russian brothers and sisters. They had so little, but they seemed so happy. How could that be? In a country in which you had to carry your own toilet paper, how could you be satisfied? I began to hear stories of Christians who for many years had to hide their meeting places. One woman used to type pages of the Bible to pass on to other believers. She put her typewriter into a wooden box, then cut two holes through which to place her hands so the neighbors wouldn't hear her typing and grow suspicious.

Those Russian Christians were so eager for the Bible and to know God better that material possessions (even toilet paper) really didn't hold much value. They were simply minor inconveniences on their journey to heaven.

Where are you headed on life's journey? Are you so busy collecting the "good things" of this life that you're missing what's really important? Are you concentrating on things you'll grow tired of? Or have you set your sights on heaven and spending eternity with Jesus?

While I was in Russia our friends treated us like kings. I learned that they felt we were far more important than any material possessions they could ever own. Someday, when we meet our friends in heaven, we'll be given crowns. But we won't keep them. In fact, we'll give them away as soon as we get them! We'll give them to Jesus, the King of kings! Nothing else will really matter.

Jim

Dec 20

Outta Gas!

God is able to make all grace abound to you, so that in all things at all times, having all that you need, you will abound in every good work. 2 Corinthians 9:8, NIV.

Family," said Father in a worried voice as he returned from knocking on the locked door of the service station, "we are in trouble."

Mother nodded solemnly and put her arm around Judson in the passenger seat of the little Datsun pickup.

Dad slid behind the steering wheel. "We're here doing God's work, but suddenly all the stations seem to be out of gas."

Judson asked, "How long can we go?"

"Fifteen minutes, at the most," answered Dad. "And home is about two hours away."

"Let's just pray," said Mother, "and then decide what to do."

After prayer Dad said, "It's not safe to stay here—let's just go." As Dad started the little pickup down the bumpy road into the African night, a light rain began to fall. Judson felt sleepy and, though he was 10, he still liked to put his legs in Dad's lap and his head on a pillow in Mother's lap.

It seemed as if only a few minutes had passed when Judson heard the engine die and felt the truck roll to a slow stop, rocking slightly, as if its front wheels were in a big pothole. Suddenly awake, he sat up. "Where are we?"

"We've run out of gas," said Mother. "But," she added, "the front half of our truck is sitting in our own garage here at home. We can push the truck in the rest of the way."

"What happened?"

"My guess is that God multiplied the gasoline in our tank, just as He multiplied the oil in the pots and pans of that widow we read about in your Bible story books," said Mother.

"All I know," said Dad, "is that we were almost out of gas back in Butare, but we prayed, and here we are—home!"

"God knew *exactly* what we needed!" exclaimed Judson.

"He always does," said Mother.

How right she was!

Carolyn

That's the Way the Cookie Crumbles

A man wandered through his town, glum and discouraged, nearly sick with worry. Rumors were flying that he might lose his job, and his teenaged son had been making some decisions that could ruin his own future. As the man shuffled down the sidewalk, past the funeral home, a sign in the window arrested his attention. "Why walk around half dead?" the sign asked. "We can bury you for $70."

A slow smile of hope crossed the man's face. It was true. He'd been walking around half dead, letting his worry suck all possible joy out of his life. His employment was something he couldn't control, so whether or not he lost his job, he had to stop worrying about it and start believing that something else would come along. His teenager's decisions were not his to make, but he could give guidance and pray for the boy.

He also remembered what he used to do, and allowed himself one hour out of each day to worry and pray. The rest of the day he allowed himself to think about only hopeful, happy things.

The events in our lives are often unpredictable, as unpredictable as the way a cookie will crumble. Sometimes all you can do is shrug your shoulders and let it go, as you do when a cookie crumbles in your hand. But you don't have to waste the cookie; eat the smaller pieces and enjoy them!

Many things are going to happen to you today, some pleasant, others not so good. But you're alive, and you will be that way for a very long time. It's your choice whether or not you live a happy life. Find something good about everything that crumbles around you today, even if the only thing good about tragedy is that you learn a lesson from it. Today's verse, **Proverbs 24:10,** is a strong one. **You are a poor specimen if you can't stand the pressure of adversity (TLB).** Evaluate each of your challenges. If you can change something about it, do so. But if you can't do anything about a challenge, lick up the crumbs and go on.   **Nancy**

Dec 22

First-Grade Pyrotechnics

There is a way which seemeth right unto a man, but the end thereof are the ways of death. Proverbs 14:12.

When I was in the first grade, my best friend was Ernie. Ernie and I did everything together. We even got in trouble together once. It happened this way.

Each morning at school we would line up, head for the door, and do jumping jacks in the backyard. That was OK if you didn't have anything better to do, but on this particular day something more interesting caught our attention. Ernie and I were at the back of the line when we noticed that the trash was burning. There really wasn't anything unusual about that—people did it all the time back then—but it wasn't usually on fire during exercise time. So Ernie and I slipped over to the trash barrel to watch the fire. We figured we could exercise some other time.

I don't know where the time went, but before you could say "We're in trouble now," exercise time was over, and the kids were walking back in. This was great! We didn't have to exercise, we got to watch the fire in the trash barrel, and the teacher didn't even care! No recess was better spent!

As we headed back up the stairs at the end of the line, the teacher said, "Ernie, Jim, I need to talk to you."

I didn't understand. If she was going to get us in trouble, why didn't she call us when we first went to watch the fire? Well, I won't repeat what happened during the next few minutes. Let's just say Ernie and I met the teacher's belt, up close and personal.

Sometimes things in life catch our attention, just as that fire caught our attention. Satan will try to take our minds off Jesus by keeping us too busy or by getting us caught up in the things of this life. Let's keep our eyes on Jesus. Like the song says, "The things of earth will grow strangely dim in the light of His glory and grace." The fires of this world will be nothing compared to the light from Jesus' face!   **Jim**

Hounded by a Hippo!

You hem me in—behind and before; you have laid your hand upon me. Psalm 139:5, NIV.

Do you know which wild African animal kills the most people? It's the hippo. Many people have thought they can outrun—or outswim—one of these clumsy-looking creatures. They don't know that the hippo is capable of becoming a short-spurt speed machine, cleverly disguised as a huge, blubbery, lumbering beast.

"Watch out for hippos!" Bizimana's father warned as the 11-year-old left for a swim with his friend Amoni in the nearby lake.

Bizimana and Amoni decided to swim to a low-lying island, surrounded by thick clumps of cattails. When they were almost there, they saw a huge hippo lurching its way through the cattails.

"Hippos!" screamed Bizimana. "Head for shore!"

Amoni was the stronger swimmer and soon left Bizimana in his wake. The hippo snorted water, submerged partially, and headed for Bizimana. The more the terrified boy pumped his arms and legs, the heavier they became—and the closer the hippo got to him. Lungs burning, Bizimana realized he must soon give up and could almost feel the hippo's jaws chomping down on his legs.

"Come on! Swim!" called Amoni, who had already reached shore.

Somehow Bizimana dragged his weary body out of the water, but the hippo stayed in the shallow waters, angrily patrolling and spouting.

Bizimana first told me this story when he was my student in Africa. "Even though that hippo was capable of swimming a whole lot faster than I could as a little boy," Bizimana said, "I believe God protected me so that hippo couldn't grab me. I know now that God had a plan for my life."

God *did* have a plan for Bizimana's life. Two years after he told me the story about the hippo, Bizimana graduated from a Christian college with a teaching diploma. The next school year he was in his own classroom with his own students, teaching them about his heavenly Father.

Only when we get to heaven will we know about all the "hippos" God protected us from so that He could complete His plan in our lives too.

Carolyn

Dec 24

Strain at a Gnat and Swallow a Camel

It was test time—algebra test time. And unlike a class that people took because they were interested in it, algebra was a class everyone had to take. If they flunked a semester of algebra, they had to take it again in the summer or during the next year or never get out of high school! So passing the algebra test was very important.

Mrs. Thornby knew this. She knew that sometimes desperation made her students cheat. So as she handed out the examinations she said solemnly, "I'm giving you two tests today. One is in algebra, and one is in honesty. If you must flunk one of them, flunk algebra. The test in honesty is much more important."

Mrs. Thornby didn't want her students to "strain at a gnat" (their grades) "and swallow a camel" (their honesty). Read how the apostle Paul put it in **2 Corinthians 4:18: We fix our eyes not on what is seen, but on what is unseen. For what is seen is temporary, but what is unseen is eternal (NIV).** The students who cheated may have looked good on the outside by making a good grade, but inside they knew they were cheats.

Our verse today tells us that what is seen is temporary, but what is unseen is eternal. This here-and-now life is temporary. Heaven is unseen, but it is eternal.

The smartest people are those who know the difference between an insect and a camel. If you get the "big things" in order, such as your belief in God, then the rest of your life will be manageable. **Nancy**

The Eyes Have It

I praise you because I am fearfully and wonderfully made. Psalm 139:14, NIV.

If you can see, you probably don't think about it too much. If you can't see, you may sometimes think about the day when Jesus will open your eyes and you'll see Him face-to-face.

Have you ever thought about what your eyes are made of? Well, there are the lens, the iris, the retina, the sclera, the cornea, the pupil, and several other parts in an eye. The pupil is an opening at the center of your eye that has a lens behind it. This lens projects the images you see onto your brain. Look into the eyes of someone around you. Isn't it amazing that you and I can see with those ball-shaped objects in our heads. They have so many parts and work so wonderfully that unless you are an eye doctor, it's pretty hard to understand.

Your eyes, of course, aren't the only part of you that's made so remarkably. Even the human hand is an awesome wonder. The ability to lift heavy, bulky objects as well as small, delicate things is amazing.

Some people think the way your eyes and all the other parts of your body function just happened by accident. Try this. Take apart a jigsaw puzzle and put it into a box. Shake the box for about 10 seconds. Now open the box. Is the puzzle put together? No? Well, close the top and shake some more . . . How about now? Is the puzzle assembled? Of course not! Well, the chances are just as good for our amazing body to fall together as they are for a puzzle to put itself together.

We have an amazing God. He's the only one who could put us together the way we are. Worship Him today for His awesome power and great love for you. **Jim**

Dec 26

Saying Goodbye to Tama, Hello to Heaven

God shall wipe away all tears from their eyes; and there shall be no more death, neither sorrow, nor crying, neither shall there be any more pain: for the former things are passed away. Revelation 21:4.

Dumb rabies," said the African veterinarian. He'd been in the area and dropped in to examine the little wire-haired terrier quivering and moaning on the thick throw rug in front of the fireplace.

Courtney gasped as the vet continued. "Your dog will be dead within 24 hours or so. Bury him deeply, and be sure to burn anything that's touched him within the past week—this rug, your clothes . . . *anything!*"

Courtney and her parents had bought Tama in Belgium on the way back to the mission field so she'd have a pet to keep her company. She and Tama had spent months playing hide-and-seek, ball, and Frisbee. She'd taught the happy little dog to sit, shake hands, and roll over. Tama had slept on Courtney's bed every night and greeted her every morning with doggy kisses. She and Tama were a team—almost like their own little family within the family.

Dad buried Tama two days later. The family immediately began a 10-day series of rabies vaccinations. Courtney tried not to cry when the nurse carefully put the needle into her stomach, but how those shots stung!

"I miss Tama so much," cried Courtney one morning. "And I'm so tired of hurting like this." She lifted her pajama shirt high enough to show Mother the black-and-blue bruises from the injections in her stomach. Then she flung herself into Mother's arms.

"I'm tired of hurting too," said Mother, wiping her own eyes. "I know how lonely you are without Tama. But darling, the good news is that Tama isn't suffering anymore. And the best news is that God will someday take away the pain in both our bodies *and* our hearts."

"Oh," sobbed Courtney, "I want to forget what it even *feels* like to hurt. I'm starting to see why heaven is so special. I *really* want to go there."

"Oh, so do I," said Mother, hugging Courtney. "So do I."

Carolyn

Get a Handle on It

John thought he was going to be a hero as the football sailed through the air toward him. It should be easy. Running sideways with one eye on the ball, arms outstretched, he prepared himself to take that ball in his arms . . . then fumbled it. The ball slipped out of his hands, and he didn't score.

As the spectators groaned, John shouted something derogatory and shook his fists at them in anger. He kicked at the turf and acted like a 2-year-old. Instead of being a hero, he was a shame. He couldn't get a handle on the ball, and he couldn't get a handle on his anger.

To "get a handle" on something means to find some way to control it; to cope with it. It's thought the saying comes from the game of football. If the ball had a handle sticking out somewhere, it sure would be easier to hold on to! Our emotions are often just as difficult to get a handle on and cope with as is a football.

Here's a suggestion for controlling your temper: Determine to control the situation, rather than letting it control you. Sometimes you have to talk to yourself to calm down. Sometimes you have to say out loud, "Stop!" And then, quietly, "Relax. Keep cool. Keep quiet. Don't say something you'll regret later."

God wants you to live your life in control of yourself. Get a handle on your emotions; learn to cope with the abundance of chemical messages your body floods you with and you will enjoy life better. It's very clear how highly God values people who can control themselves. Read **Proverbs 16:32: One who is slow to anger is better than the mighty, and one whose temper is controlled than one who captures a city (NKJV).** God values the quiet, personal decisions we make, while the world values the loud, boasting warrior who rides into a captured city at the front of a noisy parade. God speaks with a still small voice. **Nancy**

Dec 28

Pick Up Those Clothes Right Now!

Count yourselves dead to sin but alive to God in Christ Jesus. Romans 6:11.

Has anyone ever told you, "You pick up those clothes right now"? Oh, that's right; I'm sure you've never left your clothes lying anywhere in the house, have you? Well, I must admit that I have. I guess we can't blame our mothers for not liking it, can we?

I do know someone that leaves stuff lying around and their mother never gets after them. I'm talking about a snake here, and the stuff they leave lying around is their skin. You've probably heard that as snakes grow, they actually grow out of their skin. The old skin breaks at their mouths, and slowly they rub against rough objects and turn the skin inside out. They literally crawl out of their skin and leave it there. You may even have found an abandoned snakeskin. You can see every detail of the snake in its skin.

Sin is like a snakeskin. The apostle Paul tells us we need to die to sin and leave the old life behind, just as a snake leaves its old skin behind. How can we do that? Through faith! We are children of the King, and God wants us to live like it. He doesn't want us to be slaves to sin. As you and I give our lives to Jesus and begin to focus on Him, He can begin to change our desires and our hearts. It's a miracle only He can perform.

Next time you find a snakeskin, look at it carefully. Think about the snake that is living a new life with new skin. Then remember that God wants you to live a new life with a new heart. Leave the old life behind. Don't pay any attention to the devil's temptations, and watch God change you from the inside out.

Jim

Milk of Human Kindness

Milk is one of the most nourishing, complete foods on earth. Amazingly, it's the only food babies eat during their first few months of life, yet it's enough to help them grow bigger and taller. They even grow hard, white teeth while they drink only milk! This miracle happens so often we hardly give it a second thought. As the old TV commercial used to tell us, "Milk is good food."

When we show kindness to others and take an interest in them, it's just a simple thing, yet it is so emotionally "nourishing" that it helps them feel emotionally healthy. Do you remember a time when you did something careless, or maybe heard an unkind rumor that was circulating about you? Or has someone in your family embarrassed you by being irresponsible by what they say, leaving you to wonder what others are saying behind your back?

Fear and embarrassment make us feel isolated. We want to curl up into a ball and ignore everyone else. But if there is only one person who takes the time to reach out with a caring note or a few kind words, it can make all the difference. That's what we mean when we speak of the "milk of human kindness." Read **Matthew 7:1, 2 (NIV): "Do not judge, or you too will be judged. For in the same way you judge others, you will be judged, and with the measure you use, it will be measured to you."**

Anyone who has received understanding knows how nourishing it is. Maybe it was encouragement just when you needed it. See if you can give the milk of human kindness to someone today. Say something nice to someone the next time you drink a glass of milk! You will find that it will nourish your own soul, too.

Nancy

Keep One's Ear to the Ground

Cowboys have always been sort of glorified as rough-and-ready guys who could handle anything. They've been thought of as toughies who swagger into town with their hands on their guns. That's why I found it especially amusing to learn that the expression "keep one's ear to the ground" comes from something silly cowboys used to do.

Picture this scene: a hot dusty street in the middle of a prairie town. Piano music drifts cheerily out a window of a restaurant down the street. Women in long dresses and parasols step lightly along wooden sidewalks. And into the middle of this scene rides a cowboy. He's got it all—tan shirt, tan jeans, leather vest and buckskins, triangular scarf tied around his neck, fancy boots with spurs sticking out of the back, and a cowboy hat perched smartly on his head. With a practiced tug on the reins, he brings his horse to a stop, looking behind him as though he expects someone else to join him.

Then he dismounts, unties his scarf, and lays it on the ground. Before you can ask what's happening, the cowboy kneels in the dirt and places his ear to the scarf. He thinks that the scarf somehow amplifies sound. He thinks he can learn something by keeping his ear to the ground.

We say keeping your ear to the ground means to keep yourself aware of everything that's going on around you. When your ear is to the ground, you read the signals of the people around you—their comments, their facial expressions, events coming up—so you can be ready for whatever happens and not be taken by surprise.

Sometimes you interpret things correctly; sometimes you don't. Usually we get out of life what we expect to happen. That's very clear in **Proverbs 23:7: As [a person] thinketh in his heart, so is he.** If you expect people to dislike you, they probably will. If you tell yourself you're going to dislike something, you probably will. But if you expect to be pleased, that will happen.

What are you telling yourself about life? The Bible says that if we choose to think positive thoughts, we will become positive people. That's not just a harebrained idea; the Bible supports it. Say to yourself, "God thinks I'm something special." Does that make you smile?

Nancy

The Hazards of Joy

I am come that they might have life, and that they might have it more abundantly. John 10:10.

In the early 1900s an advertisement was put in several London news-papers that read like this: "Men wanted for hazardous journey. Small wages, bitter cold, long months of complete darkness, constant danger, safe return doubtful. Honor and recognition in case of success.—Ernest Shackleton."

You would think that no one in their right mind would respond to the ad. An amazed Shackleton said later, "It seemed as though all the men in Great Britain were determined to accompany me, the response was so overwhelming."

What was this crazy proposal? Shackleton was looking for men to accompany him on the National Antarctic Expedition. They never did make it to the South Pole. Was it the challenge? Were all the men who responded bored with their lives, or was it that they were looking for something bigger than themselves?

Jesus called a group of men to follow Him under similar conditions. They left their homes, carried only the clothes on their backs, faced constant attack, and most of them were eventually killed for following Him. Why did they do it? Was it the challenge? No. I think they could have found that elsewhere. It was because they had found something, Someone, bigger than themselves. They discovered the Son of God, and their lives would never be the same.

Sometimes being a Christian seems like answering Ernest Shackleton's ad. It can be rough. You get made fun of. It seems as though you miss out on some of life's pleasures, and God doesn't always explain things the way we would like Him to. So why answer the call? Well, how about eternal life? That's what the apostle Paul was looking forward to. But it's not just eternal life that God gives. Jesus said that He came to give us more abundant life—*now!* Right now!

So how about it? Will you answer His advertisement today? The fringe benefits start immediately and go on eternally! **Jim**

Scripture Index

GENESIS

EXODUS

NUMBERS

DEUTERONOMY

JOSHUA

1 SAMUEL

2 SAMUEL

1 KINGS

2 KINGS

1 CHRONICLES

EZRA

PSALMS

PROVERBS

26:41 . . . . Jan. 3	12:31 . . . . Feb. 7	15:4 . . . . Apr. 29
26:41 . . . . . . May 17	13:14 . . . . . . Sept. 26	
27:46 . . . . July 15	14:2, 3 . . . . . . Jan. 12	

MARK

14:5 . . . . Sept. 18	
1:17 . . . . Feb. 21	14:6 . . . . Jan. 9
8:34 . . . . Oct. 30	14:6 . . . . Nov. 22
9:27 . . . . Feb. 13	14:15 . . . . June 16
9:35 . . . . Sept. 11	14:30 . . . . Oct. 6
10:28 . . . . Jan. 20	15:13, 14 . . . . . Dec. 18
10:49 . . . . . . Aug. 26	15:15 . . . . . . Apr. 20
12:43 . . . . . . May 18	16:13 . . . . May 2
15:39 . . . . . . June 30	17:14 . . . . Oct. 1
	21:25 . . . . Feb. 4

1 CORINTHIANS

1:27 . . . . Aug. 19
2:9 . . . . Feb. 19
2:9 . . . . Apr. 12
2:9 . . . . Dec. 19
4:2 . . . . Feb. 22
9:24 . . . . May 21
9:27 . . . . Apr. 18
10:13 . . . . June 27
12:4 . . . . June 25
13:11 . . . . Feb. 25
13:12 . . . . Mar. 27
13:12 . . . . July 27
15:20 . . . . Sept. 7

LUKE

2:8 . . . . Sept. 20
9:11 . . . . Apr. 5
9:23 . . . . Sept. 23
10:41, 42 . . . . . Oct. 24
12:7 . . . . Oct. 15
12:12 . . . . Sept. 29
12:32 . . . . Apr. 3
16:13 . . . . Oct. 9
18:7, 8 . . . . . . May 24
21:8 . . . . June 5
21:34, 35 . . . . . Feb. 3

ACTS

4:12 . . . . July 25
4:29 . . . . Sept. 5
10:34, 35 . . . . . Mar. 3
17:11 . . . . . . Apr. 11
17:25 . . . . Apr. 21
26:16 . . . . . . Aug. 15

2 CORINTHIANS

4:2 . . . . Nov. 7
4:18 . . . . Dec. 24
5:17 . . . . Dec. 16
6:14 . . . . July 1
9:7 . . . . Aug. 7
9:7 . . . . Dec. 17
9:8 . . . . Dec. 20
10:17 . . . . Apr. 24
12:9 . . . . Apr. 16
13:7 . . . . Apr. 4

ROMANS

1:16 . . . . July 6
3:10 . . . . May 23
3:22 . . . . Aug. 23
5:8 . . . . May 30
6:11 . . . . Dec. 28
6:23 . . . . May 16
8:1, 2 . . . . . . Jan. 17
8:15 . . . . Mar. 12
8:26 . . . . Feb. 12
8:28 . . . . Jan. 16
8:28 . . . . Feb. 11
8:28 . . . . Aug. 5
8:31 . . . . Apr. 25
8:32 . . . . Mar. 1
10:17 . . . . Sept. 8
12:2 . . . . Nov. 21
12:10 . . . . Feb. 16
12:17 . . . . Mar. 24
14:21 . . . . Feb. 17

GALATIANS

3:28 . . . . Oct. 22
6:2 . . . . Oct. 11
6:9 . . . . Apr. 13

EPHESIANS

1:7 . . . . Jan. 29
1:7 . . . . Apr. 14
3:20 . . . . July 23
4:1 . . . . Nov. 15
4:15 . . . . Feb. 14
4:26 . . . . Nov. 13

JOHN

1:1 . . . . Feb. 27
1:1 . . . . Mar. 31
3:8 . . . . Nov. 25
3:16 . . . . Nov. 24
3:17 . . . . Apr. 7
3:17 . . . . Oct. 31
3:21 . . . . Nov. 3
5:22 . . . . Nov. 30
5:39 . . . . Mar. 6
6:35 . . . . May 29
8:44 . . . . Jan. 9
10:9 . . . . Oct. 17
10:10 . . . . . . May 20
10:10 . . . . Dec. 31

374